Ш hat's going on in the Kremlin? Can *perestroika* succeed? What are Gorbachev's options? Will the real Soviet economy please stand up? In addressing these crucial questions, Stanford economist John Gurley conducts a guided tour through Soviet history and Russian literature. The reader meets 19th-century peasants, 20th-century factory workers, and seemingly ageless bureaucrats. Professor Gurley is the author of two earlier Portable Stanford books, *Challengers to Capitalism* and *Challenges to Communism*.

D1736462

THE PORTABLE STANFORD BOOK SERIES

★

PUBLISHED BY THE
STANFORD ALUMNI ASSOCIATION

★

"ЩНДТ IS TO BE DONE?"

SOVIETS AT THE EDGE

JOHN G. GURLEY

THE PORTABLE STANFORD is a series publication of the Stanford Alumni Association. The series is designed to bring the widest possible sampling of Stanford's intellectual resources into the homes of alumni. It includes books based on current research as well as books that deal with philosophical issues, which by their nature reflect to a greater degree the personal views of their authors.

THE PORTABLE STANFORD BOOK SERIES
Stanford Alumni Association
Bowman Alumni House
Stanford, California 94305-4005

Library of Congress Catalog Card
Number: 90-070426
ISBN: 0-916318-42-7

10 9 8 7 6 5 4 3 2 1

This book has benefited greatly from the guidance and excellent advice I have received from editor Bruce Goldman and from the highly professional work of his assistant, Amy Pilkington. Beverly Cory reworked and shortened my manuscript in ways that readers, if they only knew what she had to work with, would applaud enthusiastically. Before that, Professor Terrence Emmons and Dr. Dorothy Atkinson, while throwing up their hands in despair (as I, the ultra-sensitive author, interpreted their written comments), nevertheless gave me invaluable advice which enabled me to turn something poor into a better product. The editorial staff took over from there.

TABLE
OF
CONTENTS

INTRODUCTION/PAGE xiii

HISTORY'S RELENTLESS COURSE/PAGE 1

IN SEARCH OF A MORE VIBRANT SOCIALISM/PAGE 25

BREAKING THE STRANGLEHOLD OF BUREAUCRACIES/PAGE 65

Why Were Bureaucrats Ever Invented? ★ The Distinct Nature of Soviet Bureaucracies ★ The Special Problems of Central Planning ★ Attempts to Reform the System ★ Pushkin's Vision of the Mighty State ★ Gogol's Powerless "Little Citizen" ★ Unveiling a Corrupt Power Structure ★ The Struggles of a Lone Wolf ★ Getting the People to Fight Back

THE SOVIET FARM: OVERCOMING A DIFFICULT HISTORY/PAGE 95

The Soviet Farm: Overcoming a Difficult History ★ The Changing Labor Supply ☆ *Where the People Are* ☆ *How the People are Doing* ★ Facing the Problems of a Declining Labor Supply ★ The Russian Worker of 1900 ★ Rural Living Standards in This Century ★ Recent Efforts at Improvement ★ Gorbachev's Agricultural Measures ★ The Peasantry: Up Close and Personal ☆ *The Dominance of Religion* ☆ *The Senseless Violence* ☆ *The Wholesale Drunkenness* ☆ *The Pervasive Anti-Intellectualism* ★ Gorky's Hope for the Future ★ A Dark View of the Working Class ★ Poverty within the Collectives ★ Revitalizing the Collective Farms

THE LEGACIES OF RAPID INDUSTRIALIZATION/PAGE 129

Lenin's NEP: A Transition Stage ★ *Perestroika* and the NEP: A Comparison ★ Stalin's Departure from the NEP ★ An "Industrial Novel" Looks at Rebuilding ★ The Growth of Central Planning ★ Accounting for the Success of Industrialization ★ Kataev: Glorifying the Worker's Spirit ★ Undermining the Worker's Spirit ★ Troubles of the Postwar Economy ★ Behind the Recent Slowdown ★ Wanted: Pride of Workmanship ★ Restoring the Socialist Spirit

THE POWER AND PERILS OF PERESTROIKA/PAGE 167

Will the Real Soviet Economy Please Stand Up? ★ Lackadaisical Labor Plus Creaking Capital Equals Long Lines ★ What Is to Be Done? ☆ *The Overall Goals of Reform* ☆ *The Particulars of the Cure* ☆ Is *Perestroika* Likely to Succeed? ★ What Havoc Do the Furies Wreak?

THE HARD REALITIES: WHITHER PERESTROIKA?/PAGE 201

Can the Working Class Rise to the Occasion? ★ Will Socialist Values Be Lost along the Way?
★ What Will Happen to Marxian Socialism? ★ How Has History Sculptured Socialism?
★ Peering over the Edge

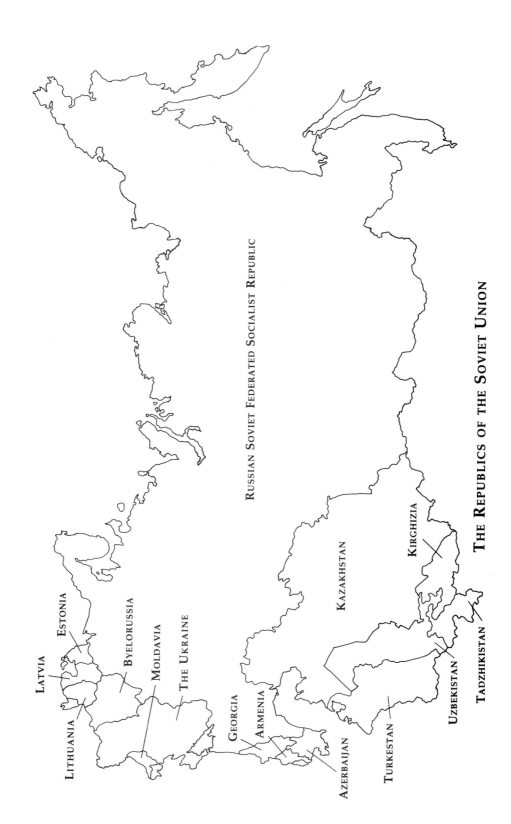

LATVIA

ESTONIA

LITHUANIA

BYELORUSSIA

MOLDAVIA

THE UKRAINE

GEORGIA

ARMENIA

AZERBAIJAN

TURKESTAN

UZBEKISTAN

TADZHIKISTAN

KIRGHIZIA

KAZAKHSTAN

RUSSIAN SOVIET FEDERATED SOCIALIST REPUBLIC

THE REPUBLICS OF THE SOVIET UNION

INTRODUCTION

Economic and social problems in the Soviet Union today are numerous. The economy is sluggish. Bloated and lethargic bureaucracies stifle initiative and drive people crazy. Some workers come to their jobs drunk, some are not on the job at all, and most produce far too little for the time spent at their posts. Consumers waste many frustrating hours in seemingly endless queues. The low quality of merchandise is the despair of all. And that is only the half of it.

Perestroika and *glasnost* are two key Russian words that refer to the Soviets' efforts, led by President Mikhail Gorbachev, to make their economy more dynamic and efficient and their society more democratic and open. This book explores the reforms comprised by *perestroika*, the alternative means of achieving them, the ultimate goals that they seek to attain, and—most significant—their chances of success.

Gorbachev's attempts at reconstruction are sharply circumscribed by the experiences and traditions of socialism in the Soviet Union and in Russia before that, and by Russian habits, beliefs, and institutions that were formed long ago and persist to the present day. A major part of the book is devoted to this historical background, for what has happened in the past powerfully limits the choices available today. The distant and near past are presented through economic data that delineate the development of the Russian and Soviet economies, and through Russian and Soviet literature. Anyone who has an eye cocked the right way quickly becomes aware, on reading the poetry, novels, plays, and short stories of the nineteenth-century Russian masters, that many of the economic and social problems of the present day are not solely Soviet or communist problems, but also long-standing Russian ones. There is also much in the more-recent Soviet literature that depicts economic and social problems under Lenin, Stalin, and their successors. Although constrained by socialist realism, these Soviet writers have deftly portrayed the society in which they lived, offering insights on such topics as super-rapid industrialization, central planning, bureaucracies, forced labor, and alienation. Their stories convey a spirit that a cold set of statistics could not. Even in the face of state censorship, these writers have managed to illumine the source of many current difficulties.

Some people hold the optimistic view that there are no intrinsic or traditional barriers to economic progress in the Soviet Union. Progress would begin the day after tomorrow, these advocates allege, if the Soviets permitted free markets to establish correct prices, unleashed individual initiative, and refrained from penalizing the winners in the economic race. Critics of this view argue that the burden of tradition holds back each of these reforms. At the extreme, some writers have proposed that the suffering of the Soviet people has its roots in Russian currents that commenced centuries ago and cannot be altered now.

Vasily Grossman expresses this pessimistic view in his novel *Forever Flowing* (1970). The story's central figure, Ivan Grigoryevich, is arrested in the 1920s for speaking out against dictatorships and limitations on freedom. For the next thirty years, he is incarcerated, spending the last nineteen years in labor camps in the Arctic. He is released after Stalin's death and makes his way back to Moscow. Throughout the story, Ivan ruminates about the terrible, unending plight of the Russian people—about their eternal suffering. His sense is that not much has changed in a millennium, and not much will. At the end of the novel, Ivan stands before an empty plot of land, where once his home was located. "He stood there—gray, bent, and changeless." That final sentence—that last word—emphasizes the controlling impression left with the reader. And the title? According to Grossman, while nothing of substance has changed in Russia for a thousand years, the forms of servitude have been continually in flux—forever flowing.

This sort of pessimism suggests a hopelessness about the possibility of doing anything dramatically positive about the Soviet economy. The forms may change, but the basic, stultifying structure will remain intact. And yet, a series of revolutions going on right now seems to be turning things upside down. Can Grossman really be right? Or should we side with the optimists in their belief that the Soviet people could begin immediately to create wealth, instead of destroying it, if the government would simply back off? Then again, given the deep Russian traditions, how can the government back off? These issues arise throughout the book.

Our main focus is the Soviet economy, but it is not possible to ignore the ethnic, religious, and nationalist clashes and confrontations within the Soviet Union in recent months, nor can we nonchalantly pass by the Soviet Communist Party's loss of its monopoly political powers. Outside the USSR, the astounding events in Eastern Europe stem largely from Gorbachev's own words and deeds, and these dramatic turns have reverberated back to the Soviet Union. All these events suggest to many observers that socialism and dictatorship have run their course, and that capitalism and democracy have won. We will consider this and alternative explanations in the final chapter.

This book is not a treatise on world communism, nor does it pretend to report on the latest happenings in the many former communist countries of Eastern Europe. Instead, it is about the Soviet economy—the economic history that shaped it, literary works that help us interpret it, and, especially, the current attempts to restructure it. Whatever further surprises are just around the corner, my hope is that this book will provide the background for a better understanding of them.

THE DNIEPER RIVER, AS SEEN FROM THE HISTORIC UKRAINIAN CITY OF KIEV.

HISTORY'S
RELENTLESS
COURSE

When Mikhail Gorbachev, president of the Soviet Union, claims that *perestroika* is a necessity of history and no whim of his, he implies that he is merely history's tool. *Perestroika* was bound to come, in accordance with history's timetable, with or without him. That's what he wants people to think.

But what do you think? Would Japan have turned out the way it did after World War II without General Douglas MacArthur? Would slaves have been freed if there had been no Abraham Lincoln? Would the Russian Revolution have occurred in the absence of Lenin? And what about the role of Churchill in saving Britain: Was he crucial? Then there are similar questions about Jesus, Napoleon, Hitler, Joan of Arc, and, indeed, about every great leader or "genius" in the world's history. Were they absolutely necessary for the events that have blazoned their names?

An affirmative nod to this last question puts you into the camp of the "great leader" advocates—those who see momentous events as the works of outstanding individuals, good or evil, who just happened to appear on the scene at the appropriate time. Without them, it is said, the course of history would have been quite different.

There is a camp on the other side of the river where people believe just the opposite: that great events produce great leaders. The inhabitants of this camp think that the course of current events is determined by all previous history; that, if we knew enough, we could prove that what is happening now inevitably had to happen; that all historical dramas need heroes and, lo!, they are found. Social history is a history of what people have done—people are not on the sidelines cheering history on—what they did on the field of action they had to do. That, at any rate, is what the "historical determinists" of the second camp assert.

★

DID ALL ROADS LEAD TO PERESTROIKA?

If we apply the viewpoint of historical determinism to the new economic policies of the Soviet Union—the policies called *perestroika*, or restructuring—then we would say that they were set by the march of events preceding them. *Perestroika* did not come about by chance, nor did it arise because some genius or great leader suddenly appeared on the scene. *Perestroika* was predestined, and when its time came, the great leader was found—or, rather, the same march of events produced both the current happening and the people needed to formulate and implement it.

Such a viewpoint fashions our judgment of Soviet economic policies from the Revolution to now. All these policies, we would be forced to conclude, were correct for their times, for each grew inevitably out of the past. Thus, Stalin's collectivization measures, starting in the late 1920s, were right for their time—just as historically valid as Lenin's New Economic Policy (NEP), which he and the party launched in 1921. *Perestroika*, too, has come according to the historical timetable.

If, on the contrary, we view social movements from the opposite shore, we might attribute the advent of *perestroika* to the fortunate, not to say miraculous, appearance of Mikhail Gorbachev. The harsh, cruel, and despotic policies of the 1930s we would identify, following the same star, with Stalin personally, who just happened to survive the

Siberian exiles imposed on him before World War I and lived, almost incredibly, through the world war and the civil war as well. That is, a series of chance events, a number of free decisions made first this way and then that way, allowed Stalin to survive. If he had not, according to this view, the course of history would have been dramatically different. Moreover, even after capturing power, Stalin could have moved in any of several directions in the late 1920s. Unfortunately for many Soviet citizens, he acted as he did owing to the luck of the draw, personality, and rivalries.

In the first view, we are confident that everything that has happened had to happen—and therefore everything has been, in that restricted sense, "correct." In the second view, we affirm that anything at all could have occurred at each stage of the historical process. One could, of course, take a position between these extremes by contending that some things were inevitable and some were not. For example, we could allege that *perestroika* was inevitable, given the historical background to these new policies; also that the basic decisions of the past regarding industrialization and collectivization of agriculture were inevitable, but that the means to achieve these goals were often mistaken and avoidable. Either this or something close to it would seem to be the approach taken by Gorbachev.

Gorbachev has referred to *perestroika* as a historically necessary and revolutionary restructuring of society. What does he mean by *historically necessary*? *Necessary* has at least two distinct meanings. It could mean "essential, most desirable, indispensable, crucial"; or it could signify "inevitable, absolutely predetermined." In the first case, there is a choice between, say, capitalism and socialism, but socialism is so superior that the choice of it becomes essential, crucial—that is, necessary. In the second case, there is no choice: History has offered us only socialism, which makes that mode of production "historically necessary"—that is, inevitable or predetermined. Or, looked at another way, history compels us to choose socialism even with a so-called choice before us.

What is Gorbachev's position on *perestroika*? In his book, *Perestroika: New Thinking for Our Country and the World*, the Soviet president at one point seems crystal clear about this: ". . . we are unanimous in our belief that *perestroika* is indispensable *and indeed inevitable,* [emphasis mine], and that we have no other option." Less clear is the following: "*Perestroika* is no whim on the part of some ambitious individuals or a group of leaders . . . [it] is an urgent necessity arising from the profound processes of development in our socialist society." A bit later, he tells us: "*Perestroika* is not some kind of illumination or revelation. To restructure our life means to understand the objective necessity for renovation and acceleration. And that necessarily emerged in the heart of our society." Finally, Gorbachev notes that *perestroika* is "necessitated by objective changes in the situation and in social moods."

By this time, it is perfectly obvious that Gorbachev wants us to know that *perestroika* is not simply his brainchild or whim, but something that has been made necessary by the recent trends of the country. That is, *perestroika* comes from objective, not subjective, conditions. The objective conditions—the whole historical background—produced both Gorbachev himself and the opening for *perestroika*. "If there had been no Gorbachev," the president states, "there would have been someone else." So there was no choice, Gorbachev tells us. But his other formulations leave uncertain the availability of alternative choices, however inferior to *perestroika* they might have been. "There was a choice; we were free to choose; but there was really no choice," he seems to be saying. A close economic adviser of Gorbachev, Leonid Abalkin, more recently pondered *perestroika* as a historical necessity. It certainly was not a random occurrence, an aberration, he thought. "I am inclined to believe that *perestroika* was inevitable. It reflects a fundamental change in the very processes we must manage. We now face a different set of technological relationships than in the past, a different scale, a different social situation, and a change in the character of the people who are participating in the process." It would seem that these fundamental changes necessitated the introduction of the reforms, and they were introduced by people who had themselves changed in the historical process and so had become capable of introducing them. Another economist in the Gorbachev circle, Abel Aganbegyan, wrote that *perestroika* "is not an invention of the leadership, not a subjective wish of a group of individuals, but a real need for our development. This *perestroika* has been prepared by the whole course of our previous history."

Gorbachev consistently maintains such a viewpoint about historical processes. For example, in referring to the roles of the United States and the Soviet Union in Europe, he said: "The U.S.S.R. and the United States constitute a natural part of the European international-political structure. And their participation in its evolution is not only justified, but is also historically determined." (*New York Times*, 7/7/89) All Marxists, in fact, think this way. Take Deng Xiaoping, the Chinese leader. In his famous speech to military commanders in June 1989, after the massacre of students and others near Tiananmen Square, Deng said that the students' uprising was bound to happen sometime; it was "independent of man's will." (*New York Times*, 6/30/89)

★

TRACING THE CAUSES OF ECONOMIC AND SOCIAL DETERIORATION

Gorbachev apparently believes that the basic directions taken by Stalin in the late 1920s and 1930s were determined by objective conditions. With regard to the program of industrialization, the general secretary insists that "we had no option." On the collectivization of agriculture, he writes: "But even many of the objective students of this period of our history [the 1930s] do not seem to be able to grasp the importance, need and inevitability of collectivization in our country." He has also said: "The specific situation in the country *made us* [emphasis mine] accept forms and methods of socialist construction corresponding to the historical conditions." These statements strongly suggest that Stalin had no other options, given the conditions of the time—isolation of the Soviet Union by the hostile world-capitalist system, the growing weaknesses of Lenin's NEP, the rise of Hitler, the militarization of Japan, and so on. Industrialization and collectivization were just as inevitable for those days as *perestroika* is for ours. Stalin was simply a tool of history.

But Stalin can be severely criticized, according to Gorbachev, for the ways he pursued these goals. As he explains in a peculiarly delicate way, "But the methods and forms of accomplishing these reforms [industrialization and collectivization] did not always accord with socialist principles, with socialist ideology and philosophy." Such deviations from "real" socialism were voluntarily chosen by Stalin; they were not imposed on him by history. They were, furthermore, deviations with undesirable, unfortunate, and sometimes tragic consequences—as, for example, the brutal measures he used to collectivize agriculture. These and other errant methods of Stalin, together with later errors by Khrushchev and Brezhnev, led to the unfavorable trends in the Soviet Union that Gorbachev, by 1985, was forced to deal with.

Gorbachev is nothing if not forthright in explaining what the recent trends have been. Since the early 1970s, economic growth rates have declined alarmingly. The Soviet Union, compared to the leading capitalist countries, is using increasingly outdated technology in much of its economy, and the quantity and quality of its consumer goods are abysmally low. Consumer services are also depressingly inadequate. Moreover, the system is not providing the right kind of incentives for enterprise managers, who have repeatedly gone off in the wrong direction, or for workers, whose absenteeism, low productivity, and poor work habits have greatly contributed to the economy's sluggishness. Social insurance, employment guarantees, free services, and wage leveling have made "spongers" of the people. Because more and more economic resources have been committed to an effort to reverse the decline in growth, fewer have been available for the social and cultural areas, which have as a consequence deteriorated. There has been a diminution of interest in social affairs, a turning inward by Soviet citizens, as they have become alienated from the larger society. Moral degradation and an erosion of revolutionary ideals and socialist values have eaten into the fabric of society, accounting for the rise of alcoholism, drug addiction, crime, and vulgar cultural imports. Party initiative has also stagnated, Gorbachev points out, and leading members have engaged in bribery, abused their power, and wallowed in luxurious living.

Gorbachev points his finger back to the cult of personality under Stalin, the erratic subjectivist policies of Khrushchev, and the complacency of Brezhnev, indicating that these culprits account for the unfavorable trends of the recent past and present. Although Stalin chose correct forms and methods in the beginning, Gorbachev declares, these forms and methods "were canonized, idealized and turned into dogma."

They became fetters, producing eventually "a braking mechanism" on the economy. The braking mechanism slowed the economy's growth and generated ever-larger bureaucracies to deal with the problems. Gorbachev also traces excessive bureaucracies and overcentralization to wars, the isolation of the country, its economic and technological backwardness, and mistaken premises and subjective decisions by certain leaders. While some of these factors narrowed the options facing the country, Gorbachev believes that some poor choices were made and, once made, defended far beyond valid limits.

As far as I know, Gorbachev has not asked what accounted for Stalin, although this question has been raised very recently in Soviet periodicals. If one uses Marxist analysis on this problem, the answer could run this way. Contrary to Marx's main expectation, the first proletarian revolution occurred in a relatively backward country. To carry out this revolution, Lenin needed a much stronger Communist Party than Marx imagined for the advanced capitalist countries, because the working classes, composed mostly of peasants, were themselves more backward and so required stronger leadership. After the Revolution and the civil war, therefore, a powerful party was on hand, but one even more powerful was now required to guide the country out of the morass—a situation infinitely worse than that visualized by Marx for the post-revolutionary period in any Western European country. In addition, the Bolsheviks inherited a large bureaucracy from the tsarist regime, which had to be enlarged even further to deal with the chaos and destruction of the civil war (1918–20) and to overcome the backwardness of the economy.

Stalin's position, as overseer of the bureaucracy and daily manager of key positions within this bloated structure, became therefore increasingly powerful. In a political fight between Stalin and his only serious rival, Leon Trotsky, Stalin won because of his powerful party position, defects in Trotsky's character, public suspicion of Trotsky as the Napoleon of Russia, and Stalin's better grasp of the realities of the day—including his drive to achieve "socialism in one country" as opposed to Trotsky's call for international revolution and his pessimistic outlook for the Soviet Union in the absence of such upheavals. Thus, a Marxist could say that it was more or less inevitable that Stalin would become the leader after Lenin's death.

★

THE MARXIAN VIEW
OF HISTORICAL PROCESSES

Gorbachev emphasizes that history narrows choices, sometimes down to one. Still, he does leave some room for free will, accidents, and the contributions—positive or negative—of strong leaders. Even so, some difficult questions remain: Why did history leave Stalin no choice but to pursue collectivization, while giving him a choice on how to carry it out? Why was Khrushchev able to act with such abandon, apparently with few historical constraints, while Gorbachev (by his own account) finds the weight of the past crushing out all options but one—*perestroika*? The only possible answer to such questions is that sometimes the weight of the past narrows our choices to only one and sometimes to a few. That answer, in fact, would not be inconsistent with Marx's view of historical processes. And there is clear evidence that Gorbachev has drawn on Marxian theory when he has recently discussed the necessity of *perestroika*.

In a work published in 1852, *The Eighteenth Brumaire of Louis Bonaparte*, Marx wrote: "Men make their own history, but they do not make it just as they please: they do not make it under circumstances chosen by themselves, but under circumstances directly found, given and transmitted from the past." Marx emphasized here that history is not some impersonal force, advancing down the playing field while people root in the stands for faster or slower progress. History is made by humans; it is social history. So if historical circumstances force us to do one thing rather than another, we must remember that we ourselves have fashioned those very circumstances.

Notice that Marx said historical circumstances deny us the privilege of making history *just as we please*. He left room for some choice. Otherwise, he would have written: "Men think that they make their own history, but in fact they act according to iron laws, not at all as they please." Instead, Marx's position was that historical circumstances press down on us, forcing us into a constricted channel for our future advances, but allowing us to move to one side of the channel or the other. We do not advance just as we please—because we are, after all, in that channel—but there is some freedom of choice within it, narrow as it might be, and we ourselves fashioned the channel.

Another way of looking at Marx's notion of history is to notice his insistence on a unity between theory and practice. The theory of socialism arises out of the very processes of capitalism; this capitalist development gives rise to a working class that enters into a struggle against the bourgeoisie, aided by socialist theory. And theory develops more fully in the light of the actual struggles.

After Marx's death, however, this unity was broken by his followers in three different ways. Some saw socialism as an aim based, not on class struggles arising from capitalist development, but on moral considerations—on what is right, equitable. Socialism was simply something highly desirable. In a second departure from Marx, others looked upon socialism as a system for the future—one that history would work out while workers and intellectuals sat back and watched. The working class and its struggles were not, according to this formulation, a necessary part of the historical process. For these followers, Marxism became mechanical, fatalistic, a set of iron laws predetermined by impersonal forces.

Still a third school arose which stressed the evolutionary—not revolutionary—path to socialism, a path that could be pursued through capitalist political institutions. In this view, it was not necessary for workers to use violent means to attain their ends; instead, the ballot box, the legislative bodies, and bourgeois freedoms could be used to gain a majority for supplanting capitalism with the new socialist society.

In these ways, Marx's conceptions were corrupted by his purported followers. One of Lenin's significant contributions, in the early 1900s, was to revive the original Marxian notion of historical processes. That is to say, Lenin reunited theory and practice by arguing that the doctrine of historical necessity does not rule out the role of the individual in history. If anything, Lenin went beyond Marx with an unusual stress on the importance of human volition, of human will, in achieving the socialist goal. Marxism became once again an active doctrine, not a passive one; revolutionary, not evolutionary; it unified human will and historical laws.

For Marx, society advances within the channel in a definite and explainable way. A society's economic development is generated by the growth of its "forces of production," which consist of workers, the current capital goods created in the past by these workers and their predecessors, and the land. During the processes of production, the workers develop their own talents, scientific knowledge, productivity, and needs, while at the same time they create new and more advanced capital goods and ways of producing final output. At each stage of development, therefore, in fashioning the present, we change ourselves and the instruments we use, making further advances possible. And not only possible but essential—because our own horizons and needs are extended through work. We demand more.

This progress, however, cannot continue unless social and ideological changes are forthcoming. In Marxist theory, the economic forces are eventually braked by increasingly outmoded institutions and practices and by social classes that no longer conform to the times—what Marx called the relations of production. Economic progress under capitalism, for example, might eventually be slowed by factors that debilitate the capitalist class, necessitating that its functions be increasingly assumed by the state if any semblance of progress is to be retained. Thus, crucial decisions about saving, investment, risk-taking, and research and development would be made less and less satisfactorily by capitalists; but the state, as the presumed savior of the system, would not be able to perform them much better. At this point, such capitalist institutions and practices as private property, private profit seeking, capitalist control of enterprises, and elaborate financial markets would no longer be essential for the further progress of the country. Indeed, they would be impediments. The capitalist class itself would be passé.

During a severe economic crisis, then, the working class would carry out a successful revolution, depose the nearly moribund capitalists, and reorganize the economy to socialism, establishing social ownership of productive assets, central planning, workers' control over production and distribution of goods and services, and institutions and incentives to promote cooperative endeavors. According to Marxism the state, complete with its bureaucracies, armies, police, and prisons, would come under the control of the working class. Eventually the values of society, its family arrangements, education, law, culture, and other "superstructural" elements would reflect the political dominance of the working class rather than the capitalists.

With the advent of socialism, therefore, all the capitalist incumbrances are swept away, some immediately and others eventually. The revolution is led by the up-and-coming social class that has developed with the new economic forces. This scenario, as Marxist thought would have it, accounts for the revolutionary transformations from slavery to feudalism, from feudalism to capitalism, and more recently, from capitalism to socialism. The Marxian lexicon denotes each of these shifts as a "qualitative change" or a "leap," distinguishing them from mere "quantitative," evolutionary changes—which also occur, but during the periods between revolutionary leaps forward.

Marxian theory prophesied that socialism would be a transition stage between capitalism and communism.[1] The latter, generally believed by Marxists to lie too far into the future to analyze in any detail, was nevertheless expected to be a classless, highly affluent, and thoroughly planned society in which members would work according to their abilities and receive according to their needs. At the previous stage, under socialism, there are still classes—a working class, a dispossessed capitalist class, and others—and distribution is mainly according to work. In the class society of capitalism, on the other hand, distribution is according to work *and* the private ownership of productive assets. *Need*, which totally governs distribution in communism, is a relatively small factor in capitalism and plays a larger, but not dominant, role in socialism.

Marxists have not closely analyzed the transition from socialism to communism, but clearly it would not be propelled by a violent class revolution—for socialism generates no class to overthrow the proletariat, and communism, furthermore, is classless. The transition to communism might, however, be called a nonviolent revolution, inasmuch as the working class and all other classes disappear and, with them, all class-based institutions, such as the party and the state. On the other hand, these transformations, dramatic as they might be, could occur gradually in a more evolutionary than revolutionary way.

What happens within the stage of socialism itself? The usual

---

[1] In view of the recent turn of some socialist countries to capitalist ways, wiseacres have changed this to say that socialism is the transition stage between capitalism and capitalism.

Marxian thought is that society gradually develops its socialist institutions and practices, ridding itself of previous ones, until it is finally poised at the gates of communism. In other words, socialism develops quantitatively until it is ready for the big leap into communism.

Gorbachev, however, has referred to *perestroika* as a revolutionary restructuring of society, which suggests that within socialism itself there may be qualitative transformations, leaps from one sub-stage to another. Indeed, this is exactly the way the general secretary has talked about *perestroika*. For example, in a speech in Murmansk in 1987, he declared: "Revolutionary creation and the embodiment into life of the great ideals and goals of the October Revolution now proceed at a qualitatively new stage. . . . " (*Moscow News*, no. 42, 1987)

The next year, at the All-Union Party Conference, he said that "what we need are new, qualitative changes in our development. . . ." (*Moscow News*, no. 27, 1988) In his speeches, Gorbachev has also referred to *perestroika* as a "radical economic reform," a "revolutionary restructuring," and a "new stage of development." He stated outright in his book that "*perestroika* is a revolution . . . it involves radical changes on the way to a qualitatively new state . . . it is a jump forward in the development of socialism." Several more such references to *perestroika* all make clear that the general secretary sees it in Marxian dialectical terms—that is, as a qualitative transformation; not a leap to a brand new mode of production, but rather to a new stage within the socialist mode of production itself.

The revolution that is *perestroika* requires the destruction of many old ways of doing things and, after that, the construction of new institutions and practices. But in this revolution, says Gorbachev, "there are no bombs exploding or bullets flying." There is however resistance, active as well as passive, in the form of "inaction, indifference, laziness, irresponsibility and mismanagement." Socialism, Gorbachev tells us, requires several such revolutions before it can crystallize. And why not? After all, capitalism needed not just the original revolutions to sweep away feudal orders, but repeated revolutions after those. In France, for example, "after its Great Revolution of 1789–93, it took another three revolutions (1830, 1848, and 1871) to carry through its aims." Much the same was true in Britain and Germany, he adds. We might note that these revolutions within revolutions were themselves quite violent. Bombs did explode and bullets did fly. And aren't bullets flying in *perestroika*, despite Gorbachev's forecast?

According to Gorbachev, *perestroika* can be achieved only through socialist democracy. He and other Marxists consider socialist democracy to be superior to capitalist democracy, partly because managers, directors, and bosses are elected by and are responsible to the working class in a socialist society—not, as in capitalist societies, to property owners. Moreover, in Marxist theory, socialist democracy places the state and all of its agencies directly in the hands of the majority class— the workers—whereas, in capitalism, this political power is held by a propertied minority. Gorbachev is acutely aware that socialist practice in the Soviet Union has moved some distance from socialist theory, away from the democratic ideal, and that this errant path has contributed to economic stagnation. That is why he is promoting *glasnost* (openness, telling the truth) and a *perestroika* in the political structure that will allow the masses of people more say in policy making at all levels. "Truth is the main thing," Gorbachev has repeated in various ways. *Perestroika* aims not to convert the economy to capitalism, but to achieve a more vibrant socialism and an acceleration of economic activity. A vigorous and expanding socialism depends on freedom of expression; it needs *glasnost*.

★

TOLSTOY LOOKS AT THE ROLE OF HISTORY AND HEROES

Gorbachev's idea that *perestroika* was in the cards and not pulled out of the air owes much to Marx, as we have seen. But a powerful Russian literary giant—Leo Tolstoy—also established this way of thinking in his epic novel, *War and Peace* (1866). Marx and Tolstoy make an awesome pair. They were at the peak of their powers during the same decades (though Tolstoy lived much longer and continued to do great work), but they acted independently of one another. Tolstoy did not know Marx's works when he was composing his own about history and heroes. From a Russian's standpoint, it is just as important to look at Tolstoy as at Marx. But Russians will insist that other literary traditions, too, are important in understanding present-day notions about *perestroika*. A look into the Russian literary background will reveal that the question of "history or heroes" goes back at least to the middle of the last century. A brief consideration of both sides of the story can deepen our understanding of where Gorbachev stands on the origins of *perestroika*.

Leo Tolstoy would have to be termed a historical determinist—at least according to his views in *War and Peace*. In this story, farfetched as it may sound, Tolstoy denies that Napoleon had any significant role in the French invasion of Russia. He was simply a tool of history, one of the least effective actors on the stage. To fully appreciate Tolstoy's heresy, we need to unearth the notes on historical determinism that he has embedded in the narrative.

The book was written in the late 1860s at Tolstoy's estate, located 130 miles south of Moscow. The story spans the years 1805 to 1813, with an epilogue that jumps to 1820. However, the centerpiece of the novel is the Napoleonic invasion of Russia in 1812, the burning of Moscow, and the French retreat and defeat later that year. In addition to Napoleon, other major historical figures appearing in the novel include Tsar Alexander I, who reigned from 1801 to 1825, and M. I. Kutuzov, commander in chief of the Russian forces against the invading armies of the French emperor. Tolstoy uses many more real characters throughout the novel, including both military figures and statesmen.

Throughout the latter part of *War and Peace*, but especially in its two-part epilogue, Tolstoy presents a variety of arguments, not all mutually consistent, to demonstrate that current military events are not ultimately determined by the whims, actions, and decisions of emperors and generals. According to one of his arguments, what emperors and generals do is not of their free will but is set by the past, predetermined. "The acts of Napoleon and Alexander," Tolstoy tells us, "on whose words it seemed to depend whether this should be done or not, were as little voluntary as the act of each soldier. . . . " Not free to act as they want, rulers are the slaves of all history. Of course, Napoleon thought he was acting freely, but in fact "he was in bondage to those laws which forced him . . . to do what was bound to be his share in the common edifice of humanity, in history." Such acts are "predestined from all eternity."

In another argument, Tolstoy again denies the power of generals to affect the outcome of war. Prince Andrey—one of the principal fictional characters—is listening in June 1812 to a group of military men debate what to do about Napoleon's invasion, when it occurs to him that there is no such thing as a military science and, hence, no such person as a military genius. "How can there be a science of war in which, as in every practical matter, nothing can be definite and everything depends on countless conditions, the influence of which becomes manifest all in a moment, and no one can know when that moment is coming." There is no way to plan in a war, for the unexpected is always happening. Andrey further reflects that a war's outcome is determined not by generals, but by unforeseeable turns in the heat of battle, that "victory or defeat depends in reality on the soldier in the ranks who first shouts 'Hurrah!' or 'We are lost.'"

Tolstoy offers a third argument against the "great leader" thesis. The course and outcome of a battle, he writes, are determined by the thousands of individual decisions made by the multitudes engaged in war. The myriad of individual decisions, which are expressions of individual wills, collide and coalesce to produce a definite outcome. These decisions may be motivated by purely selfish concerns, but taken in their entirety, they produce something in the public interest. For example, the people fled from Moscow as Napoleon's armies closed in, not to save Russia or the army or for any other grand purpose, but for their own selfish reasons—to save themselves. However, the sum of these individual decisions was to save Russia—because they emptied the city, leaving Napoleon only a fragile shell to enter. Individual decisions by the multitudes, and not the commands of leaders, sealed the fate of Napoleon.

The commander in chief Kutuzov was successful, Tolstoy lectures us later, precisely because he went with the flow, because he did not try to impose his own will but acted "in harmony with the will of a whole people." Napolen failed because he thought he alone knew what was right and what was wrong and did not harmonize with the flow of history.

Thus, Tolstoy argues, the millions who act in their own interests, without any concern for "public affairs," are the true makers of history. If people attempt to further the public interest directly—that is, try to understand and play a part in the historical drama—they will be "stricken with barrenness." "In historical events," he further explains, "we see more plainly than ever the law that forbids us to taste of the fruit of the Tree of Knowledge. It is only unself-conscious activity (i.e., instinctively acting in one's own interest) that bears fruit, and the man who plays a part in an historical drama never understands its significance." Referring to the 1812 invasion period, Tolstoy asserts: "Those who were striving to grasp the general course of events, and trying by self-sacrifice and heroism to take a hand in it, were the most useless members of society; they saw everything upside down, and all that they did with the best intentions turned out to be useless folly. . . . " Of course, the generals are Tolstoy's prime targets here.

At one point in the narrative, Tolstoy shows that generals and others trying to act directly in the public interest acted, in fact, against that interest. The example he offers occurred during the invasion. "Every effort . . . was being continually made *on the Russian side* to hinder the one means that could save Russia [i.e., retreating and drawing the enemy into the heart of the country]; and in spite of the experience and so-called military genius of Napoleon, every effort was made *on the French side* to push on to Moscow at the end of the summer, that is to do the very thing bound to bring about their ruin."

Tolstoy has given us three quite different reasons why generals are of little consequence: First, they simply act out history's commands; second, their directives are lost in a sea of uncertainty and chance happenings; and third, the real movers and shakers are the armed multitudes.

These require reconciliation. If all preceding events determine current events, what room is there for uncertainty and chance happenings? The answer is that these latter phenomena exist in our minds because of our ignorance about the relation of the past to the present. Tolstoy explains: "Why did it come to pass in this way and no other? Because it happened so. '*Chance* created the position; *genius* took advantage of it,' says history. But what is *chance*? What is *genius*? . . . These words merely denote a certain stage in the comprehension of phenomena. I do not know how some phenomenon is brought about; I believe that I cannot know; consequently I do not want to know and talk of *chance*. I see a force producing an effect out of proportion with the average effect of human powers; I do not understand how this is brought about, and I talk about *genius.*" History is, in fact, in the driver's seat, but, in our ignorance, we are compelled to use chance and genius as explanations.

But how does "history" square with all those millions of individual decisions that are supposed to determine events? For Tolstoy, these individual actions are what count, but nevertheless, each one is determined by everything that has preceded it. People may believe that they are exercising their free will and so acting voluntarily, but all are in fact compelled to do what they do. "In history," Tolstoy tells us, "what is known to us we call the laws of necessity; what is unknown, we call free will." There is really no free will, Tolstoy alleges. "If the will of every man were free, that is, if every man could act as he chose, the whole of history would be a tissue of disconnected accidents." Later, he adds more sharply: "If there is a single human action due to free will, no historical law exists, and no conception of historical events can be formed."

In a peculiar passage, which is a loophole of sorts, Tolstoy suggests that in ancient times history was made by heroes, but "at our stage in the development of humanity" history "of that kind is meaningless." Thus, what Tolstoy now presents as a "law" has apparently not always been true. And, in the future, it may not always be valid, either. In another aside, Tolstoy states that people have free will in their personal lives but not as part of the larger human community. Thus, the course of a society is predetermined, but it is up to Napoleon to decide whether or not he wishes to pick his nose—what Tolstoy would call "an abstract interest," outside of society.

These fleeting thoughts do not much diminish the author's main thesis, which squares with Gorbachev's view of the historical necessity of his revolutionary reforms.

★

TURGENEV'S SEARCH FOR HEROES

The Tolstoy of *War and Peace*, Marx, Lenin, and Gorbachev look to history—that is, social history that includes active human beings—for their answers; who looks to heroes? For an illustration of this last orientation in Russian literature, we can do no better than to turn to Ivan Turgenev, one of Russia's most celebrated writers of novels and short stories. He was born in the same year as Marx (1818), and both died in the same year (1883).[2] Like Marx, Turgenev was interested in how social change could be achieved, for he opposed Russia's serfdom and deplored her generally backward conditions as compared to those in Western Europe—especially in France, where he lived a good part of his adult life.

But Turgenev did not come up with Marx's answer of revolution; he was, at best, a gradualist and a reformer; he abhorred violence. He believed that reforms in Russia could be achieved only by outstanding individuals or intellectuals who would themselves act on their progressive ideas or would sow the ideological seeds among others who would attain the goals "from above." He searched in his stories for a hero. This sets him apart not only from Marx but also from Gorbachev, who traces the roots of *perestroika* to the economic and social past of the country and not to the lucky appearance of a hero or great leader. Of course, the Tolstoy of *War and Peace* would also oppose Turgenev's notions of what makes history. The materialist conception of history, or the necessity of social change, was completely foreign to Turgenev's way of thinking.

In his first novel, *Rudin* (1865), Turgenev raises the question of the origin of social change. He depicts a character who is potentially a great man, but who has serious deficiencies that prevent him from leading others effectively. Rudin is an intellectual and estate owner, retired at the age of 35. He is an inspirational, convincing, and clever talker, and he aspires to achieve important things (of some undisclosed, social type). He is, however, incapable of effective action; he is all talk and no go.

Late in the novel, Rudin correctly sums up his own failings: "It's words, all words! There were no actions!" A friend puts it more broadly:

---

[2] Ivan and Karl came and went as a pair,
In in eighteen and out in eighty-three.
But Ivan hunted partridges and hare,
While Karl, more glum, tracked down the bourgeoisie.

"There is genius in him, admittedly . . . but manliness . . . that's the whole problem, there's really no manliness in him. But that's not what matters. I want to talk about what is good and rare in him. He has enthusiasm; and that, believe me—for I speak as a phlegmatic man—is a most precious quality in our time. We have all become intolerably rational, indifferent, and effete; we have gone to sleep, we have grown cold, and we should be grateful to anyone who rouses us and warms us, if only for a moment. . . . He will not achieve anything himself precisely because he has no blood, no manliness; but who has the right to say that he will not contribute, has not already contributed, something useful? That his words have not sown many good seeds in young hearts, to whom nature has not denied, as it has to him, the strength to act, the ability to implement their own ideas?"

For Turgenev, a hero's new ideas are potentially powerful and capable of changing the world. Marxists would argue that more important are the historical reasons why those particular ideas were conceived at just that time, and why they were or were not destined to take root in the world at large.

In *On the Eve* (1860), Turgenev shows us a Bulgarian hero who is needed as a leader of the movement to free his country from Turkish rule. The hero, Insarov, is a student in Moscow, 26 years old, polite, frank, highly reliable, and totally dedicated to driving the Turks out of his homeland. Unlike Rudin, Insarov is an actor, engaged in the liberation movement. But he dies on his way back to Bulgaria and is thus unable to fulfill his potential.

In this novel, Turgenev makes it a major thesis that Russia herself is producing no heroes like Insarov. A young artist friend of the hero exclaims: "When is our time coming? When are we going to produce some real people?" After Insarov's tragic death, this friend returns to the theme: "Do you remember . . . what you said to me the night we heard of poor Elena's marriage, and I was sitting on your bed talking to you? You remember I asked you when we should have some real people among us, and you replied, 'They'll come.' Oh, spirit of the black earth! Today, from my pleasant remoteness, I am writing to ask

you once again: 'How about it, Uvar Ivanovich, are they coming?'"
Gorbachev might answer, "When the need arises, they will be there;
history will produce them."

In Turgenev's most famous novel, *Fathers and Sons* (1862), he
suggests a materialistic hero who emerges from the conflict between
two generations, the older aristocrats and the younger leftist intelligentsia. The father (an estate owner) and his brother represent the
traditional values of Russia, while the son, Arkady, and his university
friend, Bazarov, represent a radical approach. The central figure, the
potential hero, is Bazarov, a student of natural sciences and medicine.
Bazarov calls himself a nihilist, but, despite Turgenev's intentions, he
is not really a political radical, for politics seldom enter his thoughts; he
does not discuss any political issues of the day. Instead, he espouses the
scientific method, rejecting everything that is romantic, emotional, not
based on facts and controlled experiments. He judges the worth of
everything by its usefulness (useful for what, Turgenev does not
permit him to say), not by its beauty or emotional appeal. He has no
feeling for music, poetry, art, natural beauty, or the humanities in
general. He states that he wishes to destroy all contemporary institutions, and he is so far removed from political movements that he is
indifferent to what would take their place.

At the end of the story, Bazarov—who is giving medical assistance to peasants—contracts typhus from opening the body of a
cadaver (cutting himself in the process). As he lies dying, he whispers:
"And yet there was a time when I, too, thought of all the things I would
do, and never die, why should I? There were problems to solve, I said
to myself, and I'm a giant. And now the only problem for this giant is
how to die decently. . . . " So ends another "hero."

Turgenev looks to heroes, yet he has given us a fast talker (Rudin)
who otherwise cannot arouse himself, a Bulgarian fighter (Insarov)
who dies too soon, and a nihilist (Basarov) who doesn't know what he
wants in any positive way and who, in any case, dies before he has a
chance to destroy anything at all—except himself. This search for a
hero to save Russia, to alter the historical trend, would be laughed out
of court by Tolstoy or Marx and certainly would not meet with
Gorbachev's conception of how changes are produced in the real
world.

★
WHY THE MARXIAN
SCENARIO PREVAILS

Is it significant that Gorbachev and his comrades credit history rather than heroes for the recent turn of affairs? Some readers may be inclined to answer no—that this is a smokescreen, for it is to Gorbachev's advantage to have people believe that his hands are tied by historical forces. Then any failures of *perestroika* would be the fault of circumstances and not of the actors. Moreover, many Soviet failures of the past could be excused in a similar way.

While these considerations may play roles in Gorbachev's pronouncements, I do not think that they are of major importance. The general secretary of the Communist Party is a Marxist, trained as such in formal education and life. Marxists shun the view that everything that happens is accidental, whimsical—that it could just as easily have gone the other way. They would generally agree with Tolstoy that the whole of history is not simply "a tissue of disconnected accidents." After all, as Gorbachev sees it, the world has moved in connected ways (in dialectical processes) from slavery to feudalism to capitalism—and, in this century, to socialism. In his opinion, the Soviet Union has had to go through everything it has experienced since 1917—that is, all the major stages—to arrive at the point where it is possible to achieve a better socialist society.

I believe that Gorbachev has formulated and promoted *perestroika* only because he is confident of this Marxian scenario. If he thought that history was not producing a superior socialism and that anything could happen, he would have been much less likely to set forth on the perilous path he is now taking. Thus, we have *perestroika* and *glasnost* fundamentally because they are historically bound to lead to a more vibrant socialism in the Soviet Union. And we have Gorbachev, thinking the way he does, because history has produced him.

A Marxist like Gorbachev sees a definite pattern to past and current events, a pattern that enables him to make sense of the flow of history and to anticipate the broad sweep of things to come. A Marxist is not a diviner, but he does have a framework that releases him from viewing the world as a whirlpool of chance happenings, as a casino where everything is up for grabs. Needless to say, that framework is under tremendous strain right now, but Gorbachev and other Marxists will continue to cling to it—because they have to.

The serious problems of the Soviet Union do not await an accidental hero. The solutions, if there are any, are now in the process of being formed by the same historical forces that produced the problems to begin with. If that is true, if that is the way the world really works, then those who see it have a decided advantage over those who place their chips on heroes. That is the strongest conclusion that we can draw from this chapter.

"THE WHOLE CLASS TO THE HILLS."

IN SEARCH OF
A MORE VIBRANT
SOCIALISM

et us assume that Marxists agree: *perestroika* is a necessity. But will these revolutionary reforms retain the socialist system of the Soviet Union, or are they likely to lead to capitalism—or to some hybrid? It would be ironic if *perestroika*, as a necessity, led to capitalism, for it would mean that socialism was a requisite phase of development for the Soviet Union to reach a capitalist society. From tsarist capitalism to Marxian socialism to Soviet capitalism! Wouldn't that devastate Marxian theory?

However, Gorbachev has assured us that his programs will produce not capitalism, but a more vibrant and progressive socialism. We cannot swallow that whole without asking what the Soviet leader means by socialism. Perhaps his socialism is our capitalism. We must be on our guard because the definition of socialism has changed over time; this has been particularly true in the last few decades.

One of Gorbachev's most difficult problems is to find ways to rejuvenate the Soviet economy with radical policy changes while, at the same time, justifying his claim that the country will continue to follow the socialist road. To many observers, Gorbachev seems to be introducing capitalism into the economy, not a revved-up socialism. Is there any way to judge this? Is there a standard definition of socialism that we can compare to Gorbachev's policies? Any useful answers to these questions must rest on some understanding of how the concept of socialism evolved.

★

THE EVOLUTION OF SOCIALISM

T he history of socialism starts in the early nineteenth century. A number of leading socialists at that time were later called "utopian" because they visualized ideal communities to replace the ones in which they lived, without proposing any realistic way to get from one to the other. These socialists lived in France and Britain, and most of them—or their followers—established utopian communities in the United States. These were intended to be forerunners of many similar groupings; eventually the entire society would be transformed according to the models. Generally speaking, the utopian socialists stressed cooperation instead of the unrestrained individualism and competition that they abhorred; order, planning, and harmony were to replace the chaotic conditions of the real world; and social ownership of goods and property was preferred over private ownership. The utopians also promoted small communities, in which members sometimes engaged in both agriculture and manufacturing. Most were interested in reducing the poverty that contaminated society at large. Finally, they believed that human beings were malleable and so could become better people if exposed to the right social environment. One of the leading utopian socialists was Charles Fourier, the French social philosopher.

In the spring of 1847, the great Russian writer Fyodor Dostoyevsky joined a group in St. Petersburg that discussed social and literary issues, the former often from the viewpoint of Fourier's writings. This group, called the Petrashevsky Circle, had a printing press (for anti-government literature), read many forbidden works, and debated topics that the tsarist government considered subversive. Infiltrated by police spies, the entire group was arrested in 1849.

Dostoyevsky was condemned to be shot, but at the very last moment his sentence was reduced to four years of penal servitude in Siberia.

While the Russian authorities (and others) were convinced that the ideas of the utopian socialists were dangerous, Marx and Engels derided them as just so much foolish fancy. The utopians' "solutions," they said, arose not from real-life circumstances, but simply from the brain of some "great thinker"—from a self-proclaimed "hero." Capitalism would be overcome, according to Marx and Engels, when the proletariat (the urban industrial working class), born of and nurtured by capitalist society, overthrew the capitalist class. The utopian socialists could be excused for not seeing this, as Engels later explained, because in their day the proletariat was still in its formative stage, so it appeared that capitalism's ills could be cured only by schemes imposed from outside the system. Marx and Engels called *their* socialism "scientific" because they purported to show that capitalism itself, through its own development, would produce its own gravediggers. That is to say, capitalism produced both its problems and the solutions to them.

Despite these criticisms, some important utopian socialist ideas were incorporated in later socialist movements: planning, cooperation and sharing, a lesser role for private property, and an attack on poverty.

Later socialists attempted to create a better society for the workers, not by setting up model communities, but by obtaining the cooperation of their governments in changing some of the existing capitalist institutions into cooperative ones. Louis Blanc, a French socialist politician and journalist, believed that the state should aid the working class by establishing "national workshops," in effect enterprises that eventually would be run by their workers. These firms, he believed, would compete successfully against capitalist ones and gradually drive the latter from the stage—at which point capitalism would be defeated. Ferdinand Lassalle, a German socialist and lawyer, looked similarly to the Prussian government for the financing of producers' cooperatives. However, he did not think this likely unless the government represented all the people, which it would do only after universal suffrage was gained. So Lassalle urged his followers to organize the workers into a political party to fight for universal suffrage. The producers' cooperatives that would follow would allow workers to choose their own managers and to share in the profits. Lassalle believed that only in this way would the distinction between wages and profits disappear, and only then would the "iron law of wages," which condemned labor to minimal living standards, be repealed.

Once again, Marx and Engels felt that they had an easy target for shooting practice. According to these "scientific socialists," Blanc and Lassalle were mistaken in their implied theory of the state. This political institution did not represent all the people, nor could it. Instead, it was the instrument of the ruling class—just as most other institutions, practices, and values in bourgeois society existed essentially in the interest of this ruling class. Consequently, to appeal to the state to strengthen workers and to weaken capitalists was futile— worse, naive to the point of childish. Marx and Engels postulated that the bourgeois state had to be overthrown and replaced by the dictatorship of the proletariat, a workers' state. A dictatorship was necessary because socialism would be a class society (only communism is classless) in which former ruling classes and foreign capitalist classes would do what they could to overthrow the workers' government. A workers' state set against these hostile groups was thought necessary to protect the new socialist society.

Blanc and Lassalle, nevertheless, contributed to later socialist theory and practice in their advocacy of producers' cooperatives as necessary components of a socialist society. Even now, the Soviet Union is actively encouraging such undertakings in its drive to reconstruct the economy. Another of their contributions to socialist thought was the coupling of socialism to political democracy. Neither advocated a dictatorship of any type; their governments were to be the servants of the people. While this did not sit well with Marx and Engels, the democratic movement is right now being worked out in several socialist countries, including the Soviet Union. (Whether political democracy in these cases will be coupled to socialism or to capitalism remains to be seen.) Lassalle's movement also supplied the chief impetus for the formation of a socialist political party in Germany, which itself was highly influential in the creation of a Marxist political party in Russia during the 1890s.

Blanc and Lassalle desired to use the state for their purposes. Other radicals, the anarchists, wanted to smash it once and for all, without any comparable replacement. Still others—syndicalists and guild socialists—sought to replace the state (or reduce its size) with a workers' trade-union congress. Later Marxists, the so-called revisionists, expected to be able to act within the existing parliaments, eventually as a majority that would, by legislation, transform capitalism to socialism. Fabian socialists in England looked to the state for welfare programs and the management of a mixed capitalist-socialist economy. All these movements opposed capitalism and espoused the interests of the working classes. All, too, sought some form of political democracy and, by implication, freedom of expression for everyone. Indeed, the anarchists fought for freedom of the individual from constraints of all types; they opposed anything that infringed on individual liberty. Only the revolutionary Marxists foresaw a dictatorship of the proletariat after the revolution, which would suppress the comeback aspirations of the former ruling classes. Aside from the revolutionary Marxists, therefore, the many early socialist movements were clearly consistent with democracy and freedom of expression in pursuit of their aims.

★

TWO BASIC TYPES OF SOCIALISM

By the beginning of the twentieth century, socialism (as a theory) had assumed various forms of a revolutionary Marxian socialism, on the one hand, and various forms of a democratic socialism, on the other. Despite the many varieties, it is useful to compare model definitions of the two basic types, as they would have appeared eighty or ninety years ago.

Taking Marxian socialism first: It could be defined as a mode of production and distribution in which the working class has political power through a dictatorship of the proletariat (administered by the Communist Party); the major means of production are socially owned and managed; economic activity is largely centrally planned; a high degree of social and economic equality is sought; and international proletarianism and communism are the ultimate objectives.

The contrast is democratic socialism: a mode of production and distribution in which the working class has political power through a democratic process; the major means of production are socially owned and managed; economic activity is guided by both central planning and markets; and a high degree of social and economic equality is sought.

In comparing the two forms of socialism, we see one crucial difference: a dictatorship of the proletariat in the Marxian form and a democratic procedure for changing governments in the other. We see a similarity in that the major means of production in both models are "socially owned and managed." This indicates that industrial, commercial, and agricultural economic units may be owned by the state ("owned by all the people"), by the public in smaller political groupings, or by the workers employed in the economic units ("collectives"). In addition, the economies may contain some self-employment and private enterprise. I have listed these possibilities as socialists would rank them, from the highest to the lowest in value. There is a presumption that, in the Marxian model, the economic units would be distributed more at the upper end of this scale than they would in the democratic model. This is largely because Marxists consider socialism as a transition to a higher stage of society—communism—in which most everything is owned by all the people.

Another crucial difference is that Marxian socialism relies more heavily on central planning and less on free markets than democratic socialism does. Additionally, for the Marxian model, socialism is a transition stage between capitalism and communism, the latter being the ultimate goal. Democratic socialism does not have this final aim. Moreover, it does not attempt to support and link up revolutionary proletarian movements throughout the world in an international class struggle. The Marxian model posits armed struggle in a world of violently contending social classes; Marxism is pitted against capitalism on a worldwide scale—against the imperialist foe.

In both types of socialism, however, the working class has political power; private enterprise and self-employment have places but not prominent ones; there is at least some central planning, and a large measure of equality is desired.

Let's look more closely at two of the features of Marxian socialism that are most vulnerable to attack: the dictatorship aspect and central planning. Why is the dictatorship of the proletariat so necessary a part of Marxian socialism? Why is it so important that the Communist Party maintain a political monopoly in its representation of the working class? Marx believed that capitalism was characterized by the dictatorship of the bourgeoisie. Bourgeois democracy for him was a sham. Despite surface manifestations of real democracy for the working class—for example, being permitted to vote every few years—the bourgeoisie actually held the reins through their control over the key political positions, the bureaucracies, the military, the police, and other crucial institutions. Thus, below the misleading surface of political life, control was always exercised in the interests of the capitalist class. In the same way, there was a misleading and distorted surface to economic life. Buying and selling in markets gave the impression of economic equality, but in the sphere of production, the capitalists held the real power over the workers.

Socialism, according to Marx and his followers, would simply substitute one dictatorship for another, one political monopoly for another—in a sense, tit for tat, except that tit was a political monopoly of the majority, while tat was a political monopoly of the minority. Inasmuch as socialism would still be a class society—a transition to the classless society of communism—it was necessary for the working class to exercise such power over its enemies, at home and abroad. In the Marxian view, the dictatorship of the proletariat as exercised by the Communist Party, along with all other class institutions, would fade away as the socialist society became a communist one.

Turning now to central planning: Why has this structure, whether in its strong or weak form, so consistently been an ingredient of the socialist fare? Socialists have always looked on capitalism as being so chaotic as to subject its citizens to lives over which they have no control. Under capitalism, people are but pawns in a huge casino-like game, pushed this way and that by impersonal forces and chance, never in command of the situation, never making their own history or deciding their own fate.[1] They are continually at the mercy of unpredictable and erratic markets, of sudden changes in mass psychology,

---

[1] This seems to contradict the Marxian view of historical determinism. But history produced capitalism, and one of its chief characteristics was that workers were but pawns in a network of unpredictable markets. History made workers feel that they were objects of chance happenings.

and of shortages and surpluses that come in bewildering sequences. Planning, socialists have repeatedly said, would enable people to utilize their own personal powers to chart their course and, by so doing, to become fully human, no longer creatures shriveled and cringing before malevolent and presumably uncontrollable outside forces. Through planning, people could become dignified and worthy of the potential within them.[2]

★

A CHANGING
MARXIAN SOCIALISM

During the twentieth century, and especially after World War II, the model of democratic socialism was steadily watered down until only a pale facsimile remained. Finally, it largely disappeared. Labor and social-democratic political parties retained some socialist principles, but they became in fact welfare-capitalist parties. This was one result of the 1917 Bolshevik Revolution, which weakened many centrist movements, forcing them to choose either the capitalist or the Bolshevik side. By the 1930s, the Marxian-socialist model had triumphed over the democratic one.

But Marxian socialism itself also changed over time. The actual features of Stalin's economy became the working definition—model— of socialism among Marxists throughout the world during the 1930s and 1940s. These features included an all-powerful Communist Party existing within a huge bureaucratic structure; a central-planning system that administered most of the economy; state enterprises and collective and state farms that left little room for private endeavors; and an all-out industrialization drive, in which priority was given to industry over agriculture, to heavy over light industry, to urban areas and industrial workers over the countryside and peasants, and to ever-

---

[2]Before socialism got its start, Adam Smith, in his classic work *The Wealth of Nations* (1776), set out to demonstrate that there was indeed order in capitalism—general order out of a maelstrom of individual activities. If every person followed his or her own selfish interest, Smith said, the economy would be led as though by an invisible hand (which was, in fact, competition) to the good of the general populace. The society as a whole would gain order and derive benefit from the seemingly chaotic strivings of its citizens to gain only their own individual advantages. Socialists have never really believed this.

larger quantities of output at the expense of quality. There was also a tendency to glamorize massive projects and giant enterprises.

These pillars of socialism were not questioned until the late 1950s and early 1960s, when China under Mao Zedong took off in a different direction from the Soviets—and, it appeared at the time, successfully. The Chinese departed from the Soviets by stressing the importance of developing the rural areas with thousands of small industries and many large-scale water-control projects. They also launched massive ideological campaigns to combat bourgeois values and practices and to promote socialist ones. The rural communes established in China in the late 1950s were new socialist forms in that they were not only economic centers but political and military ones as well; they represented decentralization of decision making throughout the countryside. Furthermore, Mao and his party lauded, even more than the Soviets did, "leaps" in economic development that occurred through the mobilization of masses of peasants for communal undertakings.

Thus, by the 1960s, the definition of Marxian socialism had become more complex. A debate over the meaning of socialism took on a partisan flavor, with Chinese supporters lining up against Soviet advocates. Most Marxists probably continued to cling to the basic model of Marxian socialism that I defined earlier, or at least something close to it, but with much less certainty than before.

However, by the end of the 1970s and particularly during the 1980s, that model was seriously weakened again by a new series of events: the declining growth rate of the Soviet Union, the difficulties in China during Mao's last years, China's new directions charted by Mao's successors, the reforms proposed and undertaken in Eastern Europe, the transformation of some Western European Marxist parties toward reformist orientations (that is, Eurocommunism), and discouraging experiences with economic development in smaller Marxist countries, such as Cuba, Angola, Mozambique, Vietnam, and Ethiopia. All these events pointed to the grave problems generated by an intractable Communist Party and an overloaded central-planning system, which together dampened individual initiatives in the political and economic areas, slowing economic development to a crawl.

Consequently, some of the Marxian-socialist economies—Hungary, Vietnam, Mozambique, and China—started (under extreme pressure) to move away from their heavy reliance on central orders in running the economy, but not yet toward more democratic political processes. They provided more economic space for free markets to determine how commodities should be priced and distributed. Some gave less emphasis to large-scale state enterprises and more to smaller cooperatives and to the proliferation of shops in the service sector operated by individuals or families. In some cases, even private enterprises organized along capitalist lines were permitted.

These departures from standard Marxism suggested to many adherents of the old system that the new socialist societies might develop greater inequalities of income and wealth as those in favorable positions seized the new opportunities to enrich themselves. Moreover, with the spread of free markets and private economic activities, it seemed possible that a new capitalist or entrepreneurial class would appear, eventually to challenge not only the Communist Party in the political sphere but also the very notion that Marxian socialism was a transition stage to a classless society of the future.

Thus, the definition of Marxian-socialist society continued to change. By the late 1980s, such a society was consistent with a lessened role for central planning; various arrangements for property ownership, as long as social ownership was foremost; more tolerance for income inequalities and short-term unemployment; and less emphasis on international proletarianism and communism as the ultimate goals.

During 1989, the Marxian-socialist society throughout Eastern Europe and elsewhere, instead of continuing its adaptation to changed circumstances while maintaining its basic integrity, began to lose its very identity and to metamorphose into either a democratic-socialist society or a capitalist one. The crucial step in this disintegration was the collapse of the political monopoly held by the Communist Party. This opened the way for competition among several political parties and so for competition among social classes. Marxian socialism, which through the Bolshevik Revolution had crushed the democratic-socialist model over half a century ago, was now the vehicle for the resuscitation of that democratic form of society. There was a kind of dialectical process in all of this that might have delighted Hegel.

I began this discussion by asking if there is a standard definition of socialism by which to judge Gorbachev's contention that *perestroika* will lead to an energized form of that society. The answer, based on the long historical background of socialism, is that no country can be called socialist unless the working classes control the political institutions, a central-planning system calls at least some of the important shots, and most of the leading economic enterprises are owned and managed by workers, if only through producer cooperatives. These are the core requirements. Beyond them, we can have either Marxian or democratic varieties, each ranging from weak to strong depending on the extent of political democracy, the overall impact of central planning, the degree of equality of income and wealth, and the seriousness of the leaders toward the eventual attainment of a worldwide, classless communist system.

How can one tell when Marxian economies are moving beyond democratic socialism into capitalist waters? The sequence of events would probably be this: The economy is opened wide for private enterprise; market outcomes largely supplant central planning in determining the speed and direction of the economy; a new and increasingly influential capitalist class arises to challenge successfully the political power of the working class; income and wealth inequalities grow; and the economy begins to generate not only growth but financial crises and business cycles. If the economy is a major one, it might also behave internationally in ways to enhance the profit opportunities of its leading enterprises.

But when a Marxian economy is in transition, only partway to a democratic-socialist society, it would be difficult to tell whether it will eventually consolidate its socialist bases and opt for the new socialism, or move right on through this possibility to capitalism. Such a transitional economy might move swiftly to capitalism but then, later on, backtrack to some form of democratic socialism—or circle all the way back to Marxism. In all cases, transitional economies can find themselves at any given time betwixt and between.[3] Because there are many possible paths, it would be difficult in the early stage of a transition to

---

[3] An Argentinian economist, in characterizing his own economy, called it the worst of all possible worlds because it was "socialism without a plan, capitalism without a market." That the socialist economies, too, must watch out for this pitfall was recognized by a Soviet planner who called 1989 one of the worst years for the Soviet economy because the old system had been condemned and the new one not yet created. (*San Francisco Chronicle*, 1/10/90)

foretell the ultimate destination of a society, especially when its leaders and their spokesmen offer "clarifications."

The most confusing one was provided recently by China, where it was declared that the transformation of state-owned enterprises to privately-owned ones was a definite move toward more socialism, inasmuch as the private firms would issue stock to the public—"public issues"—and thus become "publicly owned"! Also from China, a retired general of the People's Liberation Army was reported to be complacent about the dangers of socialism turning into capitalism in his country. "There is no conflict between Marxism and capitalism," he said bluntly. "They are just two religions, like Buddhism and Christianity. What's the difference? The only thing that counts is people. People are the real force in history." When one views conflicts from sufficient heights, Buddhism could appear the same as Christianity, Marxism like capitalism. However, we may not be dealing with elevated philosophy here but, rather, with simple ignorance. The general admitted that he had never gone to school and had not read a book until he joined the army. (*New York Times*, 7/5/89)

Zany definitions of socialism have come out of the Soviet Union, too. Leonid Abalkin, a leading Soviet economist and now a deputy prime minister, recently said that any enterprise is socialist if it is profitable. (*The Economist*, 6/17/89) This was reported seriously, but if Abalkin wasn't kidding, he should have been. Even more recently, a leading Communist Party official in Cambodia was asked whether the free-market economy that the party now favored was consistent with Marxian socialism. This official smiled and said: "If people enjoy prosperity, I don't think we are deviating from Marxism." (*New York Times*, 1/8/90)

★

SOCIALISM THROUGH GORBACHEV'S EYES

Does Gorbachev have a definition of socialism? In his 1988 speech to the 19th All-Union Party Conference and in his book, *Perestroika*, the Soviet president has spoken of socialism as a mixed system of central planning and decentralized decision making.

By central planning, however, he rules out the Stalinist-type command system, in which state enterprises are told what to purchase, what to produce, and how to produce it. Instead, Gorbachev presumably wants central planning that reflects market prices and the daily decisions made "down below" within guidelines set by the planners. Further, his socialism allows both public and private ownership of property, which is consistent with most Marxists' conception of socialism, as long as the major economic activities are under social ownership. In February 1990, the Communist Party endorsed these notions of central planning and property ownership.

Many Marxists would disapprove, however, of Gorbachev's reference to "the people" as possessing political power in socialism, rather than the working class specifically. For these Marxists, the Gorbachev formulation slides too easily past the class structure that they believe continues to prevail in all socialist societies. Of even greater concern to Marxists would be his statements that socialism is "a system of true and tangible humanism"; that it is a system that "has nothing to do with equality"; and, finally, that it is a system in which strife among nations has been eliminated—a system promoting peace in the world and the right of peoples to shape their own futures. These notions would be anathema to most followers of Marx and Lenin.

"Humanism" has always suggested to a Marxist the absence of a proper class analysis of society. Such an analysis would reveal class enemies of the proletariat, which would rule out a general humanist approach. The "absence of strife among nations" and the promotion of peace in the world certainly would indicate to followers of Marx and Lenin the absence of any recognition of capitalist imperialism and of the proper striving of Third World peoples to overcome this oppression. Marxists-Leninists have always supported the "just struggles" of those oppressed by such imperialism. The notion that socialism "has nothing to do with equality" ignores, as most Marxists would see it, the fact that socialism definitely promises to eliminate property incomes and, hence, a major source of income and wealth inequalities; and it promises to eliminate the political power of a minority class (the capitalists), thereby achieving a socialist "democracy," a wider political equality—even under the dictatorship of the proletariat. Moreover, socialists have generally opposed all extreme inequalities of wealth and income, although it is true that absolute or even near equality for everyone has never been a part of Marxian socialism. Gorbachev in this regard is dangerously close to "that most metallic of names" (author Nadezhda Mandelshtam's term for Stalin) when he denounces equality.

So Gorbachev's specifications of socialism depart from the standard Marxist-Leninist definition. They are specifications that reflect a movement away from the Marxist model—toward what? Toward capitalism, or toward the more vibrant socialism that he promises?

★

AVOIDING THE TAINT
OF CAPITALISM

Gorbachev's *perestroika* promotes, among other things, self-employment and producers' cooperatives, small privately owned firms, and farmers' leaseholds, but not large-scale private enterprise organized along capitalist lines. What do these preferences and prejudices mean, and what are the reasons for them?

• In self-employment—which we can also call personal enterprise—we see a single, personal owner of a business that provides goods or services, generally the latter. The term is not inconsistent with the owner employing family members to help him or her.

• In producers' cooperatives, or collectives, the workers in the firm are both employees and owners, receiving wages and sharing the profits. The "boss" is chosen by the workers.

• A small, privately owned firm employs only a few workers, who are not supposed to be exploited by the owner, though it is not clear how the owner can avoid this.

• Farmers' leaseholds turn over state-owned land to a family on a long-term basis. The land may not be sold, but it can be inherited by the family's descendents.

• A large capitalist enterprise has an owner or owners who hire many laborers for wages. The profits go to the owners, the stockholders. The capitalist owners set the terms of employment and hire the managers, who are on wages, to supervise the workers.

Why is this last form of enterprise ruled out in Gorbachev's reforms? Because Marxists believe that, under these conditions, capitalists exploit workers, the extent of the exploitation being measured by the profits appropriated. Socialism, according to Marxists, seeks to eliminate such exploitation and, hence, cannot countenance capitalist enterprises.

The exploitation occurs because capitalists purchase labor (Marxists would say labor power) at its *exchange value* but receive its *use value*, which is higher—the difference between the two being the amount of exploitation. The exchange value of labor power is the "socially necessary labor time" required to maintain and reproduce that labor. The use value of labor is the value of commodities produced by labor, value being measured, again, as socially necessary labor time. The difference between what labor produces and what it takes (in goods and services) to (re)produce labor is "surplus value," the embodiment of exploitation. "Socially necessary labor time," which is the way Marx measured value, means that the commodity is produced under the normal conditions of production with the average degree of skill and intensity prevalent at the time. It is quantified in the number of (standard) hours embodied in the commodity.

For example, it might require twenty hours of labor to produce a hundred loaves of bread—counting four hours of labor to make good the depreciation of ovens and other equipment, another five hours of labor necessary to reproduce the raw materials used up, and eleven hours of direct labor time. But the owners can purchase labor power for the equivalent of seven hours, because that is the amount of time it takes others to produce the goods and services that will sustain the workers and their families. The surplus value, or four hours' worth of residual production kept by the the capitalists after they have paid the workers, is the measure of the capitalists' exploitation of the workers. By capitalist rules, this was not cheating, for labor power was purchased at its true value. But who wants to play by capitalist rules? Not the Soviets.

Why are cooperatives free of this capitalist taint? Although the workers in a cooperative are similarly exploited by the cooperative— by themselves!—the evil deed is canceled because the very same people receive the profits of the business. These people are both workers and owners. The cooperative does not reflect a class structure of capitalists and wage-laborers or of slave owners and slaves. Likewise, the business run by an individual or by members of a family, as a personal enterprise, is also clean in this regard.[4]

Marx's theory of exploitation, which castigates capitalist (private) enterprises, is still accepted wherever there are Marxist parties. His theory is not accepted by most economists in the capitalist world, who ask why Marx did not consider the contributions capitalists make to the production of goods and services—namely, the taking of risks, the organization and management of their firms, and the burden of saving for capital investments. Marxists contend that capitalism is inherently full of risks (depressions, overproduction, chaotic markets), just as a slave system is (runaway slaves, insurrections), but rather than paying capitalists and slaveowners for assuming these risks, it would be far better to junk the systems. Also, Marxists say, the jobs of capitalists can be performed by managers paid like all other workers; there is no justification for their claim to the profits. Marxists add that saving is no sacrifice for the wealthy (whose wealth is based on exploitation in the first place) and so deserves no special payment.

While there are other facets to this continuing argument, some suggesting the antiquated condition of Marxian economics, we need not examine them here. It is pertinent to mention, however, that Marxists now seem to be on the defensive, hard-pressed to sustain their traditional theory about exploitation, not so much from counter-theoretical thrusts, but mainly because capitalists around the world appear to be creating wealth as never before—for their own and others' benefit.[5]

---

[4]My students, for 25 years, have told me, with great glee, that people in business for themselves must, according to Marx, be exploiting themselves—as though this would refute Marx. Aside from the response that, even so, they are getting it back, the heart of the matter is that any such personal firm is not a "class" firm; it does not have capitalist and worker, except as they are combined in one person, which, if pursued, would probably get us more into Freud than into Marx. My students have also told me over the years, with the intention of justifying surplus value, that some surplus has to exist if the economy is to grow. The Marxist answer is that, while this is true, the crucial point is who owns the surplus—the capitalist or the people at large?

[5]Marxists have also become the butt of jokes about exploitation. A communist, for example, trips all over himself in explaining Marx's view to an audience: "Capitalism is a system in which man exploits man. But socialism," he boasts, "is just the opposite."

★

A CLOSER LOOK AT THE CHOICE:
CAPITALISM VS. SOCIALISM

Gorbachev would be horrified if *perestroika* led to capitalism in the Soviet Union. What do he and other Marxists have against this economic system? What do they find so attractive in socialism? Then again, what is capitalism's case against a socialist society? This question, too, is of great interest right now to Gorbachev as he tries to put some capitalist zip into the Soviet system.

In the literature of Marxian economics, we can find hundreds of charges against the "evil system" of capitalism. However, because some are similar to others, and still others are trivial, the long list can be reduced to six basic complaints.

We have already discussed the first one, namely, that capitalism is an exploitative system in which a capitalist class takes unfair advantage of the working class. This, it is claimed, results in extreme concentrations of wealth at one end and abject poverty at the other. A capitalist class, supported by state power, is alleged to control production, appropriate the workers' output, and claim a significant portion of the national income without justification. This portion is surplus value, which is divided among the capitalist-owners (as profits), the moneylenders (as interest), and the landowners (as rents).

The second charge is that capitalism is unstable. It is a system powered erratically by the private-profit motive, in which capital formation rises and falls sharply, without an overall plan. Capitalism produces booms, depressions, inflation, and unemployment, subjecting millions of people to hard and uncertain lives.

Third, advocates of socialism claim that capitalism promotes behavior unworthy of civilized human beings. It reduces human relations to the law of the competitive jungle, where everyone is both prey and predator. Such a dog-eat-dog environment encourages selfishness, cold feelings toward others, narcissistic behavior, lawlessness, and violence. These undesirable traits are not impossible to overcome, but the values of the capitalist system are so intrusive in daily life that they render efforts toward altruism largely fruitless.

In capitalist societies, people are trained to look for profitable opportunities anywhere, especially in extraordinary events such as disasters. If an earthquake devastates thousands of victims, the first question for a capitalistic person is, how can I make a killing out of that? not, how can I help the unfortunate? Forget the joy of seeing the Berlin Wall come down; instead, figure out immediately how to sell it. Waste no tears for the homeless, but calculate how to get a piece of the action as public funds are directed that way.

The fourth indictment of capitalism is that the system is warlike. Capitalism aggressively seeks profits everywhere and, if need be, defends its profit areas with force. Over the centuries, leading capitalist nations have fought innumerable wars against each other and have spread violence among peoples of underdeveloped countries. Capitalism often supports right-wing dictatorships because they support capitalism, especially investment by foreign capitalists in those underdeveloped countries. Capitalism is often more concerned with private profits than with human rights.

Fifth, socialists allege that capitalism lacks economic democracy and undermines political democracy. Within capitalist nations, economic power is highly concentrated, and this power is easily transformed into political power. It is said that political democracy is mostly a sham, for a political dictatorship—the dictatorship of the bourgeoisie—lurks in the shadows of voting booths, within the bureaucracies where the crucial decisions are made. In the same way, an economic dictatorship exists in the workplaces where exploitation occurs, even though, on the surface, democracy seems to rule and all are apparently equal as they buy and sell in the various markets.

Finally, capitalism is said to degrade work. It cheapens labor by reducing it to simple tasks. It alienates laborers from their work, lowers workers' productivity, increases absenteeism, and leads to destructive behavior. Capitalism drives workers into the only area of enjoyment left—leisure time—and so turns them into consumption-machines.

In view of the problems recently encountered by the socialist economies and their attempts to solve some of the difficulties by turning to capitalist methods, some (perhaps all) of these aged indictments are to be wondered at. Under the cover of *glasnost,* many Soviet critics of their own society have complained almost exactly along the above lines: lack of democracy, alienation of workers, a retreat from social to personal concerns, economic stagnation (if not cycles), and so on. The indictments seem to cut both ways.

Nevertheless, a great many people in the socialist and less-developed countries would likely choose socialism, with all its blemishes, over capitalism. Socialism's best case for itself is that cooperation is better than competition, planning is superior to unruly markets, equality beats inequality, stability is better than cycles, democracy in the workplace wins out over hierarchical capitalist-worker arrangements, and society—not individuals—should own the important things.

Considerations such as these account for socialism's appeal throughout much of the world during this century—and for capitalism's bad name. But the worm is turning. There has long been a capitalist case against socialism, but only in the past few decades, as socialism has floundered, has it been getting a decent reception. That case can be summarized this way:

First, socialism relies on a false conception of human nature—as selfless, altruistic, collectivist, and motivated by moral and nonmaterial incentives. Since people are not like that—and they are not sufficiently malleable to become like that in any foreseeable future—socialism is built on a shaky foundation.

Second, by stressing central planning over private markets, socialism creates huge bureaucracies that soon stifle initiative and retard economic progress. Central planning breaks down as the economy becomes more complex. Shortages of critical goods develop, shoddy merchandise is produced, and a huge black market grows up. Incentives are generally lacking in such a society.

Socialism, the third point states, not only denies individuals economic freedom (that is, the freedom to make exchanges and to own property), but also denies political and other freedoms. Freedom is indivisible: If individuals cannot own property, the state has a power base from which to encroach on all areas of a person's life.

The fourth charge is that private profit making under capitalism knows no national borders and so tends to undermine narrow nationalistic concerns. Private profit making, therefore, promotes world unity and world peace. Socialism lacks this economic motivation and tends to appeal to narrow chauvinistic feelings and superpatriotism in order to elicit from the people greater cooperation and effort in the tasks ahead.

Fifth, when capital goods and productive wealth are nationalized under socialism, no one has an interest in maintaining and improving them, so they soon deteriorate from neglect. If everyone owns productive wealth, no one owns it.

Finally, socialism creates more inequalities and privileges than capitalism does—privileges for bureaucrats and their families, for the politically favored, for the military brass. Private enterprise and competition tend to break down all privileged positions; socialism solidifies and expands them. At the other end of the spectrum, socialism tolerates much more poverty than capitalism does. There is less economic and social mobility under socialism, so the poor have fewer chances to escape their poverty.

As capitalism sees it, these are the weak spots of any socialist system and surely of Gorbachev's in particular. This is *glasnost* from the capitalist side, and Gorbachev should be all ears.

★

A LITERARY PERSPECTIVE: WHAT IS TO BE DONE?

Much of socialism is about cooperatives, poverty, and—in Marxian circles—the vanguard role of the Communist Party. This last topic pits the dictatorship of the proletariat against a more broadly based democracy, which has been a hot issue in the Soviet Union and Eastern Europe. Gorbachev, through *perestroika* and *glasnost*, is promoting cooperatives as hard as he can, claiming that his reforms will achieve acceleration of output growth and so benefit especially those at or near the bottom of the pile. He has also encouraged a fuller democracy, at first without relinquishing the monopoly position of the Communist Party, but later allowing even that to be breached.

If we listen to earlier voices on these topics, our understanding of Gorbachev's undertakings will be greatly enriched. The issues of the present day have been discussed before. Of particular interest are three works by Chernyshevsky, Tolstoy, and Lenin, all titled (more or less) "What Is to Be Done?" All three proposed solutions to Russia's economic and social problems; we can learn a great deal about socialism and Marxism through these literary perspectives.

N. G. Chernyshevsky was a radical thinker of the nineteenth century with some socialist ideas that might well contribute to Gorbachev's more vibrant society. His famous work *What Is to Be Done?* (1863) helped steer Lenin onto a revolutionary path. As a radical journalist in St. Petersburg, Chernyshevsky urged sweeping reforms of the tsarist regime and kept up this agitation until Tsar Alexander II could stand it no longer. Chernyshevsky was arrested in 1862 and imprisoned for two years before being sent eastward into 25 years of exile. While in prison, Chernyshevsky wrote his celebrated revolutionary novel, which, by some fluke, was actually published despite the author's official censure.

The story, set in St. Petersburg, focuses on a young woman and two young men who represent the coming race of "truly human people." The woman is Vera Pavlovna; the two young men, whom she marries in turn, are Dmitry Lopukhov and his friend Alexander Kirsanov.

Vera opens a successful dressmaking business, set up as a profit-sharing cooperative, that employs young girls. Later she opens a second cooperative shop, which also prospers greatly. Vera is the new, modern woman. She, not any of the men in the story, becomes the entrepreneur and provides better lives for young women within cooperative enterprises and cooperative living arrangements. She also earns a medical degree on the side, a rare accomplishment for a woman in those years. Vera wants to be free and independent so that, even in marriage, her life should continue to be her own. Vera argues that the present is the age of male brute force, to be followed by the reign of women, who are intellectually superior to men—and physically superior, too, as evidenced by their longer lives.

The cooperatives are meant to be the economic institutions of the future. Vera's firms, however, are set up at first as maternalistic private enterprises, in which the employees work for wages while Vera magnanimously distributes all the profits among the wage earners. The employees gradually begin to share in making the important decisions about expansion, investment, loan funds, and so on; they are also encouraged to experiment with various types of profit distribution, and in the end they agree to equal shares. Part of the profits are set aside as a loan fund for employees, at a zero rate of interest. (Ever since

Aristotle, Christ, and Muhammad, much of the world has considered interest to be the grossest form of exploitation. For the most part, socialist doctrine has accepted this view.) Vera's firms, moreover, establish purchasing agencies to make bulk purchases at lower costs, thereby adding to the profits. Each day someone reads enlightening literature to the young women workers, and on some nights they all go to the opera. A visitor to one of the shops is astonished by its cleanliness, efficiency, and profit-sharing features. The women workers get along nicely at work, and they live near the establishment under excellent, cooperative conditions. "The general progress of the association was gay and prosperous," the author tells us.

Dmitry and Alexander, the two young men in the story, are notable for their rational approach to life's twists and turns. Both are medical students when we first meet them, but Dmitry drops his studies to earn a living as a factory accountant. When his wife (Vera) falls in love with his friend, Dmitry feigns suicide to clear the way for Vera's continued happiness.

There is another young man that we cannot overlook. This is Rakhmetov, who comes into the story halfway through and stays for only a short time. Nevertheless, he is clearly the "superman" of the plot. He is in his early twenties, physically powerful and uncommonly intelligent. He has, with serious resolve, done heavy physical labor to build his strength and has limited his diet to virtually nothing but raw beef. He touches no wine and stays away from women. His only vice is smoking cigars—which, he argues, are necessary to quicken his thought processes. An avid reader until the age of 22, he then reasoned that he knew enough, and his reading thereafter is slight. He makes friends only with learned and powerful people and does not bother to talk to the hoi polloi. He always says exactly what he thinks, however offensive it might seem to his conversants. The author informs us: "Great is the mass of good and honest men, but Rakhmetovs are rare. They are the best among the best, they are the movers of the movers, they are the salt of the salt of the earth." (In fact, Rakhmetov is so superior and so self-assured that to many readers he is undoubtedly insufferable. Moreover, as the new socialist man, Rakhmetov's unwillingness to talk to the common people is enough to make one wish for still another generation beyond him.)

Vera sees Rakhmetov as standing above everyone else. As she says to her second husband: "The Rakhmetovs are another sort of people: they are so much concerned about the common welfare that to work for public ends is a necessity to them, so much so that to them altruistic life takes the place of private life. But we do not scale these high summits, we are not Rakhmetovs, and our private life is the only thing, properly speaking, that is indispensable to us."

In the author's eyes, Vera, Dmitry, and Alexander are superior people of the new generation, but still they are egoists, always using reason to work out what is best for themselves. Rakhmetov, on the other hand, transcends that state and is to be considered the future socialist man, at all times thinking first of others. But, as the author tells us, he is neither a principal nor a secondary character in the novel, and almost before he has a chance to do anything, he disappears for good. Why, then, does Chernyshevsky introduce him? For artistic reasons, he reveals. He wants his readers to understand that the three main characters, while they are certainly superior to the masses of people, are nevertheless within reach of the ordinary person. But Rakhmetov is something else again: He is the future toward which we should all be striving. In some far-off day, we shall all be like him. But, in the shorter run, we can rise to the level of Vera or Alexander or Dmitry if we have the desire to work for our intellectual and moral development. "Come up from your caves, my friends, ascend! . . . Observe, think, read those who tell you of the pure enjoyment of life, of the possible goodness and happiness of man. . . . Sacrifices are unnecessary, privations are unnecessary, unnecessary. Desire to be happy: this desire, this desire alone, is indispensable. With this end in view you will work with pleasure for your development, for there lies happiness." Reason and rational desire to do what is best for ourselves will lead to this bliss. In the era beyond that lies a superior, altruistic society in which, out of need, people will work for the general welfare.

Another woman in the story demonstrates Chernyshevsky's belief that cooperatives rather than charity offer the best solution to helping the working poor. This woman is Katerina, the daughter of a ruined capitalist merchant. Near the close of the novel, Katerina wonders why a few fortunate people are so wealthy while so many others have virtually nothing. She has used part of her allowance to help the poor, but is dismayed by how little good these alms did and by the baseness and deceit of many of the poor. When her father lost most of his wealth, she was relieved, in a way, because fewer people crowded around her for handouts. When Katerina learns that Vera has been able to alleviate poverty through her cooperatives, she visits one of the shops and within a short time has organized her own cooperative. Previously she had been frustrated by lack of opportunities and bored almost to death, complaining that "A young girl is so hampered in every direction . . . It is society that thwarts me." But at last, she finds satisfaction as an entrepreneur in the cooperative movement.

So far as poverty and exploitation are concerned, what then is to be done? The answer is to organize profit-sharing cooperatives and encourage everyone to rise to a new level, to shed their evil ways, and to work their way out of poverty. Do not get trapped in almsgiving, for down that road is a dead end. Bring reason and self-interest to bear on the problem, and it will be solved.

Chernyshevsky's socialism, in this novel, relies not only on new people whose behavior transcends and puts to shame our own, but also on the replacement of profit-making institutions by cooperatives, the elimination of poverty and exploitation, and the effacement of all discrimination against woman. These are the answers to the question posed by the novel's title. But all of the implied ills of society can be overcome only if the wicked come to realize that it is in their own self-interest to be good. "They were wicked," the author preaches, "simply because it was disadvantageous to them to be good, but they know, however, that good is better than evil, and they will prefer the good as soon as they can love it without injury to their own interests." Reason will lead to the creation of new conditions that will ensure that self-interest will embrace good rather than evil.

★

THE IMPLICATIONS
FOR SOCIALISM

hat messages might Gorbachev find in Chernyshevsky's answers to "What is to be done?" Certainly, Gorbachev would look positively on his advocacy of cooperatives in the new society. He might also take a lesson from the attitudes of Chernyshevsky's revolutionary "new people." Recall that this author's good society featured people who reasoned rationally, practiced sexual equality, and established workers' cooperatives that eliminated poverty and exploitation. Chernyshevsky saw the attainment of socialism in two stages, the first encouraging rational, egoistic behavior and the second embracing altruistic concerns. Above all, his emphasis was on the "new people" who would eventually arise as the old society was transcended. They would eat and exercise sensibly, live virtuous lives, enjoy high culture, and work for the social welfare. By implication, the spread of workers' cooperatives could aid in this human transformation, though the author seems to suggest that the lofty heights would be achieved mainly by willpower, by the desire and resolve of everyone to attain the better life.

In painting this scenario, Chernyshevsky brushed up against a very real problem more than a century before it appeared so starkly in present-day socialist societies. The Chinese are a good illustration of the problem: For the past decade, the Chinese regime has encouraged people to enrich themselves, to work for their own welfare and enjoyment. The communal life has been diminished; private lives have taken over. This has led to selfish behavior, widespread corrupt practices, and glaring income inequalities. Inasmuch as Marxists continue to define socialism partly in terms of cooperative attitudes—or as Mao Zedong expressed it, "serving the people"—a serious problem arises. If socialism can be attained only through rapid economic development, and if such development requires the type of behavior now promoted by the Chinese, how then can people ever be changed into less selfish, less greedy human beings? The Soviets have this problem to encounter just ahead. Chernyshevsky's new people—Vera, Alexander, and Dmitry—followed their own interests, too, but at a later stage a race of selfless Rakhmetovs was expected to appear—perhaps helped along by the beneficial influence of increasing numbers of cooperatives.

If we interpret Chernyshevsky in this way, cooperatives would play a key role in the drive of a society to full socialism. In Marxist thought, too, workers' cooperatives are definitely socialist institutions, superior to privately owned firms. In an impassioned article that

Gorbachev and his associates have pointed to many times, Lenin touted cooperatives not as the final solution but as a necessary first step. Further along the socialist road we would find enterprises owned not just by their workers, but by all the people of a local community. Beyond these would be firms owned by all the people of the nation—state enterprises in the fullest sense. Thus, from a Marxist perspective, Chernyshevsky's model economy represents only one step toward full socialism, but it is in the right direction.

For Gorbachev and his colleagues, the promotion of cooperatives and personal enterprises is intended to fill empty economic spaces—which are found, so to speak, between every pair of giant firms—with thousands and thousands of small businesses. Needed in particular are services and more services. Compared to the United States and Western European countries, the Soviet Union's services sector is a disaster area. For Chernyshevsky, small cooperatives were a step forward. For Gorbachev they are, in a sense, a step backward, for they represent a lower form of socialist enterprise, and some already established state enterprises are slated to become collectives. Lenin once wrote an article titled "One Step Forward, Two Steps Back." Gorbachev's *perestroika* policies toward cooperatives and personal enterprises would have to be seen as "One Step Back, Two Steps Forward" because, if socialism is to flower later on, the economy must fall back on these smaller enterprises to accelerate development right now.

★

A RELIGIOUS RESPONSE TO POVERTY

Leo Tolstoy, writing some twenty years after Chernyshevsky, observes similar economic problems but envisions a different road to a better society. Like Chernyshevsky, Tolstoy was persuaded that philanthropic gestures to the poor were worthless. In his book *What Then Must We Do?* (1886)—which is often given the same English title as Chernyshevsky's novel—Tolstoy recounts the time he spent among the poor of Moscow's slums. His intention was to aid them with his and other people's money and, in this way, gradually reduce their poverty and misery.

But Tolstoy found that, no matter how much money he gave or the circumstances under which he gave it, no one was helped, no one gained either work or happiness. "Such people needed to be relieved," he wrote, "not by my charity, but of their own false views of the world. . . . I did not see that in order to help them it was not necessary to give them food, but to teach them how to eat." Their misery, he thought, was within themselves, "a misery not to be mended by any kind of banknote." Among the poor, he found much drunkenness, insincerity, falseness, callousness, and depravity.

Tolstoy concluded that the failure of the project was partly his own fault. "To change a man's estimate of life, he must be given one more accurate than his own, which unhappily, not possessing myself, I could not communicate to others." He was living a life, he thought, that prevented him from understanding many of the poor's problems and their outlook. He realized that he had to reform his own mode of living before he could have any conception of how to reform the lives of others. "And so I became aware that the cause of the impossibility for us rich men to help the town poor was nothing more or less than the impossibility of our having closer intercourse with them, and that this we ourselves create by our whole life, and by all the uses we make of our wealth." In order to help, he would have to break the barriers that impeded communication between the rich and poor.

Why are the poor so poor? Tolstoy concluded that all wealth is produced in the countryside. Much of it is drained away by city people, mostly a non-working group, and it is spent ostentatiously. The cities themselves produce no wealth, but they consume much of it. The rural poor—made poor by this drain—make their way into the cities, lured by the sparkle and glitter, and become the city poor. Thus, the city non-workers first plunder the rural workers and then tempt them into the hovels of the city slums. The city non-workers are able to exploit the rural wealth-creators by their possession of money. "Money," Tolstoy warns, "is a means of violence . . . it is the most convenient means of holding in slavery the majority of mankind." Among the city non-workers are government officials, artists, scientists, educators, composers, and entrepreneurs who simply reap the harvests produced elsewhere. All live on the real labor of others, through the extraction of their wealth in the form of profits, rents, and taxes.

Of course, Tolstoy realizes that every civilized society needs the division of labor that frees some people from the real work of the world and allows them to be artists and scientists. These city people have produced many wonderful things. What is wrong with that? What is wrong is that the working people are so impoverished, through their enforced support of these non-workers, that they are not able to enjoy the artistic or inventive products. Scientists, artists, educators, officials—all of the urban predators—are divorced from the people. They serve only the rich, producing things that the poor cannot use. They should live among the workers and try to provide what the real people actually need, for what they now offer, the poor could easily do without. Not only must the urban elite give up their extravagant ways, but they must suffer to provide for the people. "Thinkers and artists," Tolstoy intones, "cannot be sleek, fat men, enjoying themselves, and self-conceited. . . . To teach how many insects there are in the world, and observe the spots on the sun, to write novels and operas, can be done without suffering; but to teach men their welfare, which entirely consists in self-denial, and in serving others, and to express powerfully this teaching, cannot be done without self-denial." Tolstoy's "self-denial" is two-pronged. First, the rich do not need anywhere near as much as they now consume. Those who really desire to live virtuously should greatly reduce these superfluous expenditures. Second, the rich should divest themselves of private property. True property is our own body; our other possessions—land, money, horses, and so on—are imaginary property. These possessions—private property—are the root of all evil; they are the means of using other people's labor. According to Tolstoy, the rich require only a few worthy examples of such self-denial by other people, plus their own willpower, to make the transformation from a shameful to an honorable life. Once they have reduced their needs and stripped themselves of property, they will no longer force others to work for them, no longer exploit and impoverish the real workers. They will have to provide for their food, clothing, and other basic needs through their own physical labor. This means, in a sense, suffering—which is essential if the poor are to be helped—but physical labor also leads to physical, mental, and spiritual well-being, and it permits effective communication between the rich and the poor. It is not shameful, Tolstoy says, to be unable to speak French or not to have read the latest novel. But "it is shameful to eat bread and not to know how it is prepared." It is doubly shameful not to prepare it ourselves.

The answer to the book's title, therefore, is this self-denial; the answer is also "suffering," as Christ suffered. At bottom, Tolstoy's answer is from the Bible, which he quotes many times throughout this book. His answer is to follow the path of Christ: Give up worldly possessions and work for the poor, for the equality and unity of all peoples.

Tolstoy's views on the role of women in the good society are in sharp contrast to Chernyshevsky's advanced thoughts on the subject. Tolstoy believed that the proper role of women, like that of men, is to engage in physical labor. For most women, however, this means bearing and rearing children—and proudly, not reluctantly. "If you are such [a woman]," Tolstoy instructs, "you will not say, after two or after twenty children, that you have borne children enough . . . because in that work you put your life, and because, the more you have of that work, the fuller and happier is your life." But those women are lost who avoid giving birth, who think of nothing but dressing up to enchant men, who attend lectures, who work alongside men in business, who do intellectual work, and who demand women's rights. (Happy indeed must have been Tolstoy's wife Sophia, who gave birth to thirteen children!)

These views on women, if Tolstoy could express them today, would elicit demonstrations and ridicule in many quarters, to mention only the mildest responses. But his notions of economics would also draw fire from all quarters. No economist today would support Tolstoy's basic theory that wealth is created only in the countryside, and that urbanites (government and church workers, artists, scientists, educators, military personnel, business people, and others) only appropriate the wealth of others. Even in Tolstoy's time, such a notion was decades out of date in Western Europe, after having been expressed by the French physiocrats in the second half of the eighteenth century and successfully attacked a short time later. Today, we would say that all current output of good and services with prices above zero, whether produced in agriculture, industry, or the services sector, contribute to the gross national product; and that the net value of those goods not consumed, such as new factories and machinery, add to the national wealth.

Nevertheless, Tolstoy had a good point—namely, that so much of the wealth produced in the countryside was siphoned off to the cities that the rural population was left relatively miserable; and that much of the wealth flowing to the cities was enjoyed by people who, in fact, did not work but rather collected "tribute" on their landholdings and other lucrative assets. In this sense, the cities exploited the countryside. However, as Marx had already declared before Tolstoy wrote *What Then Must We Do?*, the real exploiters in modern societies were capitalists who exploited not so much peasants as industrial workers. Whether or not this was entirely true, Marx had correctly identified the two new classes in modern industrial societies—the capitalists and the proletariat. Thus, in focusing on peasants and urbanites, Tolstoy was several decades behind contemporary economic analysis—which may be understandable, inasmuch as the Russian economy lagged that far behind Western Europe.

★

TOLSTOY'S LESSON
FOR GORBACHEV

I f Gorbachev were to review Tolstoy's *What Then Must We Do?*, at first glance there would seem to be very little that a modern Marxist could learn. Indeed, wouldn't a Marxist be repelled by Tolstoy's fervent faith in Christ and by his backward views of women? Still, Tolstoy was the champion of the poor peasants, and he believed that the most important economic problem of his time was how the wealthy could help these poverty-stricken souls, whether living in the countryside or as refugees in the cities. We might think that any Marxist would be of like mind, but that certainly was not true of Stalin. This dictator directed a forced-march industrialization drive that largely bypassed the peasantry—or worse, exploited them for the benefit of industry, cities, bureaucracies, and the military. When Stalin was finally finished with them, the peasants were left about where their grandparents had been.

Abel Aganbegyan, one of Gorbachev's economic advisors, related recently an experience of his in 1953, the year of Stalin's death:

> I recall that when I married in 1953 and temporarily worked in
> a textile factory in the small town of Sobinka in Vladimir
> Region, I decided to call on my wife's relatives in the village of
> Zhokhovo in the same region. This village was situated 80 km
> from the railway and there was absolutely no means of trans-
> port available to it. In actual fact there was no road in our
> understanding of the term either. There was a cart-track im-
> passable in autumn and spring and covered with snow in the
> winter. I walked almost 20 km on foot. Zhokhovo, which is
> situated 150 km from Moscow, did not at this time have
> electricity. The economy was predominantly based on ex-
> change of goods in kind and on self-sufficient consumption,
> with the shop open only twice a week and in a neighboring
> village at that. In this shop, there was virtually nothing besides
> sugar and salt, so that in the village the people baked their own
> bread, drank their own milk and ate their own eggs etc. all
> produced on their family plots. . . . The collective farm workers
> had no guaranteed income, no pension and no sickness benefit.
> Their lives depended mainly on their family plots."

Aganbegyan notes that the situation was similar in many other parts of
the country, where electricity, running water, and central heating were
unheard of, although "in the wealthier regions of the Caucasus, Kuban,
the Ukraine, Uzbekistan and the Baltic, the level of development of
agriculture and of the villages themselves was much higher."

The lot of the peasants improved considerably after Stalin's death,
but even as late as 1985, when Gorbachev came to power, they were still
second-class comrades. Tolstoy would be dispirited, if he returned
today, to find that rural life is still relegated to the back burners and that
many retired people, especially in the large cities, are living below the
poverty level. In his search for a more vibrant socialism, Gorbachev can
heed Tolstoy, observe China's success in improving living standards in
the countryside, and draw upon his own rich experiences with agricultural and poverty problems. He must know that *perestroika* will not be
a success unless it can overcome the country's food problems, and this

requires Tolstoyan concern about the lives of the people who grow the food.

An allied worry of Tolstoy focused on the great disparities of income and wealth in the population. The rich, in his judgment, were much too rich, and the poor too poor. The Bolshevik Revolution corrected some of the sources of income disparity by largely eliminating private ownership of capital goods and land—and, therefore, private profits, interest, and rents as income to the wealthy. But Stalin later created new inequalities that persisted up to the middle of the 1960s. After that, many measures were enacted to alleviate these injustices. However, when market determination of prices and output becomes more widespread under *perestroika*—along with more monetary incentives to workers and managers, opportunities for profitable family farming, and a larger scope for personal and cooperative enterprises—then income differences could widen once again. While there would be no return to the disparities of Tolstoy's day, his warning cries are still worth heeding.

Gorbachev would certainly agree with both Chernyshevsky and Tolstoy about the futility of trying to solve poverty through "handouts." The poor, whether in Central Asia or in the largest cities, will have to be helped principally by the more dynamic economy produced by the reforms—the higher paying jobs, the increased supplies of essential items, the improved health and education programs, and the like. *Perestroika* is not out to achieve better lives mainly through more generous transfer payments or more philanthropy from the richer to the poorer comrades, even though struggling pensioners will need special help.

Noting Tolstoy's concern that an urban elite lived off the earnings of the real workers on the land, Gorbachev could be excused for thinking of the tens of thousands of modern-day urban bureaucrats who, producing no wealth themselves—indeed, even obstructing its creation—nevertheless appropriate much of what others produce. It is not hard to imagine Gorbachev pondering this social relation as a Soviet form of exploitation—a drain of surplus value, not to Marx's Mr. Moneybags, but to Comrade Memo-maker.

What about the issue of women's role in a better society, treated so differently by Chernyshevsky and Tolstoy? It is unclear whether *perestroika* is going to make a dent in the male-dominated Soviet society, or even whether it intends to. Gorbachev's own views are not entirely reassuring, for he has spoken of women as "keepers of the home fires" and apparently regrets that family ties have been weakened by women working outside the home. Nevertheless, as part of *perestroika*, Gorbachev has promised reforms that would ease the double burden placed on Soviet women. Chernyshevsky's views—but not Tolstoy's—might be useful as these reforms evolve.

★

LENIN'S REVOLUTIONARY ROAD TO SOCIALISM

To achieve a better society in the near future, Chernyshevsky appealed to reason, willpower, and self-interest. Tolstoy saw the solution in a religious response by the rich to the poverty around them. Vladimir Ilyich Lenin advanced yet another answer: a strong Communist Party and revolution.

In his *What Is to Be Done?* (a deliberate copy of Chernyshevsky's title), published in 1902 when he was 32 and had already suffered a Siberian exile, Lenin brought a Marxist approach to Russia's economic problems with a plan to overthrow the oppressive regime of Tsar Nicholas II. Marxism, as we have seen, is based on an analysis of the economy of a country, its associated class structure, and its necessarily linked social and political institutions. Lenin's task was to take the Marxism that had developed in Western Europe's more advanced economies and apply it to the more backward Russian one, where industry was less advanced and the urban working force (the proletariat) was, as a consequence, much less important than the peasantry. In Marxist theory, a large and highly conscious proletariat would overthrow the capitalists when a mature capitalist system had developed barriers to and brakes on its further growth. While Lenin's Russia had none of these requisites for revolution, it did have a small but fast-growing proletariat and an industrial base, an oppressed peasantry, and many grievances and much discontent among the population. Lenin had to bring these elements together to produce an explosion.

In *What Is to Be Done?*, Lenin first established the point that in all countries, not just in Russia, the urban working class develops only trade-union demands—more wages, better working conditions, shorter hours—and is not independently able to see revolutionary socialism as the ultimate solution to its problems. The theory and practice of socialism, on the other hand, were the products of certain representatives of the bourgeois intelligentsia. As Lenin put it: "The history of all countries shows that the working class, exclusively by its own effort, is able to develop only trade-union consciousness. . . . The theory of socialism, however, grew out of the philosophic, historical, and economic theories elaborated by educated representatives of the propertied classes, by intellectuals. By their social status, the founders of modern scientific socialism, Marx and Engels, themselves belonged to the bourgeois intelligentsia." Lenin applauded and quoted the German Marxist, Karl Kautsky, who argued that "modern socialist consciousness can arise only on the basis of profound scientific knowledge. Indeed, modern economic science is as much a condition for socialist production as, say, modern technology, and the proletariat can create neither the one nor the other . . . both arise out of the modern social process. The vehicle of science is not the proletariat but the *bourgeois intelligentsia* [Kautsky's emphasis]."

Therefore, Lenin reasoned, the knowledge of socialism has to be introduced into the ranks of workers from without—not, however, by isolated intellectuals but by a vanguard party of Marxist revolutionaries, which includes representatives of the bourgeois intelligentsia and educated members of the working class. The party seeks contact with the workers, supporting their immediate demands on wages and working conditions, but at the same time educating them to look beyond these shop issues to a more fundamental solution to their problems and grievances—to socialism. The economic development process that produces industry, industrial workers, and trade unions also produces sensitive bourgeois intellectuals who give birth to socialist theory and associate themselves with workers' struggles. The historical process creates both the problems and the solutions.[6]

---

[6]During 1989 and 1990 in Eastern Europe, intellectuals, artists, and writers—ironically—were in the vanguard of the exodus from Marxism and Leninism. They assumed leading positions in interim opposition groups, in new governments, and in diplomacy. Lenin would probably not have wanted to know how correct he was.

The vanguard party in Russia, Lenin proclaimed, cannot be as loose an organization as it is in Western Europe. In Russia, because of an oppressive autocracy and the tsarist secret police, the party must be composed of dedicated professionals operating in a secretive, tightly-knit organization. If it were more open, it would quickly be broken up by police agents; if it were less professional, mistakes would lead to its demise; if it were widely democratic, it could not operate as a single, cohesive unit. Lenin pointed to the type of person who would not be suitable for the party: "A person who is flabby and shaky on questions of theory, who has a narrow outlook, who pleads the spontaneity of the masses as an excuse for his own sluggishness, who resembles a trade-union secretary more than a spokesman of the people, who is unable to conceive of a broad and bold plan that would command respect even of opponents, and who is inexperienced and clumsy in his own professional art—the art of combating the political police—such a man is not a revolutionary, but a wretched amateur!" Lenin then went on to say that he himself was once such an amateur and suffered burning shame when he later thought of his feeble and untimely efforts.

While the party must be carefully closed, trade-union organizations should be wide open and as public as conditions will allow. The workers must be taught by the party, in the course of their struggles for immediate ends, about oppression throughout all of tsarist society, not just in the economic area, and about the theory and practice of social-ism. The workers must be given an integrated view of present society if they are to understand deeply why and how they are being exploited. They should be trained to respond to all forms of tyranny, no matter which class is involved. Marxists, Lenin said, cannot do their socialist work if they limit themselves to the workers' immediate concerns.

All this advice from Lenin was for the purpose of eventually forming a revolutionary movement against the tsar. As Lenin stated a few years later, this movement would initially be composed of the workers, the peasants, and part of the rural and urban petty bourgeoi-sie (i.e., small landowners and shopkeepers)—or of "the people." This phase of the revolution would achieve democratic, not socialist, aims and would be led by "the revolutionary-democratic dictatorship of the proletariat and the peasantry." In the next phase, socialist aims would be attained by the proletariat and the poorest and most radical peasants. Thus, a successful revolution against the tsarist regime would come in two stages. And it all came true, in Lenin's eyes, when the February 1917 Revolution, which deposed the tsar under the banner of democracy, was followed by the Bolshevik Revolution in October of the same year. That the first phase was terribly brief and not entirely to Lenin's specifications need worry only the fastidious.

★

THE REVOLUTION
THAT IS PERESTROIKA

As Gorbachev strives to rejuvenate the Soviet economy, how closely is he aligned with Lenin's ideas? Clearly he would mostly agree with Lenin's implicit thesis that a successful reconstruction of society requires a revolution, a sweeping away of all the principal impediments to further development, including conservative diehards in positions of power, and their replacement with new institutions, new ways of doing things, and new leaders. Gorbachev, of course, is not attempting to overthrow the social class that presumably has the political power; he is not pressing revolution to the extent that Lenin did. But the economic and political systems that he is trying to achieve are so far removed from those under Stalin that he would seem to be justified in his rhetoric of revolution.

Gorbachev knows by heart another of Lenin's points in *What Is to Be Done?*, namely, that socialist theory emanates from the vanguard party—in this case, Gorbachev would add, from socialist intellectuals—and must be injected into the ranks of the working class. Thus, the Communist Party led the way, as Gorbachev has explained on several occasions, in formulating *perestroika* as a new stage in socialism's progress. The general secretary has been quick to note that, while the outlines of the new policies were produced "from above," they reflected what the people wanted—although their desires were probably vague and unformed.

Lenin and Gorbachev would likely agree that advanced socialist theory will arise from intellectuals and not from the working class. Even so, Gorbachev and his group have made perfectly clear that the reforms cannot be effective unless the broad masses participate in the refined formulation and implementation of them. That is, democracy and *glasnost* are absolutely essential to the success of *perestroika*, even though the general outlines of these reforms came originally from the intelligentsia, as Lenin predicted. Moreover, Gorbachev's call for more democracy is not really consistent with Lenin's view of a tight-knit Communist Party. That Party, as everyone knows, eventually usurped all power, and even though it purported to act in the interest of the working class, it effectively told that class what to do and what to think. Lenin's and Stalin's Party was as far from democracy (in Gorbachev's present use of the word) as Siberia is from Moscow. In this respect, Gorbachev has departed from Lenin, though so far he has not advertised it. Moreover, Gorbachev's "democracy," while still not fully the Western concept, has been moving closer to it, pushed by the hammer blows from Eastern Europe.

★

GORBACHEV'S PROMISE: THE PROGNOSIS

Шe began this chapter by asking if Gorbachev's program of *perestroika* is leading to the more vibrant and progressive socialism that he has promised. Through a brief review of the changing nature of socialist thought over its history, we have seen that Gorbachev is departing in several significant ways from classical Marxian socialism. Yet he clearly adheres to its ideals at the same time that he struggles to overcome some of its inherent weaknesses.

On the issues reflected in the literature: We have seen that Gorbachev promotes workers cooperatives as a means to accelerate the economy, as suggested by Chernyshevsky; he acknowledges the critical importance of improving the lot of the peasantry and the urban poor, as did Tolstoy; and he casts his program of reconstruction in the language of revolution, echoing the principles of Lenin.

There is little evidence in all this that *perestroika* and *glasnost* run along a single road leading to capitalism. It is possible that, if successful, they will do what Gorbachev keeps saying they will do—achieve a more vibrant socialism. Socialism is entirely consistent with markets. As long as the major means of production are socially owned in one form or another; as long as central planning retains an important role; and as long as the working class, through the reforms, regains the political power it once had, then so much the better for socialism. On all of this, however, we will be in a better position to assess Gorbachev's chances later in the book.

"ONE IN THE FIELD, SEVEN IN THE BACKGROUND. HOW MUCH LONGER?"

BREAKING THE
STRANGLEHOLD
OF BUREAUCRACIES

Mikhail Gorbachev has been much frustrated by bureaucratic delays in carrying out the Party's reform programs. He has been keen to shrink the bureaucracies, to reduce the power at the top and decentralize it to lower units; he has wanted more democracy throughout the society.

The bureaucratic problem is an old one in Russia. If we go back seventy years to the first years of Communist rule, we find Lenin exclaiming: "Everyone in our country is bogged down in the cursed bureaucratic morass of departments. Considerable prestige, intellect, and vigor are needed to combat them daily. Departments are shit, decrees are shit." (*The New Yorker*, 3/28/88) Gorbachev has probably not addressed the problem so profanely, but very likely he feels the same or even stronger, because since Lenin's day bureaucracies have multiplied manyfold. They are another of Stalin's legacies.

In fact, Russia has had a serious bureaucratic problem for longer than that—since long before the Bolsheviks overthrew the liberals who had ousted Nicholas II and his court. In Russian literature of the nineteenth century, the bureaucratic morass is pictured in bold relief. Sometimes we find the "little citizen" pitted against uncaring bureaucrats or against the massive, impersonal state; other times, we see corrupt officials running departments bogged down with inertia and stifling formalities. Such literary attacks have continued, right into the present century and, in fact, to the present day.

★

WHY WERE BUREAUCRATS EVER INVENTED?

One would hope that bureaucrats exist in such numbers because they serve a good purpose. Let's pause for a moment to consider that happy expectation.

A bureaucracy is a group of people whose role is to make decisions for a larger group. It always involves an elaborate hierarchy of functions and responsibilities, with each bureaucrat specializing in a particular narrow province. A bureaucracy generally adheres to a rigid system of rules so that problems can be handled expeditiously by the proper officials.

At its best, a bureaucracy operates in the interest of the people it serves and, by specializing in decision making, saves its constituents time and effort. If every individual had to participate in the making of every decision, the welfare of the whole group would certainly decline. A bureaucracy, therefore, is meant to raise the efficiency of any group of people and thereby contribute to their greater well-being.

Bureaucracies, unfortunately, often develop undesirable characteristics—some argue that these tendencies are inevitable. A bureaucracy tends to look increasingly to its own interests and to resist new developments that threaten its security and privileges. It tends to be risk-averse, unimaginative, complacent, and self-serving. It is often beholden to the past and not forward-looking. Moreover, it tends to become bloated because its clout and self-esteem increase as its members grow. At its worst, a bureaucracy works almost entirely in its own interests, reduces the well-being of the larger group, and ends up corrupt and downright oppressive. This presumably is the sort of bureaucracy that Lenin cursed out.

THE DISTINCT NATURE
OF SOVIET BUREAUCRACIES

E very country has bureaucracies. Indeed, in the broadest sense, they are pervasive in every society, because specialization in decision making is as advantageous for families, business enterprises, and the military as it is for government organizations.

The Soviet Union, however, has distinctive (though not unique) problems with its bureaucracies. First, at the national level, the Soviets have a double dose of bureaucrats—both party and state functionaries. While all countries have governmental bodies run by civil servants and political appointees, the communist countries also have Communist Party units that duplicate most of the state agencies and that are managed by members of the Party. In the Soviet Union, the Party makes policies while the state carries them out, because the Party is the vanguard of the dominant class in that society—the proletariat—while the state is simply one among many institutions that reflect the continuing class structure of Soviet society. In Marxist theory the party, not the state, leads the proletariat to victory; the party, not the state, is leading the proletariat through socialism to communism—through a final class society to a classless one.

Soviet bureaucracies are also distinctive because they must be large enough to operate a centrally planned economy. In all countries, prices and quantities of goods and services have to be determined somehow. In most countries, these numbers are largely determined by thousands or millions of individuals and enterprises in their roles as suppliers and consumers in markets for these goods and services. The markets may be in wholesale establishments, retail shops, financial arenas, supermarkets, showrooms, and telephone networks. In a decentralized system, suppliers and consumers freely operate through these markets, guided by the personal advantages to be gained or lost. But in centrally planned economies, like the Soviet Union's, many of the decisions about prices and quantities are made by central planners. These planners are located in a variety of different institutions: planning bureaus, ministries, price-setting agencies, material-supply committees, and state committees in charge of such spheres as labor compensation and quality of products. Moreover, most of the planning bodies in the Soviet Union not only exist at the national level but are replicated in the fifteen republics and, again, in the lower political units. Thus, the central planning of prices and quantities of tens of thousands of goods and services—out of tens of millions—requires millions of Soviet bureaucrats.

Although the Soviet planning system has been altered from time to time, it consists essentially of the following agencies, listed from top to bottom: the Politbureau of the Communist Party, which makes the key decisions; a central planning agency that designs annual and five-year plans; dozens of economic ministries that control agriculture, industry, and other economic activities; departments within each ministry that specialize in certain commodities; other planning agencies, such as statistical bureaus, quality-control committees, price-setting bodies, and a central bank; and, finally, the managers of agricultural state and collective farms and of the industrial and other enterprises.

When prices and quantities are mostly determined in markets by individual suppliers and consumers, many fewer bureaucrat-planners are required. However, decentralized markets for goods and services are run efficiently only if they are supported by a multitude of financial institutions, such as commercial banks, savings banks, investment banks, stock and bond markets, and foreign exchange facilities. Some of these are not needed at all in centrally planned economies, and none is needed in the profusion that we see in capitalist societies. When decision makers are spread among millions of families, business enterprises, and government units, coordination among them is achieved by a panoply of financial instruments, financial institutions, and financial markets. When, on the other hand, decision making is concentrated at the top, efficiency is achieved by a profusion of specialized planning agencies.

Thus, in the Soviet Union, we find tens of millions of central planners and very few bankers, brokers and dealers in stocks and bonds, or financial analysts. In the United States, on the other hand, there are tens of millions of financial experts of all types and relatively few central planners.

In the United States, many of the citizens' needs are met in impersonal markets, where things can be bought and sold without buyers and sellers having to confront one another in highly personal ways. In the USSR, on the other hand, these problems must generally be resolved by an individual's obtaining the OK of one or more officials, which entails face-to-face confrontations, anxieties, and sometimes acrimonious exchanges. To Soviet citizens, bureaucracies seem even more copious than they actually are, and a headache to deal with. Moreover, when a bureaucracy is particularly top-heavy in decision-making power, citizens have to start at the powerless bottom and wait out the flow of memos upward and then back downward—which of course adds to the pain.

A third distinctive feature of Soviet bureaucracies is that they extend so deeply into the personal and working lives of the people. Elaborate bureaucratic structures have been erected for the surveillance and control of people in their conversations, their writings and readings, their social lives, and their pleasures. On the job, people are subject not only to the hierarchical structure of the enterprise, but also to the bureaucracy of trade unions and the Party itself, which always has a presence at the plant. A vast network of labor camps and prisons—though less extensive now than in the past—awaits both criminal and political offenders; this network is itself a huge bureaucracy that every inmate has to adapt to. Additionally, there are government bodies to check up on corruption, thefts of state property, waste, embezzlement, bribery, speculation, and whatnot. Ordinary consumers, facing constant and widespread shortages of goods, find themselves in confrontation with clerks in state-run shops much more often than consumers in societies where prices, not surly clerks, are the "antagonists." All this is bound to give the Soviet citizen the impression, mostly correct, that bureaucracies are simply everywhere—in every walk of life, in every corner of the land.

Another distinctive feature of Soviet bureaucracies is that, annoying and frustrating as they are, there is nevertheless a strong Russian tradition that people look to the top for answers to their problems or at least for sympathy for their miseries. It was not unusual in the old days for people to suppose that an oppressive action by the government would not have happened if the tsar had only known about it. That sort of thing was also said about Stalin. For more than seventy years, this attitude has been reinforced by the Marxist-collectivist response to solving problems: Look to the group, to the collective, to the officials in charge. The Soviet people today rely heavily on decisions and actions taken collectively, on answers given by the bureaucracies.

Incidents of this dependency, which may reveal a systemic trait, were reported many times from Afghanistan, where Soviet field commanders showed little initiative in their war against rebel forces and were reluctant to make decisions on their own without approval by their superiors in the bureaucracies above. (See, for example, *New York Times*, 2/15/89.) These field commanders no doubt had their own unexpressed feelings about the military bureaucracies controlling them, but they nevertheless bowed to them out of a deep tradition of respect and awe, even though improvisation probably would have been advantageous in their battle situations.

The acclaimed sociologist Tatyana Zaslavskaya wrote that the Soviet system creates "helpless people [who are] only able to follow directives from above." She added that such people were incapable of performing satisfactorily in a modern economy with its high technological requirements. If the bureaucracies do not have all the answers, the problems simply go unsolved.

Finally, Soviet bureaucracies have a winning record in fending off economic reforms that have threatened to clip their wings. Since the beginning of Soviet rule, but especially since Stalin's death in 1953, there have been repeated attempts to reorganize, diminish, or circumvent the industrial ministries that so potently intermediate between the planners and the basic enterprises. Each time, these particular organizations have beaten back the challenges, and in so doing have gained strength.

★

THE SPECIAL PROBLEMS OF CENTRAL PLANNING

Central planning and bureaucracies lumber along hand in glove. Central planning is an integral part of the Marxist conception of a socialist society. Marx viewed capitalism as an anarchic system in which everyone is subject to the blind forces of the market, in which society has no conscious control of its destiny. The worst of architects, Marx said, are superior to the best of bees, because they form a structure in their imagination before erecting it in reality, while bees are guided by instinct only. Architects plan. Human society can transcend its present chaos when it gains control of the material world, constructing plans in advance, consciously and coherently formulating its future. Hence: central planning.

Observing capitalism at work, Marx noted that, within any given firm, goods at all stages of production were freely exchanged—not bought and sold—and that, while there were many areas of specialization within the firm, a set of central managers planned and coordinated the entire operation. Observing also in capitalism the evolution of ever-larger enterprises, Marx made an inspired extrapolation: The economic organization in a socialist society would be akin to one gigantic firm, in which central planning would specify the production of each product, its distribution among other units of this gigantic firm, and all the coordination and meshing necessary. No markets would be employed; there would be no buying and selling; no commodities would be traded for money; there would be no money. Needless to say, Marx's version of central planning was an extreme one, and it had to be modified by later Marxists to allow for at least some market activity, the buying and selling of certain commodities and services, the widespread use of money, and the consequent limitation of central planning's domain.

It is difficult for most of us, living as we do in a market economy, to understand how anyone ever came up with the notion of central planning in the first place and why others paid any attention to it. However, central planning did play a positive and key role for the Soviets during the 1930s. The planning apparatus mobilized the population for clearly stated tasks and ultimate aims, and it established the means of getting from here to there. Central planning, when done well, has a potentially useful role in socialist economies; but in actual practice, it has been something that few people want to touch even with a ten-foot pole.

Most readers of this book probably consider central planning to be impossibly complicated, logically flawed, and quite unworkable. Because I suspect this, I want to show a simple, logical, and workable system of central planning. Although the model is highly simplified, it will nevertheless bring out many of the main features of Soviet planning over the years. It will also deepen our understanding of what the Soviets have tried to achieve and the sources of their failure. Since ten is a nice round number, I'll construct the model in ten steps.

Let's suppose that people eat only bread. The first step for the planners is to set the prices of wheat, flour, and bread. These fixed prices may be related to recent free market prices in the domestic economy or to prices on international markets. The second step is to establish the lowest industrial wage rate so that adequate amounts of bread can be purchased by the lowest income families. Industrial wage rates are then scaled upward from that minimum, according to skill, education, productivity, seniority, or other criteria. The third step is to set the prices of industrial goods on the basis of labor costs, established in the preceding step, plus material costs (which, when traced back, are essentially labor costs), plus a profit margin and sales taxes. These prices are official, controlled prices, which can be changed by the planners when conditions warrant. The industrial sector consists of state enterprises and perhaps cooperatives, some of them producing manufactured consumer goods (such as clothing) and the others producers' goods (raw materials, machines).

In step four, the planners set the prices of necessities (children's clothing) relatively low, and prices of luxuries (mink coats) and injurious goods (alcohol and tobacco) relatively high. A low price is below the level that would be established on a free market; at such a level, demand would exceed supply. Therefore, coupons or some similar device would have to be used to ration the short supplies. The objective in setting low prices and some rationing scheme is to ensure that the goods are evenly distributed among the population. A high price is above the equilibrium level—that is, supply would exceed demand. This high price could be protected if the planners order reductions in the production of these commodities or if they hold the excesses off the markets. The objective here is to discourage consumption of these goods. The enterprises producing the necessities might have to be subsidized by the government; the firms producing the luxuries and injurious goods might have above-average profits (which would, in effect, be taxed away in step five).

In the fifth step, the central planners allow state enterprises to retain part of their gross profits for depreciation allowances, workers' and managers' bonuses, and the welfare of workers. The remainder of the profits (generally most of them), along with any sales taxes, would go to the state budget. The incomes of industrial workers consist of their wages (from step two) plus bonuses, less income taxes (if any).

The sixth step concerns all agricultural workers. Suppose that the rural areas are organized into collective and state farms, and that these farms produce only wheat. The gross incomes of the farms are equal to the wheat produced times its price, as established in the first step. "The price," however, is not a single price but a structure of wheat prices: one low price at which the farms must sell a certain quota of the wheat crop to the government; one medium price at which the government purchases above-quota wheat; and one high price, which prevails in cooperative or free markets. Agricultural net incomes are equal to the gross incomes less non-wage costs and funds for depreciation, welfare, and investment. The residual or net income is then divided among the peasants according to the work points accumulated by each family. These work points are based on the type of work done and the number of hours worked. In state farms, the workers receive fixed wages instead of dividing a residual income, as in the collectives. These wages can be closely related to the industrial wages, already established in step two.

The central planners have now set the incomes of both industrial and agricultural workers. These incomes are sufficient to purchase bread from state and cooperative stores or in the free markets, and to purchase manufactured goods—say, clothing. If the workers have any income left over, this excess can be deposited in savings banks at some fixed rate of interest.

The seventh step is to organize the state budget. This budget receives sales taxes, income taxes, the profits of state enterprises (after bonuses and other disbursements), and the difference between the low prices paid by the state for agricultural products and the higher prices at which they are sold in the cities and elsewhere. Budget expenditures comprise national defense, government administration, funds turned over to a Construction Bank for allocations to new investment, spending for social goods (education, health) and welfare, and subsidies. The last cover the losses of some state enterprises that are selling necessities at relatively low prices or are operating inefficiently. If the state purchases crops at high prices and sells them at low prices, the subsidies would be inflated accordingly. The planners attempt to balance the state budget—total income receipts equal total expenditures.

The eighth step is a bit tricky. The central planners have to determine how much each enterprise should produce for consumers and for use by other enterprises. Thus, a farm and bakery produce bread not only for consumers but also for state enterprises and cooperatives (for their cafeterias and animals). A clothing factory produces cloth for families and also, say, for bakeries (for aprons) and for itself (for covering of looms at night). In a more sophisticated economy, coal goes to steel firms, steel goes to machine tool firms, and so on. These interrelations form a matrix of inputs and outputs, some of the outputs going directly to consumers and others becoming inputs elsewhere in the production system. Central planners, by constructing these matrices, in effect instruct each enterprise what to buy, what to produce, and how to produce it. (The prices of the inputs and outputs, recall, were fixed by the planners in steps one and three.)

In the ninth step, the central planners establish performance indicators for industrial firms and for collective and state farms in order to meet the requirements of the overall plan. The planners' aim here is to induce the managers and workers of the production units to raise labor productivity, lower costs of production—in general, operate efficiently—and meet the targets of the plan. The performance gauges include physical quantities of the outputs, limits on total wages, profit targets, quality standards, rates of technical change, and much more.

As mentioned in step five, enterprises send most of their profits to the state budget, which leaves them without funds for new investment. However, one type of budget expenditure (step seven) is the allocation of funds back to the enterprises for purchases of new structures and durable equipment. A Construction Bank can be used as the intermediary between the state budget and the enterprises requesting investment funds. Typically in central planning, the distribution of new capital expenditures among enterprises has no necessary relation to the profits earned by the various enterprises. The central planners, then, in this tenth and final step, must devise an investment plan to guide them in these allocations.

Between the central planners and the thousands of production units, other intermediaries will be formed. These have generally been known as economic ministries, each of which is in charge of some area of the economy. In addition, provision will be made for distribution and selling networks, retail and wholesale. Enterprises typically do not sell their outputs directly to consumers and other firms. Instead, the state allocates some of the outputs as inputs to other firms, and it takes the goods destined for consumers off the hands of the enterprises and places them within the distribution and selling networks. Central planners have to provide in the plan for exports and imports of goods and services. They might also set up labor exchanges where information about job openings and other labor conditions is available.

Now, that looks possible, does it not? I have constructed an entire central-planning system that seems internally consistent, logical, workable. In fact, such a system did work sufficiently well for the Soviets in the 1930s to transform their economy from a mainly agricultural to an industrial one, to raise the standard of living for some of its people, and to prepare with some success for war.

The weaknesses of the system were slow in developing, but by the 1970s, central planning was in serious difficulty. The principal snag was the lack of sufficient information held by the planners: They never knew enough, and what they came to know was generally late. This was not a major disadvantage when the economy was rudimentary and had only a few principal aims, as was the case near the beginning of Soviet development. But when the economy became increasingly complex—in the number of goods, enterprises, farms, variety of consumers' demands, multiplicity of job classifications, scientific and technological advances—the planners' problems mounted exponentially. Difficulties multiplied at each step along the way, as planners had to specify the matrix of inputs and outputs among a rapidly increasing number of production units and with an exploding number of commodities.

Some of the prices that were fixed, the subsidies that were granted, the types of goods produced, the methods of production—these decisions and more got entrenched in the system and gained constituencies; they became difficult to change. Near the beginning, this rigidity did not matter so much, but as time went on, what was being done departed more and more from what it was optimal to do. Thus, the price of bread remained the same for decades, even though cost conditions, demands, and other factors changed markedly. The problem is that central planners have a powerful interest in keeping as many points of stability as they can, for any single change in an interdependent system calls for thousands of other changes.

Since it always seemed better for central planners not to rock the boat, the economy fell farther and farther behind the capitalist world's advances in technology. As time went on, the Soviets were churning out increasingly outmoded machinery, electronics, and industrial products. The Soviet labor force may have had its own faults, but its productivity had no chance to rise to international standards with the almost laughable equipment available.

Many other weaknesses of central planning became more pronounced as enterprise managers, workers, consumers—everybody—learned how to beat the system, and not only learned how but had increasing incentives to improve their own positions at the expense of the state, and often at the expense of others.

★

ATTEMPTS TO REFORM
THE SYSTEM

When the central planning system becomes unwieldy and inefficient, it can be reformed in any of several ways. Such reforms may endanger the bureaucracies associated with central planning, although the extent of the danger depends on the type of reform imposed. One type of reform, *reorganization*, usually involves the reshuffling of ministries and national planning offices. This process can imperil some bureaucrats but provide opportunities for others—or for some of the initially displaced ones.

In a second type of reform, *decentralization* of decision making within a given planning structure, some decisions are transferred from the authorities at the top to those at lower levels, closer to where the decisions are implemented. This reform, too, will place some bureaucrats at risk but enhance the prestige of others.

Still another set of reforms falls in the realm of *decontrol*. These measures are designed to remove some decisions from the central-planning structure and lodge them in the hands of enterprise managers, families, or other small groups near the bottom of the pyramid. For example, some reforms have sought to relieve state committees of setting prices on certain commodities, turning this function over to open markets or to negotiated contracts, where demand and supply conditions could interact to establish the prices. Other reforms of this type have aimed to reduce the control of central authorities over the collection and reallocation of enterprises' profits, with the intention of allowing enterprises more discretion in the use of their surpluses. Such decontrol measures directly threaten the economic bureaucracies across the board.

A final type of reform, used sparingly in the past, is now near the forefront of the Gorbachev economic initiatives. This can be termed *desocialization*, in which higher levels of socialization are transformed into lower ones, such as state enterprises to cooperatives or state farms to collective farms, and nonsocialist entities are encouraged, including private plots in agriculture, personal enterprises, and private (capitalist) firms, both domestic and foreign. These measures pose great dangers to bureaucracies within the planning area, for the reforms strengthen the private sectors of the economy, weaken the most advanced forms of the socialist sector, and decrease the need for central planning.

It is possible for the four types of reform—reorganization, decentralization, decontrol, and desocialization—to be turned upside down and used to strengthen the economic bureaucracies. That is, reorganization could call for more bureaucracies. There could be strengthening of centralized decision making, or more control by central planners as decision-making powers outside the planning structure are reduced, or a further socialization of the economy as private activity is curtailed and higher socialist forms expanded. In all these cases, the bureaucracies would generally be the winners, though some bureaucrats might lose out to others.

After Stalin left the scene, several forays were launched to reconstruct the bulky economic machine that the dictator had erected during the 1930s and 1940s. Khrushchev introduced reorganization measures in 1957 designed to dismantle the national ministries that were organized by branches of production, such as the ministry of automobiles, the ministry of coal, and the ministry of transport construction. Each of these branches was organized from the top (Moscow), and each supervised its activity from the national down to the local levels.

In place of these vertically organized ministries, Khrushchev established over a hundred regional economic councils to supervise all the leading industrial and construction enterprises in their regions—automobiles, coal, transport construction, and other major industries. Thus, power was taken from the Moscow ministries and transferred to the horizontally organized regional councils of the country. Khrushchev expected to achieve greater economic efficiency through a more rational coordination of the various economic activities within each region. This was definitely a reorganization, but also to some extent a decentralization reform.

During the Khrushchev years, the state planning office (Gosplan) was reorganized several times, until continuity was severely damaged. There was, at the same time, a strengthening of central controls over agriculture: Some collective farms were converted to larger state farms and others were amalgamated into larger units; start-up farms in newly opened crop areas (from the opening of virgin land) were largely state farms; and the peasants' private plots came under stricter controls and more discriminatory treatment. All of these measures were of the "perverse" type noted above, that is, they all tended to strengthen the bureaucracies that administered planning in these areas.

Khrushchev's initiatives at first raised farm production substantially, but the constant reorganization eventually harmed it. The overall result of the reform packages was a sharp fall in the growth rate by the early 1960s. A disastrous harvest of 1963 added to the economic difficulties. Within five years of Khrushchev's introduction of the regional economic councils, the old bureaucracies reasserted themselves. Khrushchev was removed from leadership in 1964, and the new leaders, headed by Leonid Brezhnev, fully restored the old bureaucratic structure.

The second major effort to reform the system after Stalin's death was initiated by Brezhnev and the prime minister, Alexei Kosygin, starting in 1965. These so-called Kosygin reforms recentralized economic power in Moscow in 23 industrial ministries; called for more scientific attention to five-year plans; created new state committees, including one to set prices of major commodities throughout the country and another to centralize the distribution of producer goods; gave enterprises somewhat more leeway to handle their own affairs and to earn bonuses; revised many prices to enable most enterprises to operate profitably, and allowed more prices to be negotiated between buyers and sellers; and partially freed state and collective farms from central administrative interference, making their operations more profitable.

These reforms, while re-establishing a central decision-making structure—undoing Khrushchev's work—were nonetheless intended to send more decisions down to lower levels within tight general criteria laid down by Moscow. If they had been successful, the reforms would have reduced the power of the re-established ministries, central planning agencies, and other state committees. They would have diminished daily interference by ministries into the affairs of enterprises and farms.

However, the reforms were delayed and then applied hesitantly and inconsistently. Ultimately, they proved unsuccessful. This was, in part, owing to their poor formulation, but also to the delaying tactics of the central ministries, which were protecting their turf. The ministries and agencies found it possible to assimilate the reforms into the old administrative structure and thus reduce their intended impact. The paltry results of the Kosygin reforms were, furthermore, due to the failure of the reformers to revamp the Party, the bureaucracies, and enterprise management—in general, their failure to change radically the institutions that were supposed to implement the new measures. Some critics have pointed to the inherent weakness of any set of reforms, such as the Kosygin ones, that are applied to only a small part of economic and social life—reforms that reflect technical *perestroika*, so to speak, without *glasnost*. Such reforms, no matter how competently they are designed, always end up in the trash can because they fall into the same old unwilling hands.

Another set of reforms occurred in 1973 under Brezhnev. These were fashioned to reorganize the planning structure once again—

another attempt to squeeze more efficiency out of essentially the same lemon. It would be asking too much of the reader to follow me through the many mergers of bureaus, the renaming of others, the new duties assigned to still others, the elimination of sub-units, and the cosmetic touch-ups of this facade and that. Reorganization and some decentralization were the broad types of reform measures introduced in this early Brezhnev shakeup. After the shake, what survived were organized opposition and centralized foot-dragging.

A later set of reforms, preceding the Gorbachev initiatives, came in 1979, when Brezhnev once again attempted to raise the efficiency of what continued to be fundamentally the same system. The general goal was the same as before: to produce more and better with less.

Among other measures, these reforms encouraged enterprises to rely more on their internal funds and bank credits and less on handouts from the state budget. Thus, instead of free budget funds, firms would have to use either their own funds, and so sacrifice interest that they otherwise could have earned, or borrow at explicit rates of interest from banks. This element of the reforms was more than reorganization or decentralization; it was an attempt at partial decontrol—the removal of some decisions from the planning structure and their lodgment in the basic enterprises.

Like the Kosygin reforms, Brezhnev's 1979 reforms were only partly applied, watered down, or subverted. Some never got off the ground. In the end, they failed to significantly improve economic efficiency.

The central bureaucracies have repeatedly worked to turn aside any reform that threatened to reduce their clout and privileges. They have accomplished this by procrastination, assimilation of the new into the old, complication of what was relatively simple, and outright violation of the new regulations.

Bureaucratic inertia and roadblocks, though, cannot explain fully the failure of the post-Stalin reforms. They failed, as we have seen, partly because they were designed incorrectly, partly because they were poorly implemented, and partly because they elicited opposition, not only from ministerial bureaucracies but also from social groups in the population who stood to lose or who were frightened by the prospect of radical change. Failure must also be attributed to the absence of broad democratic input into the formulation of the reform measures. Bureaucracies were not the only flies in the ointment.

The prime lesson from all of these efforts is that a bloated and inefficient bureaucratic system is almost impossible to change in the absence of a revolt by the people at large—in the absence of a successful policy of *glasnost*. The Russian people, over many, many decades, have come up against unresponsive and oppressive officials; been intimidated by state power; and felt their own powerlessness to rectify wrongs. And yet, they have frequently displayed respect—or at least awe, a reverential fear—for such authority and so have been reluctant to rock the boat. These conflicting attitudes, along with vivid characterizations of bureaucrats, can be found repeatedly in Russian and Soviet literature. By sampling a few of these works, we can gain some insight into this side of Russian and Soviet life.

★

PUSHKIN'S VISION
OF THE MIGHTY STATE

One memorable portrayal of the "little citizen" against the state is found in Alexander Pushkin's narrative poem *The Bronze Horseman* (1833). The poem's central figure, Yevgeni, is a poor clerk who lives in St. Petersburg, the magnificent capital city built on the banks of the Neva River—at great cost—under the orders of Peter the Great.

After a torrential storm, the high waters of the Neva River inundate the city. Yevgeni's true love, who lives on an island nearby, is drowned in the flood. The next day finds Yevgeni, with tormented mind, wandering in confusion. We witness a month of such wandering about the city; Yevgeni does not go home, but lives on handouts, sleeps on the embankments, and dodges stones thrown at him. One night he awakes in a dripping rain and raging wind. He sets off wandering and soon finds himself in Peter's Square, confronting a towering figure: "eminently dark and high/Above the railed-in rock, with arm outstretched,/The Image, mounted on his horse of bronze." This is the statue of Peter the Great on his steed, commissioned by Catherine and executed by Falconet. "How terrible/He was in the surrounding murk!

What thought/Was on his brow, what strength was hidden in him!"

Yevgeni, now mad, walks around the mounted figure and flings a curse, a taunt, at "the lord of half the world." And then Yevgeni, imagining rage on the turning face of the dead tsar, begins to run at breakneck speed. "His hand aloft, the Bronze Horseman rushes/After him on his ponderously galloping mount;/And all night long, wherever the madman ran,/The Bronze Horseman followed with a ringing clatter."

From that time on, whenever Yevgeni finds himself in that square, he lowers his eyes, doffs his cap, and takes a circuitous path around the powerful tsar.

It was, of course, a natural disaster that swept Yevgeni's happiness out to sea and drove him mad. But it was a natural disaster in a highly vulnerable city that had been autocratically decreed by "the State" and built at a terrible human and material cost. The disaster was, in this sense, imposed on the poor clerk by a decision from above. And, in the aftermath of the disaster, this hapless individual could only imagine himself pursued by the mighty mounted power, until he was reduced to subservience.

★

GOGOL'S POWERLESS "LITTLE CITIZEN"

A short story by Nikolai Gogol, "The Overcoat" (1842), provides an eloquent indictment of lower officialdom as well as a sympathetic treatment of the poor and downtrodden ordinary citizen of nineteenth-century Russia.

The "little citizen" in this story is Akaky Akakievich, a lowly copy clerk, who sacrifices a full year's worth of his poor comforts just to buy himself a new overcoat. The joyous day when Akaky picks up his new coat from the tailor ends hours later in humiliation and despair. Late that evening, while walking home from a party that his co-workers have organized to celebrate the heralded purchase, Akaky is mugged and robbed of his overcoat. He runs to a night watchman who must have seen the incident, but Akaky's frantic appeals fall on deaf ears— and that is just the beginning of his troubles with an officious and indifferent bureaucracy.

The next morning, after much effort, Akaky sees the borough police commissioner, who suggests that the loss was his own fault for being out so late and offers no indication that the police will do anything to help. On the advice of a colleague, the pathetic clerk takes his case to an "important personage" said to have good contacts. Although this official is not busy—just chatting with a friend—he keeps Akaky waiting for a very long time, just to demonstrate his importance. Finally, the little clerk is allowed to present his sad tale. "'My dear sir,' [the official] answered sharply, 'don't you know the proper channels? Do you realize whom you're addressing and what the proper procedure should be? You should first have handed in a petition to the office. It would have gone to the head clerk. From him it would have reached the section head, who would have approached my secretary and only then would the secretary have presented it to me. . . .'" When Akaky stammers something about secretaries being unreliable, the important personage, enraged, stamps his foot and shouts angrily about insubordination. "And Akaky Akakievich froze completely. He staggered, his whole body shook. And he was quite unable to keep his feet. . . . They carried him out almost unconscious."

On his way home through a blizzard, Akaky becomes chilled, runs a high temperature the next day, and soon dies. "They took Akaky Akakievich away and buried him. And Petersburg went on without him exactly as if he had never existed. A creature had vanished, disappeared. He had had no one to protect him. No one had ever paid him the slightest attention."

But did he disappear? A ghost begins to haunt certain neighborhoods of the city at night, pulling overcoats off the shoulders of the inhabitants, one and all, whoever they might be. One night this ghost turns his attention to the important personage, who is riding in a carriage. "Suddenly the important personage felt someone grab him violently from behind." It is of course Akaky's ghost. "'I've caught you at last. . . . It's the coat I need. You did nothing about mine. . . . Now I'll take yours!'" After that, the ghost is seen no longer.

Gogol has given us a portrait of an arrogant, rank-conscious, lazy, and mostly insensitive minor officialdom. I write "mostly" because the important personage does have some regretful thoughts about his terrible treatment of Akaky. But it is difficult to imagine that these officials could ever solve a case, even if they were blasted out of their chairs by explosives and set in motion. This is a bureaucracy that pays little heed to the cries of those desperately in need of help, or to those who are merely below them in social rank.

★

UNVEILING A CORRUPT
POWER STRUCTURE

Gogol's comic play *The Inspector General* (1836) is also of great interest as a backdrop to the present-day problems of inflated and unresponsive bureaucracies. As the play opens, the governor of a small provincial town announces the expected arrival from St. Petersburg of an inspector general, who will be arriving incognito with secret instructions. He advises the town officials to shape up, apprehensive himself about what the merchants and townspeople will tell the inspector general. "I don't know what they are going to do. For some reason they don't seem to like me. I can't imagine why. I'm sure if I've robbed anybody I've done it very good-naturedly."

Two town gossips learn (by way of the postmaster who routinely opens and reads all the mail) that a young man from St. Petersburg is staying at the inn; undoubtedly he is the expected inspector general. The gossips further reveal that he has already been in town for two weeks. The governor is unnerved: "Two weeks! (*Aside:*) The saints have mercy upon me! Then he was here when the sergeant's wife was flogged! And when the prisoners were starving for lack of food! And he's seen the dirt in the streets; and he was here when they had the riot at Pachechuyev's taproom. My gosh, what a scandal!" The governor once more demands that they all clean up their departments. Turning to a police official, he says: "Hereafter you remember your rank! A little graft is all right, but don't steal any more than you're supposed to steal!" He turns to the police captain: "Tell all the officials, if the Inspector General asks them whether they're contented, they're to say, 'Perfectly, your Excellency!' And if anybody isn't contented I'll give him something afterwards to be discontented about. . . ."

We then learn that the supposed inspector general is in fact only a minor civil servant, Khlestakov by name, on his way home from a disastrous gambling fling. During a puzzling visit from the governor, Khlestakov catches on that he has been mistaken for some sort of high official and decides to go along. For the rest of the day, he immensely enjoys the charade, inspecting all the town's institutions, bragging of his prominent connections, courting the governor's daughter, and taking bribes in the form of "loans" from the town officials.

Meanwhile, the town merchants are vying for some attention. They complain to the supposed inspector general about their governor: "He's the most unprincipled Governor in all Russia, sir. He ruins us with his demands for tribute, sir. . . . He comes into our shops, and if he sees something he likes, we must send it home for him . . . and he never pays a kopek for it."

Filled with self-importance because he thinks his daughter will be marrying the inspector general, the governor summons the scoundrel merchants and scolds them threateningly: "You had the nerve to complain of me! Who was it, I'd like to know, that hushed the matter up when you built that bridge, and charged the government twenty thousand rubles for materials that didn't cost you a hundred? . . . It was I, that's who it was! If I hadn't winked at your graft you'd all be in Siberia by now, and you know it." The merchants promise expensive wedding presents: more graft.

The bubble bursts when the postmaster breathlessly enters, waving a letter written by Khlestakov to a friend, boasting of his strange good fortune. Naturally, the postmaster has opened it and now reads it aloud to everyone in the room. Khlestakov writes nasty, insulting things about the officials. The letter goes on: "The joke is that these people seem to have taken me for an official of some kind—an Inspector General, or something. So I have decided to leave town before they discover that . . . I am nothing of the kind." Bewilderment! They are struck dumb! They are ruined! They will never get their money back! The governor finally says: "What a blockhead I am! How could I . . . be such a colossal, blithering idiot? . . . He's tricked us. . . . Look at me, everybody . . . the prize ass of all Russia."

Gogol laid bare the corruption and oppressiveness of municipal officials in Russia more than a hundred years ago, in a satire that he probably hoped would lead to some reforms. Yet we hear echoes of the same issues in Soviet society even today.

THE STRUGGLES OF
A LONE WOLF

nventions or technological progress are used by a number of Soviet authors to highlight the obstructionist tactics of bureaucrats. One example is Vladimir Mayakovsky's 1930 play, *The Bathhouse*, in which an inventor of a time machine is frustrated over official delays. Perhaps more famous is Vladimir Dudintsev's *Not by Bread Alone* (1956), written shortly after the end of World War II. The novel was not published in the Soviet Union until after Stalin's death, when Khrushchev allowed a thaw in the icy atmosphere in which writers had labored. It was an immediate success and sensation, but later came under attack from Party stalwarts—in a typical response from bureaucratic organs that sought to defend the Leninist faith.

In this work, the hero is a fighter par excellence against a bureaucracy that the author calls "the invisible empire" or "the monopoly." His name is Dmitri Lopatkin, and he teaches physics in a city in the Ural Mountains. When he suddenly gets an idea for an invention, Lopatkin leaves his teaching post to devote full time to designing and promoting his brainchild: a machine for casting drainpipes by the centrifugal method. Do you think that Dudintsev could have thought of a more prosaic, less glamorous invention? After all, drainpipes! Lopatkin is now going to spend the best years of his life on thousands of drawings for draining away something or other through pipes. What is the author trying to tell us?

For Lopatkin to get his machine approved and into operation, he has to confront and overcome various bureaucracies: in the district capital, in Moscow at the State Institute for Projecting Foundry Equipment, the Central Scientific Institute of Foundry Research, and a ministry that oversees these and other engineering units. His main adversaries are Drozdov, a ministry official in Moscow; and a professor, who has invented a similar (though inferior) machine and is "in" with the relevant bureaucracies.

Early in the story, Drozdov tells Lopatkin that he is going to have a tough time because he is a lone wolf. "The lone wolf is out of date. Our new machines are the result of collective thought." Later on, Drozdov remarks that Lopatkin is up against it because that is the fate of an individualist; the going would have been much easier if he had been a member of a collective. Still later, Lopatkin hears Drozdov repeat the same old Marxist refrain:

> "Look here, Comrade Lopatkin, . . . you are a truly tragic figure embodying within yourself . . . a whole epoch, which by now is irretrievably past and gone. You are a hero, but a solitary one. . . . You do not understand that we can do without your invention, even if it is a genuine, a great discovery. We can do without it and, just imagine—without even suffering any loss! Yes, Comrade Lopatkin, without suffering any loss, because of our accurate calculation and the planning which insures us a steady advance. . . . Our designers' and technicians' collectives will find a solution. And this solution will be better than yours, because collective research always leads to the quickest and best solution of any problem. The collective is superior to any individual genius."

When Lopatkin objects, Drozdov insists that solitary geniuses are not necessary in a socialist society. "There is no capitalist here to buy your ideas, and the people have no use for primitive passions that jolt the economic routine. We shall reach the desired decisions gradually, without panic, at the required time, even at the required hours!"

After this rebuff, Lopatkin spends months writing letters of complaint and criticism to various officials and newspapers, until he is summoned before a stern-looking deputy prosecutor. She accosts him: "What *is* all this, Comrade Lopatkin? . . . Some people advance Soviet science and industry, doing creative work, and others fling dirt at them. How does that strike you?"

Lopatkin sets out to explain what he has been up against:

> "It's a monopoly. They do not allow any leaps forward, only a gradual, scarcely perceptible ascent. And they strike at everyone who thinks differently. . . . Their aim is to stay put in their easy chairs and to go on getting richer. But a discoverer of new things is serving the people. A discoverer always thinks

differently in any sphere of knowledge. Because he has found a new and shorter way, he rejects the old habitual one."

This is beautiful sarcasm, inasmuch as Marxist theory is built on "leaps forward," yet (as Lopatkin explains) these are outlawed in the Soviet system, and only gradual, planned advances are allowed. Only the individual inventor or entrepreneur, not the collective planning agencies, embody the Marxist principal, implies Lopatkin.

On another day, Lopatkin contemplates the scene in the ministry. From one room, he hears a clatter of typewriters; in the next, a conference is going on; and in a large hall, he sees about forty desks, with an official seated at each one. "Like an enormous ship, the Ministry was running full speed before the wind; all the seamen were conscientiously standing their watches; no one wanted to be bothered with a harebrained project of a machine for the casting of iron pipes—a project not included in any plan." A pipe dream like his, if taken on by the bureaucracy, would cause too much disruption in the routine.

Actually, Lopatkin does not always meet defeat in his skirmishes with the bureaucracies. They give the go-ahead to his machine a few times; a few officials encourage him to persevere; and others give him good advice on strategies and tactics that might work. Lopatkin's course is an undulating one: Periods of depression regularly follow periods of optimism. During the up times, he can see that some bureaucrats have human faces and good hearts; during the down periods, they all seem to be scum.

At one point, Drozdov's young wife Nadia leaves her husband to dedicate herself to Lopatkin and his cause. She surreptitiously supplies him with money, performs secretarial duties, and does serious research for him at the Lenin Library, discovering ways to improve his machine. Lopatkin and Nadia become not only lovers but partners—co-inventors—in the drainpipe project. During one of Lopatkin's "up" periods, when he is given an office and a group to work with, he turns over to Nadia all the details of the project.

This is his undoing. Accused by the government of revealing secrets to an unauthorized person, Lopatkin is convicted and sentenced to eight years in a Siberian labor camp. Freed after serving just a year and a half, he returns to Moscow and finds that, in the meantime, a competing machine has been built and put into operation—but, to the embarrassment of the bureaucrats involved, it proves to be inefficient and costly to operate. Others within the bureaucracy continue to work on Lopatkin's machine and succeed in getting it installed in the city where Lopatkin once taught. When it proves to be a great success, heads roll in the ministry. Lopatkin is honored and given a sinecure as head of a designing office, for the purpose of developing an improved machine for several other industries. One of Lopatkin's severest critics tells him:

> "Today you are the victor. And we are all amazed at the way you went through hell and high water. But your nature, dear comrade, is selfish. You are a lone wolf. [How many times has Lopatkin heard that one!] Before I met you I would have said that in our country it was impossible to fight alone. I still say it is difficult. The collective helps you, defends you, takes care of you, and gives you material support at the right time. But you kept out of the collective."

He offers a toast to Lopatkin, suggesting that the inventor could now relax, purchase a new car, a TV set, a weekend cottage. Lopatkin replies in a ringing voice, echoing Christ's response to the Devil: "Man lives not by bread alone, if he is honest." The inventor visualizes a long, difficult road ahead, focusing intently on what he must do, oblivious of Nadia at his side. A lone wolf to the very end. Or is he now a bureaucrat?

Thirty years after Dudintsev's novel was published, in February 1986, Gorbachev spoke before the 27th Party Congress of the problems that inventors face in getting anything accomplished—corroborating Dudintsev's particular criticisms of the system. Here is Gorbachev:

> The Ministry of the Machine Tool Industry has impermissibly held up the manufacture of unique hydraulic motors enabling extensive use of hydraulic techniques in mining and elsewhere, to increase labor productivity several-fold and to improve working conditions . . .

This kind of attitude to new inventions is not infrequently based on the ambitions of some groups of scientists, on departmental hostility towards inventions 'by others,' and a lack of interest on the part of production managers in introducing them. It is no secret that even the examination of invention applications is sometimes an ordeal that drags on for years.

★

GETTING THE PEOPLE TO FIGHT BACK

During the early postwar years, it was not difficult for Dudintsev and many others to discern that bloated and conservative bureaucrat organizations were damaging the prospects for the Soviet economy. But to see 20 or 25 years earlier that this was in the cards, that already the bureaucrat was forging the brakes that would eventually slow everything to a crawl—to see all that, as the Soviets' premier poet Mayakovsky did, was really astonishing. As early as 1927, when Stalin was still battling for power, this prescient poet penned a verse, "Paper Horrors," that correctly forecast the tangle of memos that would ensnarl the Soviets and, in the end, degrade them.

> Men's pride, subside, be forever forgot!
> To a dot humanity's future tapers.
> Man is gradually becoming a blot
> on the margins of enormously important papers.

Mayakovsky envisioned people losing their brains as they become clerical assistants for "paper turned boss." Papers bursting from portfolios force people out of their apartments and then "sit at tables and dine." The poet has a final word of advice to the workers:

> I'd unfurl a storm of rioting banners—
> Tear papers with my teeth and, indignant, yell:
> "Every inch of useless paper, proletarians,
> Hate like your enemy, abhor like hell!"

A century before Mayakovsky's diminished soul appeared in print, the poor clerk in Pushkin's poem certainly felt oppressed and humbled into submission by the state's power over him. Yet the "bronze horseman" represents only an abstract power, a symbol of authority; it could hardly be called a bureaucracy. And Mayakovsky portrays almost equally abstract "little citizens," frightened out of their wits by the natural and human forces pounding on them.

Gogol's copy clerk, on the other hand, encountered actual bureaucratic faces, real people who were largely unresponsive and insensitive to his pitiful misfortunes; and Akaky himself was someone we recognize on the street from the author's portrait of him. Thus, Gogol gives us a more realistic picture of a bureaucracy—small-town though it is—than Pushkin allowed himself to do.

Gogol's *The Inspector General* highlights the corrupt bureaucracy of a town, including its interference with and ultimately its oppression of the town's business interests. His bureaucrats attempted to solve the inspector-general problem in the only way they knew how—by offering bribes, disguised as loans, to the supposed official. By the same token, Gogol's businessmen, although terribly put upon by the town officials, have themselves descended into the criminal world of graft and embezzlement. We can imagine that the rottenness of the bureaucracy has spread to everything it has touched. There is only one ray of light: We in the audience should leave the theater with some sympathy for that poor devil of a governor, who at least humbles himself before his family and subordinates. Is there a fairly decent bureaucrat after all?

I find it important that, in one way or another, all those victimized fought back: Pushkin's Yevgeni with taunts; Gogol's Akaky with ghostly vindication, and his townspeople with protests and behavior that aped their oppressors' low conduct; Dudintsev's Lopatkin with persistence. Moreover, Mayakovsky's proletarians are exhorted to consider the paper mountains as their enemies and to do battle against them.

But it is equally important to hear the bureaucrat Drozdov, in *Not by Bread Alone*, tell Lopatkin that collective work done in the bureaucracies is likely to achieve much better results than work done by individuals outside these agencies. He truly believes in the advantages of careful planning over the more chaotic work produced by outsiders.

It is also important to recognize that Gogol's clerk sought out bureaucrats for an answer to his overcoat calamity and that Pushkin's clerk was drawn, as if by a magnet, to the Tsar Peter—even though both of these "little citizens" harbor resentment and ill will toward the very people they are compelled, by habit, to count on.

In this literature, then, we see two forces pulling in opposite directions. One draws the people to authority—to the bureaucracy, the collective, the group—for protection and relief. The other compels them to fight these formidable foes, these officious higher-ups, in order to free themselves. Those forces in opposition can be reconciled, and Gorbachev's aim of a better socialist society can be achieved, if the Soviet workers are able to organize themselves so that their own strength displaces that of external authority figures. In their own strength the workers can find the protection and relief they seek, and with their own strength they can overcome the bureaucrats.

We had, earlier in this chapter, a litany of failed attempts to reform the troublesome bureaucracies. Now Gorbachev is trying again. The long history of failure of reforms, or only partial success at best, has to be sobering for him. However, he seems to be acutely aware of the many roadblocks that can be erected against him and has tried to anticipate them through attacks on the bureaucracies, the encouragement of greater mass participation in decision making, and the more efficient design and implementation of the new policies.

The key to success is *glasnost*. Reforms aimed at reconstructing the economy have to be designed carefully; they have to be understood by most Soviet citizens and approved; and they must be implemented honestly and judiciously. What better way to do all this than to involve "the people" at every stage of *perestroika*? Open up. Empower the "little citizen." Encourage mass discussions of the reform proposals; let the reforms basically come "from below" and not be imposed "from above." Once the working classes become involved in debating and deciding these issues, their own understanding of the means and ends of *perestroika* will grow, and very likely the proposals that emanate from this democratic process will have their endorsement. The implementation of the reforms is not likely to be held up by bureaucracies that have been shorn of their most conservative officials and that have to face widespread and insistent public support for moving ahead with *perestroika*. *Glasnost* will clear the air of the bureaucratic stench. *Perestroika* without *glasnost* is a basket case.

The most cogent lesson of this chapter is that the working classes have to get their act together—with the help of Gorbachev and the Party—if anything good is to come of the *perestroika* reforms, and, indeed, if socialism itself is to be reinvigorated.

"Wake up, Fedot! [common peasant name]
The sowing campaign is upon us!"

THE SOVIET FARM: OVERCOMING A DIFFICULT HISTORY

The leaders of the revolutionary reconstruction now underway in the Soviet Union are all agreed that *perestroika* will not succeed without a marked improvement in the daily lives of people—at home, at work, at school, and at entertainment and cultural centers. Increasingly, the Soviet people have experienced poor and inadequate housing, some of it lacking even electricity, running water, and central heating. It is the "worst social problem of the country," according to Abel Aganbegyan, one of Gorbachev's close economic advisors. At the same time, Soviet society is experiencing a diminution of workers' interest in their jobs, rising rates of absenteeism, more theft of public property, and very low labor productivity.

The education system has received declining shares of public expenditures; teachers are notoriously underpaid; and many schools are not properly equipped. The health system has been neglected: There are too few health centers; doctors and nurses receive far too little income; and many hospitals are poorly equipped. Cultural centers need upgrading. People in their daily lives have encountered increasing crime, corruption, speculation, bribery, use of drugs, abuse of alcohol—and, in concert, more political apathy and alienation from the society as a whole.

One challenge of *perestroika* is to make at least a modicum of progress in these areas while at the same time significantly improving the basic economic situation. Almost everything has to be done at once. As Aganbegyan notes, "*Perestroika* in our society affects everything and everyone. It is universal, many-sided and all-embracing." In Marxist terms, while *perestroika* primarily revolutionizes the economic base of society, it also transforms the entire superstructure—politics, ideology, religion, law, and other non-economic areas.

★

THE CHANGING
LABOR SUPPLY

Ш here people are. About 290 million people now live in the Union of Soviet Socialist Republics, close to 40 million more than in the United States. Around 75 percent of them live in the seven so-called European republics: the RSFSR, or Russian Soviet Federative Socialist Republic (the largest by far), plus the three Baltic republics of Estonia, Latvia, and Lithuania, and the Ukraine, Byelorussia, and Moldavia. Only 6 percent of the population resides in the three Transcaucasian republics of Azerbaijan, Georgia, and Armenia. The remaining 19 percent live in the five Central Asian Soviet Socialist republics of Kazakhstan, Kirghizia, Tadzhikistan, Turkestan, and Uzbekistan. Of the fifteen republics, the RSFSR has the most people— 147 million—and Estonia, with only 1.5 million, has the least.

During the postwar period, the annual rate of growth of the total population has declined rather steadily, from over 1.5 percent in the early years to less than 1 percent in recent times. The projection for the average annual growth rate during the 1990s is a mere 0.7 percent. Since 1979, the population of the seven European republics has risen by only half of 1 percent per annum, while that of the five Central Asian republics has exploded by 2.3 percent per annum, over four times as fast. The population of the three republics in the Caucasus area has grown at a rate between these extremes, by 1.5 percent each year. The Central Asian populations are expected to continue their very rapid growth during the next decade or two, while growth rates in the European republics will slow to levels barely above zero.

Russians comprise only one-half of the Soviet population. Other Slavic peoples (Ukrainians, Byelorussians, and so on), Turkic peoples, Caucasians, and dozens of other ethnic groups make up the other half. Twenty percent of the population profess the Russian Orthodox religion, while around 10 percent are Muslims, and about 8 percent adhere to various other faiths. The remaining people (over 60 percent) are assumed to be atheists.

The working-age population in the Soviet Union includes all women from 16 to 55 and all men from 16 to 60, the older ages being the official retirement years—though many people continue to work beyond the cutoff age. In the earlier postwar period, the working-age group grew by 1.5 percent per year, but a sharp drop occurred starting around 1980. During that decade, the annual rate of growth for this group fell precipitously to only 0.4 percent. The projection for the 1990s is somewhat better but still significantly below 1 percent. Population of working age is actually declining in the European republics; it is exploding in the Central Asian ones. Since much of Soviet industry is in the European republics and much of the future gains of labor are in the Central Asian republics, a serious problem is developing—especially since the people of Central Asia have not willingly moved into the European republics; their industrial skills are deficient; and many lack facility in the Russian language. One answer is to put more capital investment and industrial training programs into Central Asia in the coming years.

★

How the people are doing. The Soviet Union produces about half the goods and services that the United States does. Its GNP is around $2,500 billion; thus, with a population of almost 290 million, the Soviet GNP per capita is approximately $8,600. Because many of the goods are for military use, for investment in capital equipment, structures, and inventories, and for other non-consumer purposes, consumers receive as income only 60 percent of the above figure (or $5,200). Their wages and salaries amount to $3,700 per person, other income and contributions to welfare funds comprising the rest. At the official exchange rate of $1 = 0.6 rubles, the last figure in rubles would be about 2,220. Very roughly speaking, we can say that the average monthly wage of the Soviet worker is 200 rubles (or about $330 at the official rate).

This sort of reckoning applies, of course, to the Soviet Union as a whole. In fact, some areas have much higher incomes than others, a situation that is common to all large countries. The Baltic republics of Estonia, Latvia, and Lithuania have higher-than-average incomes, and the five Central Asian republics (populated mostly by non-Russians) are far below the average. As a group, the Caucasian republics of Georgia, Armenia, and Azerbaijan fall just short of the average. The largest republic, the RSFSR, is significantly above the average. The richest republics have about twice the income per capita of the poorest.

More worrisome for the Soviet authorities is that the wealthiest republics have been growing more rapidly in income than the poorest. For instance, in the five richest republics (the three Baltics, RSFSR, and Byelorussia), income during the 1980s grew at an average annual rate of about 3.5 percent, while in the five poorest (all in Central Asia), income grew by only 0.5 percent each year. If we assign the index number of 100 to the top five and 50 to the bottom five for 1980, then by 1990 the numbers become about 140 and 53, which shows the absolute gap widening alarmingly. Of course, there are many more people in the top five than in the bottom five—165 million against 50 million—but population, as I noted above, is growing much more rapidly in the latter republics.

★

FACING THE PROBLEMS OF A DECLINING LABOR SUPPLY

In the past, economic growth has depended heavily on ever-new supplies of labor, land, and capital goods. In the last decade, however, new labor supplies have been forthcoming in steadily decreasing amounts; even these are being generated in areas away from much major industry, and the growth rate of capital goods has had to be trimmed to leave more room for greater supplies of consumer goods and services. Land is still available, but much would be costly to raise to satisfactory productivity levels. Thus, Soviet economic growth has recently had to depend much more than previously on quality improvements—on a more educated and healthier labor force, more modern capital goods, improved management techniques, and enhanced work efforts through stepped-up incentive systems for both workers and managers. In addition, improvements are needed in both the distribution of commodities and the markets and retail outlets where they are purchased.

The Gorbachev program of *perestroika* recognizes these problems. Measures have been enacted to raise population and working-age growth rates, to increase technical education, to improve the health system and the mental and physical well-being of the population, to offer greater work incentives, and to improve the quality of the goods produced. There has certainly been no lack of effort expended to accelerate *intensive* growth (based on quality improvement in human and non-human capital), now that *extensive* growth is much less promising.

Great progress could be made, even in the absence of fresh supplies of labor, if the attitudes of workers could be improved, their lethargy overcome, their sobriety and general health assured, their responses to life's problems made more rational through education and technical training, and their alienation from each other and from society overcome. If workers were to become really interested in their work and develop a warm team and national spirit, wondrous things could be done!

★

THE RUSSIAN WORKER OF 1900

We can gain a useful perspective on present-day concerns about the quality of life by looking at the Russian people and the country's labor supply around the turn of the century. It is a good starting point from which to view the changes that have occurred and to assess what more needs to be done.

Around 1900, the population of the Russian empire was only 140 million, compared to 290 million today. That seems like a huge increase, but it represents a growth rate of only 0.8 of 1 percent per year, just half of the population growth rate from 1850 to 1900. Still, 140 million was a tremendous number of people at that time, for the U.S. population was a mere 76 million, Germany's about 53 million, France's only 32 million, and Britain's less than 30 million. In terms of people, Russia was larger than Britain, France, and Germany combined.

However, Russia did not produce a gross national output (GNP) commensurate with the country's population. The productivity of the Russian labor force around 1900 was far below that of the United States and the European powers. For example, the average GNP per capita of Britain, Germany, and France, taken together, was 3.5 times higher than Russia's; the U.S. level was more than eight times higher. Forty years earlier, at the time of the emancipation of the serfs in 1861, Russia was also far behind these four industrial countries, but not so much as it would be at the turn of the century. In those forty years, Russia lost ground in relation to the leading Western nations, even though her own national output rose substantially, by more than 2.5 percent per year. That is because Western Europe and the United States made unusually large industrial gains during that same period.

However, during the last half of the nineteenth century Russia also began an industrialization drive, which continued, with a few interruptions, up to World War I. Railroad construction started around 1860, accelerating in the decade 1865–1875 and again in the late 1890s and the years leading up to the 1914 war. Total industrial output began its climb from a very low level around 1860; its ascent was halted during the next fifty years by several business slumps—essentially the same ones that hit most of the industrial countries. Things came together between 1883 and 1913, when industrial output grew on the average by 4.5 to 5 percent per year, quite a bit higher than the growth rate of output overall. Still, even on the eve of World War I, Russia had not become a great industrial power, despite her impressive gains during the preceding half-century.

The labor supply after 1860 rose by an average of 3 percent a year. Labor productivity registered good gains, and, as a consequence, real wages on balance rose for the industrial labor force. But it was not easy going, and in any case real wages were never generous. After 1860, these working incomes rose for a while, but as peasants were released from the land and began to move into the labor force, wages declined. There was a decided turnaround in the late 1880s and the 1890s. An industrial downturn starting around 1900 sent real wages tumbling, but the economy's recovery after 1905 created favorable conditions for the workers once again.

Throughout all these ups and downs, the wage rate was never high, particularly before the 1890s. It was depressed by the power of employers to fire workers at will, to fine them for all sorts of infractions, to impose unfavorable systems of payment on them (such as payment in goods rather than cash), and to replace them with machines. Wage rates also suffered because of government measures that outlawed labor unions until 1906 and, even after that, subjected them to numerous restrictions. Finally, many workers were not totally dependent on factory wages because they maintained contact with their villages and hence with a backup source of sustenance. This allegedly scaled down workers' demands within the industrial sector and hence contributed to the relatively low factory wages. In addition to being poorly paid, workers were kept toiling for long hours—on the average twelve to thirteen hours each day, not counting travel or meal times. This grueling workday was slowly eased by factory legislation and by employers' accumulated evidence that shorter hours did not usually lead to lower output. Thus, the average working day at the outbreak of World War I was down to ten hours.

Even with the expansion of industry during the latter half of the nineteenth century, fully 85 percent of the Russian population was still rural at the turn of the century. While rural poverty had decreased since the emancipation of serfs in the 1860s, it continued to be serious and widespread. Almost three-quarters of the Russian people (aged ten and over) were illiterate—a much higher figure than in Western Europe and the United States, where, around 1900, fewer than one-quarter of the people in France, Austria, Britain, and the United States were unable to read and write. Everywhere in Europe, women had higher rates of illiteracy than men. This problem was especially acute in Russia, as was the illiteracy rate among peasants.

Russia was comparatively no better off at that time in matters of health and sanitation. Infant mortality in Russia was more than twice the level in Britain and more than three times that of Sweden; no Western European country had so bad a record as Russia's. The countryside, once again, was especially bad; for much of the period, there was only one doctor for every 20,000 rural inhabitants. But the cities were also disaster scenes periodically, with typhus, cholera, or smallpox epidemics breaking out every few years, with terrible housing shortages dictating miserable and filthy living conditions, and with much unemployment during the industrial slumps.

Nevertheless, from abysmally low levels, improvements were made in both urban and rural nutrition and general health standards; and with these gains, the overall rate of mortality declined. Since the birthrate remained high, population surged during the decades surrounding the turn of the century.

With agricultural and industrial output gains, advances in real wages, and improvements in health and sanitation, the Russian people were better off after 1900 than they had been in prior decades. Of course, some Russians were considerably better off than those piled up at the bottom of the heap. One percent of families received something like 15 to 20 percent of total income, and their share of total wealth was even greater. Educational opportunities, superior health services, cultural activities, travel, and other pleasures—all of these were near-monopolies of the chosen few. While some peasants stayed where they were born—out in the sticks where not much was going on—many migrated to newly opened territories, often out of desperation, and others found their way into the hovels of city slums.

Added to the assorted miseries of the Russian people was the problem of excessive drinking. Extreme intoxication was not uncommon among both city-dwellers and peasants; many deaths were attributed to this social illness. The government attempted to curtail the consumption of vodka and other alcoholic beverages, but such restrictions always met with great resistance; the government also depended heavily on indirect taxes on alcohol—a third or more of its total revenues around 1900 came from this source. Nothing much ever resulted from these anti-drinking campaigns. Workers continued to spend large fractions of their incomes on this addiction. Russian and

Soviet literature is liberally sprinkled with instances of drunkenness and with evidence of the damage it inflicted on many people, the guilty and innocent alike.

★

RURAL LIVING STANDARDS IN THIS CENTURY

S ixty years after the turn of this century, the percentage of Russian people living in rural areas had fallen from 85 to about 50 percent—not a startling decline considering the industrialization that had occurred in the meantime. Even today, at least a third of the Soviet people live in the countryside and 20 to 25 percent of them are engaged directly in farm production. Those figures are quite a bit higher in many of the poorer republics, including those in Central Asia and the Transcaucasus (except Armenia). For the country as a whole, at least 90 million people continue to reside rurally—not many fewer in absolute numbers than 90 years ago! The main reason for the continuing large rural population is the very low productivity of farmers in the face of requirements for large supplies of food. In the United States, fewer than 5 percent of the population are able to provide the food for the entire nation.

While the lives of the peasants were far from idyllic around 1900, the Bolshevik Revolution in 1917 shook the countryside to its roots, and the civil war from 1918 to 1920 exacerbated an already desperate situation. Lenin's New Economic Policy that followed restored former living standards, low as they were, to most peasants; however, several years after Lenin's death in 1924, Stalin began the collectivization drives that resulted in widespread killings, internal deportations, the slaughter of animals, and terrible human suffering. As Osip Mandelshtam described it in his poem "Stalin," in two lines that cost him his life, "All we hear is the Kremlin mountaineer/The murderer and peasant-slayer." That was the low point; some improvements followed, but on the whole the lives of peasants were little or no better at the time of Stalin's death in 1953 than they had been forty years earlier.

We should recall Abel Aganbegyan's story about visiting his wife's village in 1953. In his description, that village—to which he had to walk the last 12 miles—seems like something out of the dark ages: no electricity, no shops, subsistence-level farming. While this village was typical of much of the Soviet Union at the time, there were some rural areas where living standards were much higher. Still, Aganbegyan's account is a good reminder that for half a century after 1900, revolution or no revolution, rural poverty continued to be widespread. And even ten more years—those following Stalin's death—made little difference to many peasants.

However, there were notable improvements during the 1960s and 1970s in rural living standards. The Soviet government, first under Khrushchev and later under Brezhnev, set out to narrow the large gap between city and countryside—and, more generally, to reduce the extreme income inequalities that were the legacy of Stalin's policies. To these ends, over the course of several years the government raised wages for the lowest-income groups, especially workers in the services sector; raised the minimum wage by one-third for urban workers and by one-half for rural workers; raised minimum pensions for disabled workers and minimum benefits for survivors; established a national social-insurance system for peasants; lowered taxes on low-income families; and promoted equality by locating more capital investment in the poorer regions. As a result of these and other measures, income inequalities were greatly reduced; in particular, living standards in the countryside now are not much below those in the cities.

The policies promoting greater equality occurred within a context of national economic growth. Since Stalin's death the Soviet people, both in the cities and in the countryside, have enjoyed rising income levels—though the growth process has been slowing down rather ominously in recent years. In the agricultural realm, the real wages of state farm employees have more than doubled since 1965, and the incomes of members of collective farms have increased by much more than that. Farmers working on private plots and in private agriculture generally have had good gains, too.

The rising incomes throughout the economy have led to ever-greater demands for all types of goods and services, including food items. Because the retail prices of major food products have been kept constant or permitted to increase only slightly, the result has been shortages of many agricultural goods—and this despite the fact that absolute supplies have also risen for most items. Food shortages persist mainly because, at such relatively cheap prices, supplies haven't grown enough to match the expanding demands.

If retail prices were allowed to rise to equilibrium levels, the queues would disappear and with them the "shortages." That is, the quantities demanded would decline at the higher prices, and the higher equilibrium prices would stimulate supply. This state of affairs would not necessarily indicate that people had no further needs to satisfy, for, at the equilibrium prices, they would gladly purchase larger supplies if they had more income. But, with their present incomes and the prices prevailing, people would be, for the moment, content with their purchases. No queues, no lost opportunities, no ration coupons—just limited incomes and limited supplies.

The Soviets do not have to search in foreign countries for lessons on how to change disequilibrium prices to equilibrium ones. During most of the First Five-Year Plan, 1928–32, many prices were controlled by the state at relatively low levels. At these levels, since demand exceeded supply—often by very large amounts—the most essential commodities were rationed in order to insure their fair distribution. Purchase of these rationed goods required both money and coupons. When the low-priced commodities were not rationed, money, time, and patience were required, for long queues developed quickly in front of any store rumored to have such items. Rationing was introduced for bread in early 1929, and the system soon spread to most foodstuffs and to many manufactured consumer goods. These conditions called forth free and black markets in which goods could be purchased at prices far exceeding the official ones, in one case legally and in the other case illegally. As supplies later increased, the excess of demands over supplies narrowed, and it became possible for the state to raise prices to equilibrium levels, or close to them, without having to go sky high. Nevertheless, these retail price increases, which occurred over a few years, were substantial—necessarily so to enable the state to lift the rationing regulations. Rationing on such goods disappeared; many consumer commodities were priced (high) near equilibrium levels; long lines in front of stores were no longer ubiquitous; and free and extralegal markets tended to fade away. By 1937, the controlled prices on foodstuffs were generally quite close to free-market levels.

These price correspondences were not universal, inasmuch as the state continued to make mandatory purchases from the collective farms at artificially low prices and to set below-equilibrium prices for many industrial products. Moreover, some consumer items were price-controlled on the low side. Still, the overall situation was that goods were there and purchasable if consumers could pay the prices. Later on, much of this progress had to be reversed as war expenditures created excess demands once again at the controlled prices. The German invasion in June 1941 brought on stiff rationing, widespread controls, and the other familiar signs of an economy at war.

Much of the industrialization of the 1930s was paid for by the peasants, whose food products were procured by the state at low prices, often leaving members of collective farms at standards of living so low as to threaten survival. The state then sold these procured items at higher prices in the towns and cities, the differences becoming revenues for the state budget—often by way of "turnover taxes" (roughly, sales taxes) added on to the procurement prices.

★

RECENT EFFORTS AT IMPROVEMENT

The contrast between the policies under Stalin and those that developed after Stalin's death is quite startling. Under the later and still-current measures, procurement prices paid by the state to the agricultural sector for major food products have been generally higher than the retail prices at the state stores. Moreover, the state has sold manufactured goods—such as machinery, fertilizers, and gasoline—to the farms at prices below cost. These interventions have involved the state in subsidy payments, adding greatly to recent budget deficits. Even so, procurement prices have not been high enough to cover the expenses of production on many collective farms, which has meant losses for these farms and the incurrence of debt. From time to time, the state has cancelled the long-term debt of the collective farms, thereby subsidizing them even more. All of this has been in the interest of reversing the harsh policies under Stalin that kept peasants' lives precarious and their living conditions so unsatisfactory. To make this U-turn, though, the state has seen its own budget conditions reversed—

going, in effect, from taking in substantial taxes (from the price differentials) to paying out large subsidies when the price differentials were turned the other way.

Mostly owing to these and other policies favoring agriculture, food production has grown, though food imports have risen as well. Over the past few decades, the nutrient content of the Soviet diet has been equal, or very nearly so, to that of the United States—in per capita food energy (calories), protein levels, and specific vitamins and minerals. However, half of the calories in the Soviet Union come from grains and potatoes, which is twice the level prevailing in the United States. Soviet consumers aspire to higher-quality food, which the economy has not been able to provide. Further, since income distribution is still unequal geographically and ethnically, certain subgroups in the Soviet Union have serious deficiencies in their diets.

The agricultural situation in the USSR is far from satisfactory in other respects, too. Labor productivity continues to be low—perhaps only 10 to 25 percent of U.S. performance—and Soviet agriculture generally is plagued by many inefficiencies. These can be traced to a number of different sources, including bloated bureaucracies that interfere in decisions that should be made at local levels. In addition, agriculture suffers because of poor roads, inadequate storage facilities, and shortages of trucks and railcars; these deficiencies largely account for the 20 percent of agricultural output that is wasted each year as it moves from the fields to the consumers.

Uncertain supplies of key inputs, such as fertilizers and machinery (which is generally in short supply and frequently breaks down), are another cause of low productivity. Also, many of the younger, more skilled, and more ambitious workers leave the countryside each year for the cities. Moreover, the pay of farmers has not been linked closely enough to performance, which has resulted in a lack of personal incentives for doing something extra or working harder and longer.

Finally, as we have just seen, in an attempt to stimulate farm production and at the same time to keep food prices low for urbanites, the government has paid higher prices for agricultural products than it has received in selling them through the state stores. The result is a huge subsidy to consumers and agriculture, amounting to about 15 percent of state budget expenditures. This has contributed to the large Soviet deficits and hence to inflationary pressures throughout the economy.

Many of these failings have been known for years, and Soviet authorities have made repeated attempts to cure them. As one Soviet expert wrote: "Since 1965 the Soviet government has expended an enormous number of rubles on agriculture through procurement price increases, food price subsidies, increased supplies of inputs such as fertilizer, and capital investments in agriculture and in the industries that supply agriculture." He could have added the measures to raise living standards in the countryside, the encouragement of private plots, the many attempts to decentralize decision making, the added monetary and non-monetary measures to attract and keep skilled labor in the rural areas, and the encouragement of "contract teams" or brigades. These are relatively small-scale units that enter into contracts with the collective and state farms to complete designated tasks, such as raising livestock, growing crops, and operating machinery. The contracts specify certain payments of produce or services to the farms, but the contracting units are given much freedom on how to meet their obligations, and anything produced over these amounts is theirs. The main idea is to give members of collective farms and employees of state farms greater income incentives to work harder and more efficiently.

★

GORBACHEV'S AGRICULTURAL MEASURES

It is clear that Gorbachev, upon assumption of leadership in March 1985, did not suddenly announce a brand-new program to stimulate agriculture. Almost everything he wanted to do was already contained in previous decrees, including especially the Food Program of 1982 that was put together under Brezhnev's direction (aided by Gorbachev himself, who was at the time the head of agriculture). This program drew on earlier efforts reaching back to 1965. Gorbachev, when he became general secretary of the Party, gathered together various existing strands for his own program to raise farm labor productivity. This program stressed more investment in rural housing and the infrastructure, including education, to make the countryside more attractive, especially to younger, more-skilled workers; higher-quality farm machinery and equipment; better quality control of output; a rapid extension of collective contracts with small groups of farm workers; pay more closely linked to performances; resettlement policies of labor from areas of labor surpluses to areas of deficits; and so on. Are these measures the right ones? Are they likely to work?

A recent U.S. government study that set out to explain the annual net value of Soviet agricultural output (crops and livestock) from 1968 to 1987 postulated that six factors were important: the size of the capital stock, the labor supply, material inputs (e.g., fertilizers and herbicides), the level of technology, government policy, and the weather. What especially required explanation were the sharp downturn in agricultural output in 1979, 1980, and 1981 and the general recovery after that. Was the weather the main cause in both cases?

The study found that the weather had very little to do with the downturn years. The authors claim that these were mainly caused by the slowdown in the economy as a whole, which in turn stemmed from poorly designed and ineptly administered government policies in those years. The Brezhnev Food Program of 1982 then helped to turn things around. However, generally poor weather during 1983–87 held back the gains that otherwise would have occurred—and these "losses" were substantial. The downward trend in the labor supply since 1983 (total hours worked) also reduced the gains that otherwise would have been registered in agricultural output. On the other hand, the gains since 1982 were helped along by relatively favorable government policies.

Another finding of the study, which—if accurate—would have important implications for the Gorbachev initiative, was that putting additional capital into agriculture has a relatively small impact on output—more precisely, a 1 percent increase of capital leads to a mere 0.17 percent gain in farm output. A complementary finding was that additional labor inputs into agriculture have a substantial impact on output—namely, a 1 percent gain of labor means an 0.83 percent rise in output. This suggests that labor inputs have about five times more power than capital inputs. Because the growth of labor inputs has been declining since 1983, this factor has tended to reduce output gains, too. When these findings are considered together, they seem to spell trouble for Soviet agriculture in the coming years, and for the Gorbachev program.

The authors of this study concluded that the future looks favorable only if the weather is at least average, gains in labor productivity more than offset declines in labor inputs, and material inputs into agriculture continue to grow as in recent years. This assumes that government policies will continue to be favorable—especially that the policy of encouraging team contracts will continue and expand.

In other words, the Gorbachev program should not count too heavily on turning agriculture around with more farm machinery and fertilizers, even though these help. It should continue to expand the measures designed to raise incentives and efficiency—and pray for favorable weather.

Something is fishy here. Either the study is faulty, which I am willing to rule out, or it reveals much more about Soviet inefficiency than it purports to say. All studies of agriculture that I know—in the United States, Canada, Europe—show that output has expanded mightily from inputs of capital equipment. After all, U.S. agriculture is noted for its heavy infusion of farm machinery and its rigid economy of labor. Capital has replaced labor in a big way, and farm output has prospered greatly.

This study of Soviet agriculture suggests the opposite: Put in more labor and go relatively easy on the capital. That result could reflect the awful truth that the Soviets have been grossly inefficient in introducing capital into the countryside—so clumsy that it hardly mattered for the growth of output. If so, the study is a valuable lesson in the inefficiency of Soviet planning in the farm area.

The lesson for Gorbachev, then, is not to go easy on capital infusion, but to reorganize radically the way this sector is administered.

★

THE PEASANTRY:
UP CLOSE AND PERSONAL

How Russian people lived around the turn of this century can be told, as I have just done, with some data and comparisons to the present. A more memorable approach may be to look at the lives of ordinary people—workers and peasants—as depicted in literature written around that time and more recently. For the earlier period, we will look at Maxim Gorky, who describes in his autobiography the lives of the people he knew as a boy and young man during the latter part of the nineteenth century. We will also consider two short stories by Anton Chekhov that depict the lives of peasants around the same time. These selections will add much to our understanding of where the Bolsheviks started as they pursued a socialist society after 1917. Then a look at a modern story about life on collective farms will shed light on some of the persistent problems Gorbachev must overcome.

Gorky's three-volume autobiography, written between 1910 and 1921, in fact covers only the first twenty years of his life. In *My Childhood*, *My Apprenticeship*, and *My Universities*, Gorky tells of being deposited with poor grandparents after his father's death and working at various menial jobs and apprenticeships from the age of nine. During this period, Gorky was never more than a few steps from the Volga River and the people involved with it. Both the river and the people shaped his development immeasurably.

Certain themes recur throughout the three volumes. One is the heavy influence of religion on young Gorky's friends and relatives. Another is the terrible toll that alcohol imposed on so many lives. A third theme is the combination of tenderness and sadistic cruelty that marked a great number of personal relationships. Finally, we must note the continual battle this boy waged to overcome almost insuperable barriers—mainly a virulent anti-intellectualism—along the path to his eventual position as one of Russia's most illustrious writers and the first to focus on his country's new industrial proletariat. During Gorky's first twenty years, he encountered mostly common laborers, craftsmen, and peasants; the factory workers came later in his life. Nevertheless, seeing the way these people lived and thought is useful in understanding the Soviet workers of today.

★

The dominance of religion. Gorky's young years were powerfully shaped by his grandparents, especially his grandmother. This massive woman was a religious fanatic. She prayed constantly, telling God every detail of the day; she claimed to see devils and lost souls; and she admonished even animals and insects for insufficient devotion to God. She lived in a world of mythical figures—gods, goblins, spirits—which was almost completely removed from the reality of her daily life. She did not distinguish between reality and myth and couldn't even get her Christian myths right; her explanations of things were entirely superstitious; her stories were all fairy tales. She attributed the early deaths of most of her eighteen children to God's fondness for these babies: "He kept taking them to be his angels." When her husband lost all the money he had—little as it was—she attributed the loss to God's unhappiness over their failure to "help the poor or take pity on the unfortunate." This weird belief prompted her to take young Gorky out in the middle of the night to leave coins and biscuits on the windowsills of the small houses of the impoverished—an act that reduced her own family to absolute economic misery. Despite all this, the young boy worshipped his grandmother and felt "that she belonged to a higher species than anyone else, and was the kindest and wisest person in the whole world." He thought her "saintly" and relished her many interesting stories, probably just because they were so divorced from reality. Later on, even when he changed his mind about the religious life and the make-believe world, he never rejected the person of his grandmother.

The younger boy's grandfather had his own God, a very cruel one who punished right and left. This God aroused fear and hostility in the boy: "He loved no one, watched everything with a stern eye, and above all else saw in men nothing but what was foul, evil and sinful. Clearly he didn't trust men, was perpetually waiting for them to repent, and loved punishing people." The grandfather was a fatalist, who attributed everything that happened either to God or the devil.

Religion dominated the lives of most of the people Gorky knew. For a time, when he lived with a great aunt, he felt the entire house was permeated with the family's vengeful God. "God was dragged into everything that went on in that house, into every little nook and cranny of their meaningless lives, which as a result acquired a certain significance and importance, however superficial: they seemed to be praying every single hour to some higher being." This great aunt and her husband talked about nothing but sin and death, both of which ruled their lives.

As a young teenager, Gorky was an apprentice in an icon workshop, where of course religious topics were discussed, sometimes endlessly. The workshop attracted Old Believers who told young Gorky about the Nikonites, the German Lutherans, and the many other religious sects found along the Volga. Later, in other jobs, the thirteen-year-old met many workmen who were caught up in religious myths and fairy tales; they struggled desperately in the real world and used fictional stories to transport them away from reality. "I noticed (and how many times!) that anything that was unusual, fantastic, often obviously clumsily concocted, pleased the people much more than serious stories about the real truth." Similarly, in the icon workshop, Gorky found favor with the workers when he told them terrifying tales. "Even the older men clearly preferred fantasy to fact. I realized very well that the more improbable the event, the more fantastic a story was, the more attentively they would listen to me. On the whole reality did not interest them and they all peered dreamily into the future and turned a blind eye to the poverty and ugliness of the present."

For a time, Gorky admired and respected the Old Believers who persevered against all odds; later on he realized that these people were really stupefied by their beliefs. "They were kept in the graveyard of their own obsolete beliefs by the sheer inertia of their memories, by their morbid love of suffering and oppression. But if one tried to deprive them of any possibility of suffering, then this would destroy them and they would disappear like clouds on a fresh windy day."

When he was fifteen, Gorky became involved in left-wing discussion groups in dissident movements. In these circles, he met religious doubters and outright atheists—people who contrasted sharply with the workmen and peasants he was living among. The contrast, in fact, was so stark that Gorky decided he could no longer live with people who "dressed themselves like priests in vestments of lies and hypocrisy."

★

The senseless violence. Despite their religious beliefs, the people Gorky knew were often sadistically vicious, even toward family members and best friends. When Gorky was only a few years old, his grandfather, for punishment, would flog him into unconsciousness. At other times, this same "wicked person" showered him with gentle attention. His grandfather also beat his wife horribly. "Once . . .

when she went up to him with her soft cajoleries, he quickly swung around and cracked her on the face with his fist, making a crunching sound. Grandmother staggered back, her hands pressed to her lips, then she straightened up and said softly and calmly: 'You fool. . . .' She spat out blood at his feet. . . . "

One of Gorky's uncles beat and tortured his wife to death, and repeatedly attempted to murder Gorky's grandfather. When Gorky's mother remarried, her new husband was soon beating her. There was continual war within this family, yet it was a family still, and all the suffering inflicted by one person on another, all the odious conflicts, "died away just as quickly as they flared up."

As a teenage apprentice, Gorky was flogged so viciously by his master that he had to be taken to the hospital. By that time, he writes, he was thoroughly familiar with the widespread inexplicable brutality, "the aimless, senseless cruelty, practiced merely for amusement and not for any material gain." For example, the merchants near the icon workshop tormented animals just for the fun of it, and they purposely gave false directions to people new to the area simply to watch them suffer. A worker, furiously angry with another, would chop up an animal and deposit it at the foot of his foe. These people "had an insatiable desire to laugh at other people, to hurt and embarrass them . . . [they were] always trying to make laughing-stocks of one another." They frequently addressed one another with terms of abuse: old fool, crazy woman, ill-mannered lout, stupid ninnies, filthy bitch. The peasants that Gorky later lived among swore violently at each other, did not trust one another, and all had "something of the wolf in them." They were always ready for a fight, even over trifles. Were they human beings or howling wild animals?

After some reflection, Gorky attributed all this inhumanity to the miserable and terribly boring lives of these poor people, who sought diversion by any means, including sadistic torture.

★

The wholesale drunkenness. Many people in Gorky's life often drank themselves silly—or vicious. Most of his relatives, even his grandmother (that "saintly" person), consumed vodka like water. As a small boy, Gorky thought that his grandmother, when drunk, became "all the finer for it." Several years later, however, he could see how she disgraced the family and had to be locked away in the attic during her drunken bouts. Smury, the cook on a Volga boat where Gorky worked as a dishwasher, had an insatiable thirst for vodka. "He used to start drinking in the morning, as soon as he got up, and polish off a bottle in four swigs. Then he would sip beer until evening . . . he would drink glass after glass." The cook warned young Gorky that vodka was the work of the devil and to stay away from it, though he himself was incapable of acting on his own advice.

As time went on, Gorky became ever more aware of the frequency of drunkenness among workers and peasants. "It tormented me to see how much vodka men drank, how disgustingly they behaved when they were drunk, and how unnatural their relations were with women." He described wild drinking parties, drunken prostitutes, "plastered" workers, people who delighted in getting others roaring drunk, and people who aspired to higher positions in life but fell, sodden with vodka, into the gutters. He once saw a gang of workmen getting cargo off a sinking ship, and he was struck by how hard and long they labored, seemingly with good cheer. Then he learned that, in addition to their regular pay, they had been promised nine gallons of vodka for a good job—which they later downed in a pub.

★

The pervasive anti-intellectualism. During the brief times that Gorky's mother was with him, she gave him a grammar book, made him memorize poetry, and later sent him to school. But it was Smury, the ship's cook, who introduced Gorky to literature and continually urged him to read. He loaned Gogol's *Taras Bulba* to the boy, then Scott's *Ivanhoe* and Fielding's *Tom Jones*. When the ship docked, Gorky, now hooked on reading, would seek out books that he could buy for a few kopeks. By the time he became an apprentice in the icon workshop, reading for him was a necessity. Books had become "as indispensable to me as vodka to a drunkard."

But anti-intellectualism confronted the young boy at every turn. He was caught reading a novel by his master in the icon shop. This man "lectured me for a long time on the subject of harmful and dangerous books: 'Some people who read books blew up a railway once and tried to murder someone.'" Nevertheless, Gorky continued to read surreptitiously. "I used to read in the shed, where I went to chop the wood, or in the attic, which was just as cold and uncomfortable. Sometimes if a book interested me or if I had to read it quickly I used to get up in the night and light a candle. But the old woman (his great aunt) noticed that the candles were growing shorter overnight and started measuring them with a kindling stick.... "This woman physically destroyed many of his books. He replenished his stock with Balzac, Hugo, Goncourt, Scott, Pushkin, and Turgenev.

Still, he had to listen to many warnings about the dangers of reading. He was told: "Only God knows what sullies the springs of the holy spirit. Perhaps that's your sin, you people who read books. I don't read books or anything made of paper ... I'm a simple, *living* person." Another friend told him that books are written "to befuddle you." Later, a baker who employed him voiced his disapproval of Gorky's passion for books: "You'd be better off sleeping than reading." At the same time, others continued to encourage him, and by the time he moved into revolutionary circles he was among friends who accepted his passion.

★

GORKY'S HOPE
FOR THE FUTURE

At one point, Gorky stops to ask himself whether it is worthwhile recording this barbarous life in nineteenth-century Russia. He finds that the answer is yes, "because that was the real loathsome truth and to this day it is still valid. It is that truth that must be known down to the very roots, so that by tearing them up it can be completely erased from the memory, from the soul of man, from our whole oppressive and shameful life." Later, he returns to the same theme: "Why, you may ask, am I telling you all these abominations? So that you should know, my dear sirs, these are not things of the past— far from it! ... I will not be sentimental nor conceal the terrible truth with the tinsel words of a beautiful lie. We must go forward into life! We must take from it into our hearts and heads everything that is good and humane so that it becomes a living part of us."

Gorky is hopeful that these horrors can be overcome. "Life is always surprising us—not by its rich, seething layer of bestial refuse—but by the bright, healthy and creative human powers of goodness that are forever forcing their way up through it. It is those powers that awaken our indestructible hope that a brighter, better and more humane life will once again be reborn."

Gorky informs us that the miserable and degrading conditions of the 1880s were about the same thirty or forty years later, when he was writing his memoirs. While we would not be justified in extending such wretchedness to the present day, we should nevertheless note that some of these ignominies, probably in lesser degree, have continued into our own time.

One of Gorbachev's initial programs was an anti-alcohol campaign, which was quickly withdrawn after widespread protests. There have been many reports, since *glasnost* was officially launched, of a remarkable revival of all sorts of superstition—from soothsayers, palmists, and Indian meditators to dozens of religious sects and celestial gurus. What Gorky observed apparently went underground after the Bolshevik Revolution, only to re-emerge with Gorbachev's more-tolerant policies.

Can we also discern an open revival of cruelty in the taunts and terror unleased by one ethnic group against another? It is not out of left field to suggest that these menacing manifestations severely limit rational responses to Gorbachev's *perestroika* programs, and hence threaten to derail the entire movement toward an improved economy.

★

A DARK VIEW OF THE WORKING CLASS

Anton Chekhov's short stories echo Gorky's themes of cruelty, alcoholism, superstition, and just plain ignorance. Peasants, especially, are portrayed as little more than beasts in many of his stories, but this dismal view extended beyond peasants to town-dwellers as well.

In a long story, "My Life: The Story of a Provincial" (1896), Chekhov tells the tale of Misail Poloznev. Born into a noble family, Misail is fully expected to make his career doing intellectual or white-collar work, but instead chooses to become a house painter. His father, outraged and embarrassed, disinherits him: "Anybody, even the most abject fool or criminal, is capable of manual labour; such labour is the distinguishing mark of the slave and barbarian." This is all right with Misail, who despises the sham of so-called intellectual work and believes that it is most important to earn one's daily bread without being a burden on others.

Misail is repelled by his town of 60,000; he considers his acquaintances boring and repulsive; most of the townspeople are ignorant and lead disgusting lives; and the town itself, he thinks, is barren of culture. "I did not know one honest man in the town," the narrator-son confesses. Everyone takes bribes, drinks to excess, and wallows in corruption.

Moving to a suburb where he works menially for others, Misail now discovers the seamy side of their lives as well. "Those of my fellow-citizens, about whom I had no opinion before, or who had externally appeared perfectly decent, turned out now to be base, cruel people, capable of any dirty action . . . Rarely did a day pass without swindling."

Misail marries Mariya (affectionately, Masha), a woman born to the intelligentsia, but who sympathizes with his rebellious views. Together they move to an estate acquired from her parents, aspiring to become farmers, grow their own food, and build and make whatever else they may need. It is not long before Misail loses his initial enthusiasm for the rural life. "Field labour did not attract me. I did not understand farming, and I did not care for it; it was perhaps because my forefathers had not been tillers of the soil, and the very blood that flowed in my veins was purely of the city. . . . The peasant who turned up the soil with his plough and urged on his pitiful horse, wet and tattered, with his craning neck, was to me the expression of [a] coarse, savage, ugly force, and every time I looked at his uncouth movements I involuntarily began thinking of the legendary life of the remote past, before men knew the use of fire." Just as Misail's father looks down on manual labor, Misail himself denigrates the work of the peasant.

Masha, too, begins to see the peasants as savages. In her view, they cheat each other, steal whatever they can from the young married couple, drink themselves dumb, are coarse, and live like wild beasts. Still, Misail sees something positive in their lives: "There really was filth and drunkenness and foolishness and deceit, but with all that one yet felt that the life of the peasants rested on a firm, sound foundation. However uncouth a wild animal the peasant following the plough seemed, and however he might stupefy himself with vodka, still, looking at him more closely, one felt that there was in him what was needed, something very important," which was his belief in truth and justice. (This almost has to be some sort of a Chekhovian joke, for the evidence in the story leads us precisely to the opposite conclusion. Either that, or Chekhov is giving us notice that Misail is rapidly cracking up!)

Misail and Masha eventually divorce and abandon the rural scene. At that point Misail and his sister take a place together in town, but they soon decide that they can no longer live there. "We talked of the fanaticism, the coarseness of feeling, the insignificance of these respectable families . . . and I kept asking in what way these stupid, cruel, lazy, and dishonest people were superior to the drunken and superstitious peasants of Kurilovka, or in what way they were better than animals. . . . " Misail ponders the lives he has seen, recalling:

> . . . all [the] people I knew who had been slowly done to death by their nearest relations. I remembered the tortured dogs, driven mad, the live sparrows plucked naked by boys and flung into the water, and a long, long series of obscure lingering miseries which I had looked on continually from early childhood in that town. . . . What good had they gained from all that had been said and written hitherto if they were still possessed by the same spiritual darkness and hatred of liberty, as they were a hundred and three hundred years ago? . . . So these sixty thousand people have been reading and hearing of truth, of justice, of mercy, of freedom for generations, and yet from morning till night, till the day of their death, they are lying, and tormenting each other, and they fear liberty and hate it as a deadly foe.

In another short story, "Peasants" (1897), Chekhov maintains a somber view of these rural residents. This story focuses on the extended Chikildeyev family, three generations living together in squalor in the small village of Zhokovo. We see the family through the eyes of one son, Nikolay, and his wife, Olga. They have been living and doing menial labor in Moscow, but illness has forced them to quit their jobs and return to the village.

Almost immediately on returning home, Nikolay hates what he sees and smells. "When Nikolay . . . saw the whole family, all those bodies big and little stirring on the sleeping platforms, in the cradles and in all the corners, and when he saw the greed with which his old father and the women ate black bread, dipping it in water, it was borne in upon him that he had made a mistake in coming here. . . . The tea smelt of fish; the sugar was gray and had been nibbled; cockroaches ran about over the bread and the crockery. It was disgusting to drink the tea, and the conver-sation was disgusting, too—about nothing but poverty and sickness."

The scene darkens even more as Nikolay watches a drunken brother beat his wife so fiercely that others have to pour water over her to revive her. Many of the peasants drink heavily; they are often in a stupor, stumbling and falling down, and celebrating something or other with vodka for days on end.

Chekhov writes of the same drunkenness and violence that Gorky observed in his youth—and the same religious fervor as well. Olga is a religious zealot who sees God's hand in everything, and other family members call on the "Mother of God" continually to intercede on their behalf. At one point in a religious celebration, Chekhov writes, "all seemed suddenly to grasp that there was no void between earth and heaven, that the rich and powerful had not seized everything, that there was still protection from abuse, from bondage, from crush-ing, unbearable want, from the terrible vodka." But there is no indication that this understanding makes the slightest difference in their earthly lives.

In the rest of the family, we see prostitution; we see a cross grandmother who freely employs violence and vulgar language against the children; and we see illiteracy taken for granted.

When Nikolay dies of his illness, Olga decides to return to Moscow with her daughter. As she prepares for departure, she thinks that at times "it seemed as though these people lived worse than cattle . . . they were coarse, dishonest, dirty, and drunken; they did not live at peace with one another but quarreled continually, because they feared, suspected, and despised each other. . . . Yet, they were human beings, they suffered and wept like human beings, and there was nothing in their lives for which one could not find justification."

Chekhov's tales corroborate fictionally the actual observations of Gorky about the lives of ordinary people around the turn of the century. If these views are anywhere near accurate (some scholars challenge them), they make it easier to understand why the Bolshevik Revolution had to be centered in the largest cities, home of the urban proletariat, and not entrusted to the peasantry and small-town inhabitants. Gorky and Chekhov also make it clearer why Lenin insisted, even with primary reference to the urban workers, that a strong vanguard party was absolutely essential to formulate and impart socialist ideas to the masses. We have already noted the implication of legacies from this era for Gorbachev's own revolution.

★

POVERTY WITHIN
THE COLLECTIVES

G orky's and Chekhov's accounts of life along the Volga and in villages deep within Russia depict the way people confronted their daily tribulations, some rising above adversity but most broken by it. These peasants and workers did not live pleasantly or harmoniously just prior to the 1917 revolutions, but neither did they more than a half century later. During those tumultuous 50 years, the Bolsheviks seized power, Lenin and Stalin came and went, and Russia was turned into an industrial and military giant. Still, the peasants languished.

While I could document this with statistics, the dismal truth is made quite plain in a story that takes place in 1962, almost a decade after Stalin's death. The author is Fyodor Abramov, who wrote about life as it really was on collective farms—unlike other Soviet authors who depicted nothing but happiness and dedication in the rural areas.

Abramov called his story "The Dodgers" (the Russian title, "Vokrug da Okolo," means to beat about the bush). When published in 1963, the story was at first praised but almost immediately thereafter attacked for its pessimism and distortion of typical village life. One critic said that it was the writer's duty as a Soviet to help such backward farms and not focus exclusively on the seamy side of life. In his "stark realism," Abramov gives us a picture of ordinary people's daily lives that is astonishingly similar to what Gorky and Chekhov presented—yet Abramov was writing 60 or 70 years later.

The story takes place on a collective farm in northern Russia in the early 1960s. The central figure is Mysovsky, Chairman of the "New Life" collective farm and formerly a district official for almost thirty years.

Mysovsky has made a bad decision in not ordering the farmers to gather in the hay from three hundred acres of meadow during the recent dry weather. Now it is raining cats and dogs, and the hay is in danger of being ruined—and with it the plans of the collective farm for purchasing its necessities. On a Saturday in August, then, the Chairman is making the rounds, trying to drum up members for a special workday on Sunday. Mostly what he finds is lack of interest in the collective's problems, malingering, and excuses aplenty (thus "The Dodgers," or "Beating around the Bush"). Everywhere he turns, he is reminded of people's continuing battles against poverty and hard drinking, and their abiding concerns for their own private work and affairs. Not many are willing to bring in the hay on what should be a day of rest.

The reader cannot help but notice the many signs of poverty in this *kolkhoz*, even after 45 years of socialist economic development. The poverty does not seem much different from what we encountered in the Gorky and Chekhov stories. Poverty is poverty. One old man is described as living like a beast. We meet a widow and her four children, all in desperate need of a pension but without such support. Women are sent out into the countryside to gather wild mushrooms to supplement the families' meager rations. Another old woman is begging for bread. The village has had radio reception only since the previous year. Most members are without what they all yearn for—a cow. The *kolkhoz* is without milk. The clubhouse is in serious disrepair. The lodgings of most members are simple and crude, without much cheer. There are interesting exceptions: A bureaucrat has a much better house than average. Some of the people who have escaped the collective farm to work elsewhere in the vicinity continue to maintain relatively large homes in the village. But the general run of things is not at all good.

Next, drinking! (What else?) The head of the building unit, a skilled carpenter and excellent blacksmith, turns drunk and sullen. "And then this most valuable of all men on the farm—the Chairman's main support, you might say—started to drink. [The Chairman] tried every way to find out from him what had upset him. But he kept silent. You couldn't get a word out of him, and there was a real danger that the cattle sheds would not be finished. Once the foreman had got his nose stuck into a bottle, what could you expect from the others?" Pressured to unload his grievances, the foreman evidently considers his many woes and confesses to one of them: He has no "identity card" or internal passport and hence does not feel like a man. (These cards were issued to every citizen over 16 in urban areas in 1932, but not to peasants. Consequently, their freedom of movement was greatly restricted. Only in 1976 were such cards issued to rural residents.)

The foreman is not the only alcoholic; the leader of a brigade within the collective farm is constantly in her cups. Another woman apologizes when she can't offer a drink to the Chairman: "I ought to be able to offer you something better than tea, my dear guest! But grandma hasn't got anything stronger. There was a drop here, but my grandson wheedled it out of me. The day before yesterday he sailed in here drunk. 'Come on, old woman, give us a drop of wine or I'll set fire to you.' 'You drunken sot,' I said, 'aren't you ashamed to talk to your grandmother in that way?' Then I gave it to him—better to keep out of trouble." Even the Chairman, on Saturday night after he has made his calls, goes to the bar and drinks himself silly.

It is during those liquid hours that he promises—this he is later told, for he remembers nothing the next morning when he comes to—"30 percent" to any collective farm member who works on Sunday. (This presumably means 30 percent of the gross gathering.) As soon as this word gets around, it is enough to send everyone into action, and the job is completed in record time. Work for the good of the collective is one thing; work for private gain is quite another!

This, of course, does not surprise the Chairman—once he hears what he has offered. The evidence is all around him: the goof-offs, the feigned illnesses, and the ingenious excuses when it comes to collective tasks versus the tremendous energy going into private schemes for personal gain. The Chairman notices, for example, that one member has row after row of onions in his garden. "No, that's not for myself," the farmer says. "We grow that to sell." The Chairman begins to lose patience.

> "But what about your conscience—is that all right? Don't you find any difficulty in indulging in private business in your old age?"
>
> "Sure it's difficult. It's difficult getting hold of horses. See how heavy the onions are this year. But it's no good asking the foreman for transport—without a bottle he just doesn't hear."
>
> "And do you give him one?"
>
> "I do. At first I used to give him one for the horse's tail, but now he demands one for each hoof. It comes pretty dear."
>
> "Now listen to me, comrade Devyaty! You shut up this shop as quick as you can. If you don't we'll shut it for you."
>
> "You won't shut it," objected Pete, just as calmly as before.
>
> "We will. You just see! What do you think, then—that we're going to stand by and watch while you operate a private business under the very roof of the *kolkhoz*? If *you* haven't got a conscience, we'll find ways."

Perhaps this encounter with private initiative was at the back of the Chairman's mind when, later that evening, he tied one on at the bar and came out with his 30 percent offer. Anyway, as the Chairman looks around the next day at all the marvelous activity, he reflects that the scene "was like something out of the early days of the *kolkhoz*, when the countryside was still bursting with a surplus energy." Thirty percent, he realizes, eliminated painful conferences, shouting, bawling. But he also knows that he could get in plenty of trouble with the district officials for having introduced such private incentives into the collective environment. He will have to face that music.

While Abramov shows the same poverty, indolence, and inebriety we saw in Gorky and Chekhov, he suggests that much of this could be overcome if private initiative were encouraged. The Chairman in the story tells us pretty plainly that much of the poverty is caused by the very collectives that he himself helped organize thirty years before.

★

REVITALIZING THE COLLECTIVE FARMS

Abramov's point was certainly subversive at the time he wrote "The Dodgers." It was not permissible to suggest that the collective farms were not the solution to rural poverty but actually the problem. While Gorbachev would allow such thoughts to be aired these days, he definitely would not subscribe to the full implications of Abramov's idea. Nevertheless, Gorbachev has already proceeded some distance along this path by paving the way for much agricultural work to be done by small contract teams within the collectives, as described earlier in this chapter. Each team enters into a contract with its collective that specifies the job to be done and the monetary rewards for doing well. These arrangements, and the personal incentives built into them, are expected to raise labor productivity substantially and put more food into the state, collective, and free retail outlets. Also, de facto private property is now allowed through farmers' leaseholds.

Skeptics have questioned whether these rural reforms are leading the economy away from socialism and toward capitalism. As I have noted previously, it is Gorbachev's intention to achieve a better socialism, not some form of capitalism. It is undoubtedly his opinion that Soviet agriculture can remain socialist if the newly organized teams continue to operate through collective and state farms. In China, Deng Xiaoping and his associates chose to destroy the rural communes that Mao had created in the late 1950s. Gorbachev evidently would not want anything like that to happen in the Soviet Union, but strong forces have already pushed him into other forbidden territory and may do so again.

Of course, it is true that the reforms in the Soviet countryside are encouraging private initiative and, at the same time, demoting the larger socialist units by favoring the proliferation of family and team work units. Thus, although these measures may result in Gorbachev's more vibrant socialism, they also point to a lower degree of socialism in the countryside. They represent a step backward for the purpose of attaining a more dynamic agricultural sector.

So *perestroika* in the countryside is intentionally reducing the extent of socialism in order to gain efficiency. To have an agriculture that is both socialist and efficient, personal, team, and private activities must be guided and modified by social obligations that are internalized in (not imposed on) the individuals pursuing such gains. Rural workers, therefore, must be dedicated not only to their own and their family's welfare, but equally to the aims of their collective. These aims—these social obligations—include the following: to aid members of the collective who are disadvantaged by reason of old age, ill health, lack of skills, or family crises; to behave compassionately (not ruthlessly) in all market transactions with others, so as to ensure that one's gains are not made by unduly injuring others; and to participate in the provision of goods and services that are not forthcoming through individual and family pursuits. Efficiency with a social conscience—that is the goal.

But, after contemplating Gorky, Chekhov, and Abramov, this all sounds terribly utopian. The task of inculcating social values like these into the rural population over the next several years (the patience for *perestroika* will run out before that!) seems not only impossible but hardly worth attempting when an easier solution is at hand—Abramov's 30 percent.

It would be no trick at all to allow *perestroika* to lead to capitalism—and many people around the world, including some in the Soviet Union, would applaud such an outcome. But to carry out *perestroika* within an enriched and more efficient socialist society is something else again. If that should come to pass, we can say, along with Tolstoy, that history simultaneously produced both the problem and the answer in Mikhail Gorbachev. Is history up to it?

"The 27th Conference of the Communist Party of the Soviet Union. Our Course—Acceleration."

THE LEGACIES
OF RAPID
INDUSTRIALIZATION

The most important economic accomplishment of the Soviet Union was its transformation from a predominantly agricultural and rural country to a major urban-industrial nation within only three or four decades. The new Soviet government had to extricate the country from the European war, begin to reconstruct a ravaged economy, and then fight a two-year civil war against anti-Bolshevik Russians and their foreign supporters. After that, a period of economic retreat was necessary to allow the country to catch its breath. Then Stalin pulled the trigger of his starter's gun, and the entire population during the 1930s began a frantic race for industrialization. World War II intervened, followed by the disheartening task of picking up the pieces and mostly starting all over again.

The facts about these prewar and postwar performances are a necessary basis for our understanding of the current *perestroika* effort. From the retreat of Lenin's New Economic Policy (NEP) to Stalin's astonishing and abrupt turn toward a revolutionary set of economic directives, previously unimagined by friend or foe, to the reconstruction and further industrial development of the country after World

War II—these are the paths we will tread as we follow the course of the Soviets' gigantic leap into industrialization.

★

LENIN'S NEP:
A TRANSITION STAGE

After the October Revolution and the civil war, it was clear that socialism could not be established with a snap of the fingers. Marx considered socialism to be the successor to a fully developed capitalism—an overripe one—not a system to be imposed on a semi-feudal and semi-capitalist society. In Marx's view, after the proletarian revolution swept away the capitalist class, the working class would be able to erect a socialist economic base. The large industries, the infrastructure, the skilled labor force, the advanced science and culture—all would be there for the new socialist government to build on for its own future. But for a working class to establish socialism on a base of impoverishment and backwardness required much more than a toppling of the old regime. For one thing, a transition stage between the old society and the future socialist one was needed. But what kind of transition?

The civil war, 1918–20, forced the new government into economic policies that proved to be only war-related and not viable in the long run. These included measures of rigid centralized controls, administrative orders from top to bottom, direct requisitions of grain surpluses, and compulsory mobilization of civilian labor. Such an inflexible system, which stifled initiative and turned many people to illegal markets and nefarious bargaining, could not survive the end of hostilities. The disbanded soldiers, oppressed peasants, and half-starved urbanites expressed their anger at the new regime—at the intolerable living conditions—through violence, demonstrations, and general lawlessness. The Kronstadt uprising of sailors just outside Petrograd (St. Petersburg) in March 1921 capped these outbreaks of dissatisfaction and convinced the party that it had to make radical changes, not only in the policies of the civil-war period, but also in some of the nationalization measures of 1917–18.

The changes became known as the New Economic Policy (NEP),

which Lenin formulated in speeches and writings during 1921 and 1922. The NEP came to represent the transition stage between the old and the new. Lenin, in a report in March 1921, spelled out the meaning and necessity of the transition:

> There is no doubt that in a country where the overwhelming majority of the population consists of small agricultural producers, a socialist revolution can be carried out only through the implementation of a whole series of special transitional measures which would be superfluous in highly developed capitalist countries where wage-workers in industry and agriculture make up the vast majority. Highly developed capitalist countries have a class of agricultural wage-workers that has taken shape over many decades. Only such a class can socially, economically, and politically support a direct transition to socialism. Only in countries where this class is sufficiently developed is it possible to pass directly from capitalism to socialism, without any special country-wide transitional measures.

Lenin added that the Bolshevik Revolution could succeed, in the absence of supporting revolutions in the West, only by an agreement between the proletariat, which has the political power, and the peasantry. That is, if the small and relatively weak Russian working class could not be strengthened by triumphant workers in Western Europe, it would have to be backed by the Russian peasantry. In the absence of both conditions, the Revolution would be doomed. The NEP was designed above all to establish this link between the two classes, for "the state of affairs that has prevailed so far," Lenin said, "cannot be continued any longer."

This meant a turning back toward capitalism. The grain surpluses would no longer be snatched out of the peasants' hands. Instead, a tax would be imposed that would allow agricultural producers to retain increasing amounts of their crops: The more they produced, the more they would have left after paying the tax. Newly established markets would then allow unrestricted sale and purchase of the surpluses. Although it was first thought that food could be bartered directly for manufactured goods, buying and selling with money soon took over and wiped out that dream. A money economy, it was finally conceded, would be restored, and with it the banking and financial systems. Peasants would be given security of land tenure, their right to hire wage-labor would be granted, and a free labor market would be permitted. A free labor market implied that wages would be negotiated between workers or their unions and the enterprises, and that employers could discharge excess workers. Egalitarian payments for labor services were sacrificed. Lenin also recommended that links be established between the proletariat and the peasantry by drawing on the help of foreign capitalists, who might find it in their interest to loan money to and invest in the USSR.

The NEP proposed capitalist markets for labor and much of retail trade, but socialism would prevail in other realms—banking, large industries, railways, foreign trade, wholesale trade. As it turned out, capitalism made many inroads even in most of these areas. There would be a healthy competition between the two systems, although socialism, of course, was expected to win out, since it held all the political face cards. In the meantime, agricultural output would recover, and, if industry revived, there would be manufactured goods to be exchanged for the food surpluses of the peasants.

"If industry revived"—Lenin pointed out that industrialization was essential in two respects. First, by providing technical equipment, tractors, other farm machinery, and electrification to the peasants, industrialization would expand the consciousness of the peasants as well as their capacity to produce. Second, the growth of industry would provide the consumer goods necessary for urban-rural trade. Through these two uses, industry would help transform tradition-bound peasants into modern workers and the economy into socialism.

A year later Lenin announced that the NEP was succeeding—but slowly, very slowly. The trouble was that the Communists—4,700 strong in Moscow—did not know how to rule or how to get things done. The huge bureaucracy was leading them around by their noses. As Lenin remarked, "I doubt very much whether it can truthfully be said that the Communists are directing that heap. To tell the truth, they are not directing, they are being directed." The key feature is people, Lenin said; it is not fussing around with reorganizing departments and forming new ones. The Communists now in responsible positions cannot run the economy; they lack culture; they are fooled by crooks and rascals. Let us choose the proper people and then we'll succeed!

The NEP was principally aimed at the revival of agriculture; it was not originally an industrial measure. Nevertheless, it was accompanied by initiatives to invigorate small and rural industries (private and cooperative), to lease to private management firms that were previously nationalized, and to plan for the future development of large-scale industries. Legislation placed limits on the number of wage-workers private owners could employ—limits, that is, on capitalism. Moves were also made to eliminate inefficient firms and to group others into "trusts" for greater efficiency. State trusts were made to operate "on principles of commercial accounting with the object of earning a profit." They were told, in other words, to shift for themselves. Generally, the effort was centered on light consumer industries and not so much on heavy industries.

The industries that recovered most quickly under the NEP were small rural and artisan enterprises. Recovering somewhat more slowly were the consumer-goods industries. Heavy industry, such as metallurgy, engineering, and chemicals—those producing capital goods—suffered the longest. Industrial workers, who were presumably the class in power, were weakened by aggressive managers acting like capitalists and by widespread unemployment reflective of capitalism. These workers had been favored during the 1917–21 period, and they would again be favored under Stalin's rush to industrialize the country. But the NEP had its face turned to the countryside and the peasants. Some said that NEP stood for "new exploitation of the proletariat."

Another criticism of the NEP was that it was creating a new class of capitalists—rich peasants (kulaks), speculators, private entrepreneurs, commercial traders—and was re-establishing a class of wage-laborers who owned little else but their labor power. According to many critics, the NEP was also creating gross inequalities of income and wealth. At one end, the new "Nepmen" reaped an ungodly harvest from profitable opportunities; at the other, workers labored for little or, worse yet, were unemployed for long periods of time. Still other criticisms focused on the relative neglect of heavy industry, the development of which was claimed to be the true route to socialism. Instead, too much attention was given to light industry—and, of course, to agriculture. And virtually no work was done on establishing a central plan, which seemed to have been pushed aside in favor of markets and more markets. The critics thus made their case, but the supporters of the NEP continued to insist that the peasants' cooperation with the urban workers was crucial to the success of the new state and that heavy industry and central planning simply had to take a back seat for the time being.

There is no denying that the NEP had many successes. The economy had reached its low point in 1920–21, when production in both manufacturing and agriculture was far below the levels of 1913. From the beginning of the 1920s until the start of the First Five-Year Plan in the fall of 1927, the economy for the most part regained its prewar levels and even surpassed them in the last few years. Table 1 records the overall indexes for industry, agriculture, and transportation for three key dates. All the indexes were higher in 1927–28 than in 1913, though the industrial one only barely. The table also presents some of the detail of the industrial sector. The production of these items had plummeted by the early 1920s, but all had made good comebacks

TABLE 1
PRODUCTION DATA, USSR
1913 to 1927-28

	1913	1920 or 1921	1927-28
Production Indexes (1913 = 100)			
Industry	100	20	102
Agriculture	100	64	118
Transportation	100	22	106
Industrial Production Data			
Coal (in millions of tons)	29	9	35
Oil (in millions of tons)	9	4	12
Steel (in millions of tons)	4	close to 0	4
Cement (in millions of tons)	1.5	close to 0	2
Electricity (in billions of kilowatt-hrs.)	2	0.5	5

by the close of the NEP, although oil, steel, and cement ended only slightly above their 1913 levels.

★

PERESTROIKA AND THE NEP: A COMPARISON

Ш e can find many similarities between the NEP and the *perestroika* measures. Both policies reduced the extent of socialism in the economy. The NEP did this by making room for private enterprise, which included the hiring of wage-labor, in agriculture, manufacturing, services, and trade—that is, throughout the economy, except in those areas called the "commanding heights" (heavy industry, banking, communications). *Perestroika* has been less generous to private enterprise, though limited activities in this area were allowed in March 1990. It has, instead, reduced socialism by encouraging *personal* enterprise in the services sector and cooperatives there and elsewhere. In agriculture, contract teams—a hybrid of private and personal enterprise—have also expanded rapidly. Despite those differences, the main thrust of the two reforms was the same: boost individual initiative by retreating from the most-advanced socialist positions.

Another similarity is the more favorable attitude toward capitalist ways of getting the job done, even though this has not yet been extended under *perestroika* to include the approval of large-scale domestic capitalist enterprises. Under the NEP, not only were private enterprises permitted, but the call went out to "learn from capitalism"—that is, to learn its efficient ways. Foreign capitalists were invited into the country to demonstrate their production and selling methods in real-life enterprises, though very few accepted. The promoters of *perestroika* have similarly encouraged the study of capitalist enterprises and markets in the United States, Europe, and Japan; and they, too, have opened the Soviet Union to more foreign capital. In both cases, the stated intention was to retreat or readjust so as to position the economy for a drive into a more successful and dynamic socialism.

During the NEP years, many entrepreneurs, rural capitalists, speculators, traders, and others enriched themselves, as Bukharin in

1925 enjoined them to do. At the other end of the scale, a "reserve army of labor" (made famous by Marx in his indictment of capitalism) sprang up, into which flowed the unemployed and the displaced. Thus, growing disparities of incomes and wealth were a feature of the NEP. While *perestroika* has not had time to reproduce this phenomenon, there have nevertheless been rumblings about the "obscene" wealth being acquired by operators of recently established cooperatives and by other greedy opportunists. The *perestroika* contingent will no doubt have their own "Nepmen" to deal with before too long.

The differences between the two programs, however, are numerous and deep enough to warn us against drawing up a simple equation between them. With respect to private enterprise, as I have noted, *perestroika* has not yet gone as far as the NEP did. Above all, the two starting points were very dissimilar. The NEP represented a retreat from a temporary set of measures, called "war communism," largely forced on the new regime by the civil war. In other words, the NEP was a step backward from an unsecured and a not very advanced position. On the other hand, *perestroika* is the reconstruction of an economy that has settled into a bureaucratic-socialist easy chair and has long been set in its ways, despite repeated attempts to jar it loose. Furthermore, the two economies were hardly comparable in regard to production levels. At the time of the NEP, Russia's economy was a minor-league player among the industrial nations of the world. The present economy produces a national output second only to that of the United States and surpasses the United States in the production of a long list of industrial commodities.

Another sharp difference between the NEP and *perestroika* is that the former was aimed principally at reinvigorating agriculture, while the latter has been more broadly conceived. The NEP set out to establish links between what the leaders hoped would be a more-prosperous, more-satisfied peasantry and the urban working class. *Perestroika* has not been concerned with the problem of social classes. Instead it has hit at the bureaucracies without calling them a new social class, and it has not appeared to favor the peasants over the proletariat or the reverse. (This is not to ignore a number of the NEP leaders, especially Lenin, who were as dismayed as Gorbachev apparently is over the power of the bureaucracies.)

The NEP had a clear set of priorities: agriculture first, light industry second, and heavy industry last, although these were altered somewhat after 1926. *Perestroika* has been more balanced, which means that it has given more weight to heavy industry than the NEP did. Moreover, *perestroika* has focused intently on replacing old technology with the latest scientific advances, especially in advanced industrial technologies—such as miniprocessors, computer numerically controlled machine tools, and flexible manufacturing systems. Today's Soviets have to scrap much equipment that is costly to maintain and inefficient to operate. The NEP was not faced with technological explosions and so was less concerned with catching up.

Finally, during much of the NEP period, a great many prices were established in relatively free markets, thus reflecting pressures of demand and supply. There was, therefore, little need during the early years of the NEP for a full reform of the price structure as a prerequisite for a successful economy. The contrary is the case now. Many Soviet prices are far out of line with basic market conditions; some have been set at the same levels for decades. The *perestroika* program is, in this respect, more difficult to carry out, because prices—and many other economic institutions—have been established for so long that they have virtually become icons; it takes almost a religious conversion to dump them.

★

STALIN'S DEPARTURE
FROM THE NEP

What happened to the NEP? It was gradually subverted by the Communist Party from about 1925 on and then finally killed by Stalin. Up to 1925 or 1926, the growth of the economy had been generated by the revival of industries and agricultural crops that had been depressed by war and the controls accompanying it. By returning the old productive facilities to their prewar levels, and by unleashing private enterprise in designated activities, the Soviets got a lot of mileage on the growth charts. But once the recovery was largely completed, another course had to be considered if growth was to continue. The course chosen led toward large-scale investment in industry and a greatly stepped-up program to supply new capital equipment and structures, not just to restore existing ones. Once private activity reached the level at which, in the eyes of many Party leaders, it threatened socialism itself, that activity came under increasing criticism and, ultimately, increasing control. Of the two forces propelling the economy forward, one had run its course and the other came under heavy attack. Economics and ideology joined hands to encircle and then to smother Lenin's NEP.

The attack on the new capitalists (the Nepmen) came in a number of guises: taxes on their profits, charges on their trading, accusations of evil intentions (as in raising prices and hoarding), creation of consumer cooperatives and state stores to undercut them, and the reduction of procurement prices by the government for their wheat. Gradually, price reductions and controls were extended to key commodities, which led to "shortages," and these in turn to charges against speculators, hoarders, middlemen—and Nepmen generally.

The decision to raise the tempo of industrialization meant a big boost for central planning, which many party stalwarts believed was essential, especially since it was expected to be centered in the socialist sectors of heavy industry, mining, and transportation and communications. A step-up of central planning would almost certainly be an attack on private markets and hence the Nepmen; thus, the rising class of private entrepreneurs and traders got it coming and going.

Stalin's decision to scrap the NEP came in the midst of an accumulation of problems, partly brought on by the government's interference and harrassment of private activity and partly by the nature of the NEP itself. The problems were those of continuing high unemployment, a slowing rate of growth, reduced marketings of agricultural crops (squeezing the urban areas, the military, and exports), and, it was believed, the rising power of rural and urban capitalists. Stalin's "great change" was also based on Marx's vision of a socialist society, which included public ownership of productive assets, central planning, and a large industrial base. The last desideratum was reinforced by Stalin's nationalist concerns—that, without a heavy industrial base, the Soviet Union would have to import such goods, paying for them with agricultural and mineral surpluses, and thus becoming a mere appendage to the world capitalist system. Stalin's theory that socialism could be built in one country, without the support of Marxist governments in the West (whose advent was doubtful at best), further buttressed his decision, for it suggested that no good would come of waiting. The feeling of urgency was deepened by such external events as Britain's breaking of diplomatic relations in 1927, Japan's growing militarization, and the memory of recent military interventions by the capitalist powers. The all-encompassing and abrupt nature of the great change, when it came, was probably dictated by Stalin's belief that gradual changes from a predominantly agricultural economy to a full-fledged industrial one would not have worked. Each facet of the total program depended on the existence of many other parts, so that it was essential to do almost everything at once. The transformation required a qualitative "leap," not a sequence of small steps. Finally, the great departure from the NEP was helpful to Stalin in building up his power base, putting him right in the center of a vital movement and, at the same time, isolating his rivals from the main currents of society.

★

AN "INDUSTRIAL NOVEL" LOOKS AT REBUILDING

The spirit of the NEP years is reflected in much of the Soviet writing of that era. Fyodor Gladkov's novel *Cement* (1925) is considered a classic among the so-called industrial novels—that is, stories about the joys and pains of building an industrial socialist society.

The year is 1921. Gleb Chumalov has just returned home after three years of service with the Red Army in the civil war and is now devoted to getting a badly damaged cement factory back into operation. During his absence his wife, Dasha, has become a leader of women in the local Communist Party and is no longer the clinging, dependent housewife he once knew. The story is about Gleb's and Dasha's largely successful efforts—each made independently of the other—to mobilize the workers; to survive a Party purge; to overcome inept, distant, and corrupt bureaucrats; and, finally, to get the cement factory humming once again. It is also the story of Gleb's and Dasha's efforts to come to terms with the radically changed conditions that have reshaped their lives and their marriage. In the end, the two young people go their separate ways. One can conclude that personal happiness, or at least some of it, has been sacrificed for some greater cause.

The author describes the near-starvation conditions that prevail in this town after the war. Many former factory workers have become herders of goats in the hills, speculators on markets short of supplies, or simply scavengers. Early on, while chairing a meeting, Gleb looks over the many faces in front of him: "It seemed to him that, although they were really different, yet there was a common trait in all of them, which made them into one. What was it—this something, living yet vague, that strains one's gaze and strains one's mind in an effort to define it? One wanted to find a word for it, but there was no word for it upon his tongue. Then suddenly he understood: it was hunger."

Even when the town begins to rise above these desperate levels, starving people from other areas descend on its inhabitants in search of food. They turn up in wild-looking crowds: "Men, women, children. Babies cried, choked and sobbed. Someone was groaning dully. The women were picking lice out of each other's hair. The men were searching for vermin in their shirts and the seams of their trousers. The faces of all of them were bloated. . . . And from the dirty, stinking, ragged mass, hoarse voices would cry, 'Starving! . . . We come from the Volga—from the famine country . . . Starving!'" This environment of deprivation produces a violence of language and behavior—sudden demands to line people up against the wall and shoot them, much swearing, and so on.

The novel also depicts, in the midst of daily cares, the dedication of many workers to the building of a new, socialist society, and their intense desire to see it spread around the world. At the same time, we see the many obstacles that the workers face, not in achieving their grander aims, but in simply putting a cement factory back on its feet again. To get anything important approved requires that Gleb or someone else run through a bureaucratic maze consisting of a factory committee, an economic council, a Soviet executive committee, a bureau of industry, a cement trust, distant decision makers, and a host of impenetrable secretaries and assistants protecting these important people. The maze seems designed to swallow the supplicant. In search of one crucial approval, Gleb hopes to traverse the maze in one week but actually returns to the factory an entire month later.

When Gleb appeals to functionaries for wood (needed as fuel for the factory) and for an OK to move ahead in obtaining the wood, Badin, the Chairman of the Executive Committee of the Soviet, seems sympathetic. But Badin himself runs afoul of the bureaucracy in the person of Shramm, the Chairman of the Economic Council. Shramm refuses to respond to the appeal, contending that the Council receives its tasks and plans from the Bureau of Industry only. Badin counters:

> "You're hiding behind the back of the Bureau of Industry in order to shelter your Economic Council. But do you even know what's going on on the two floors of your premises? From your written reports it seems that you are doing nothing but auditing and inventories, over and over again. You've an uncountable number of departments and sub-departments with a staff of two hundred persons—but you haven't given us the smallest amount of real creative work."

Shramm replies that the most important thing, in his view, is "to conserve the patrimony of the State without tolerating any doubtful undertakings." Badin, trying to get at the wood question, then asks him how the District Forestry Committee is working. "I have nothing to do with that, or, rather, only indirectly. They are under my control, but they have their own apparatus." Badin next asks him about the delivery of wood to the districts. "That is not the business of the Economic Council; that is the affair of the District Fuel Committee." Well, what about re-starting the cement factory? (Back to square one!) "That is not my business; that's the business of the Bureau of Industry. We cannot carry out this plan unless they sanction it." Shramm adds that the Economic Council does not accept proposals from outside the normal channels. "These schemes which are sent to us, we file for posterity without examining them. We are enemies of all questionable enterprises and plans. We must cure our Comrades of their leaning to all kinds of adventures, which will be the best safeguard against disorganizing enthusiasms." Is it any wonder, this being the Soviet system, that Shramm is arrested a few months later?

An interesting sidelight of *Cement* is the criticisms voiced by a few of the workers against Lenin's NEP. A friend tells Gleb that she worries about the NEP because it looks like a reactionary policy to her, the restoration of capitalism:

> "Does it mean," she asked, "there would be markets again? Again the bourgeoisie? Do you want our factory to be given as a concession to the capitalists? . . . Concessions, restaurants, markets . . . Kulaks, schemers, speculators . . . I suppose you'll tell me something consoling about the Workers' Co-operatives? The Food Tax . . . The Co-operatives . . . Perhaps that is necessary. But not retreat, Gleb, not that! Anything but that! Heroic exploits for the immortal revolution! That's what we want! To deepen, to light a universal fire; not to abandon conquered positions, but to seize new ones. That's it!"

At another time, a Party official expresses his concerns about the NEP to an ordinary workman:

> "There's a terrible whirlpool, and we're all in it. We're going to be subjected to a dreadful trial, worse than civil war, ruin, famine and blockade. We're in the presence of a hidden foe who is not going to shoot us, but will spread before us all the charms and temptations of capitalist business. We control the whole of the economic system. That's certain enough. But the petty trader is crawling out of his hole. He's beginning to get fat and reincarnates in various forms. For instance, he's trying to install himself in our own ranks, behind a solid barricade of revolutionary phrases, with all the attributes of Bolshevik valor. Markets, cafes, shop windows, delicacies, home comforts and alcohol. . . . The foe is mean, cunning and difficult to catch. We must forge a new strategy . . . we have radically to change ourselves, harden ourselves, fortify the Bolshevik in ourselves for a long, lingering siege. . . . "

These people were already worrying, in the very first year of the NEP, about some traders and speculators getting rich, about cafes serving vodka to all hours of the night, about luxury items being displayed in store windows when many people were starving, about corruption. What was the good of all our sacrifices, they wondered. "Was it that blackguards and vampires should again enjoy all the good things of life, and get fat by robbery?"[1]

You can be certain that many people in the Soviet Union today, including Politbureau members and other high officials, are asking similar questions about Gorbachev's own policies, which, as we have seen, bear certain strong resemblances to the NEP. Won't they lead back to capitalism? And after all our sacrifices for a socialist society?

Another interesting feature of *Cement* is that Gladkov comes down solidly on the side of sexual equality—following in the footsteps of Chernyshevsky. The women in the story are generally strong and independent. Dasha in particular is an emancipated woman. At the end of the story, she decides that she will live apart from Gleb, at least for a while. As she leaves, Gleb wants to plead with her to stay. "He had no power to utter such words because Dasha had taken this power from him. This was no ordinary woman standing before him now, but a human being, equal to him in strength—one who had taken upon her shoulders all the burden of the past years. Dasha was not just a wife; she was a woman with vigorous hands, without her former attachment for home and husband." Later, she tells him: "'It's not our fault, Gleb. The old life has perished and will not return. We must build up a new life. The time will come when we shall build ourselves new homes. Love will always be love, Gleb, but it requires a new form. Everything will come through and attain new forms, and then we shall know how to forge new links.'"

Well, Gleb loses Dasha, but he gains a cement factory. The melody of marriage is gone, but what remains is "a tender singing hum from

---

[1] At the beginning of the NEP period, Demyan Bedny, a poet who supported the Bolsheviks, spoke—albeit cynically—of the value of the Nepman:

"Just watch them, comrade . . . with an owner's eye . . .
　　And let them pasture on the busy street,
These cattle; let them batten and feed high,
　　And so make rich and juicy meat.
Let their fleece grow. But do not let your wits
　　Go gathering wool, or they'll give you the slip.
And threaten not with knives, just with a whip.
　　And when the time is ripe, then we'll be quits,
And the whole flock's thick pelts be ours to clip."

the pistons and wheels" of the engine room. "This severe and youthful music of metal, amid the warm smell of oil and petrol, strengthened and soothed Gleb's being. These gentle songs seemed to re-echo within his heart." Mawkish though it may seem to our ears, this paean to industrialism is testimony to the spirit that was to be a driving force in the Soviet Union for the next two decades.

★

THE GROWTH OF CENTRAL PLANNING

During the First Five-Year Plan, as we saw in Chapter 2, Stalin established a definition of socialism that prevailed for the next thirty years. One element of that definition was comprehensive central planning. This element has been widely criticized recently, both inside and outside the Soviet Union. "Markets" are the new good guys, "planning" is now the villain, and *perestroika* aims to move the economy toward the side of the good guys.

How did planning ever become associated with socialism? The answer lies, as we have seen, in Marx's view that capitalism is a chaotic system in which the workers lack control over their lives. The capitalist mode of production, as Marx saw it, lunges upward and then falls into depression in regular cycles, exploiting workers on the way up and releasing them into the reserve of the unemployed on the way down. Capitalism is without a plan, Marx asserted, and the workers without security. Later on, Engels suggested that capitalism contained within itself the seeds of a planned economy. These seeds were in the corporate form of business, which widened production beyond the purely privately operated firm to a larger group of (equity) owners. Engels speculated that such corporate giants would be gathered into even-larger units ("trusts"), which would be the nuclei of the socialist economy. With such units socialized, planning would not be difficult.

When the Soviet Union, in response to this background, generated in 1925 an early version of an overall plan, Leon Trotsky declared that the figures in the plan were "the glorious historical music of growing socialism." This glorious music might have accompanied the tender singing Gleb heard in the engine room of the cement factory.

If we study the experiences of Soviet and other socialist countries, we find that central planning has taken many forms. Socialist economies generally prefer direct planning over the indirect planning that sometimes occurs on an economy-wide basis in capitalism. For example, to prevent commodity prices from rising, direct planners would impose or reinforce price controls, while indirect planners would, for example, raise interest rates to moderate aggregate demand and hence counteract the upward pressure on prices. The Soviets have mostly followed the first path.

Central planning might be highly centralized at the top. Alternatively, many of the decisions could be made at regional or local levels. The Soviets have used a mixture of central and local decision making, though they mostly favor top-level centralized planning.

Central planning in the Soviet Union has almost always been command rather than indicative planning. Command planning produces a clear plan that must be followed as closely as possible by ministries, enterprises, banks, and all others down the hierarchical ladder. Indicative planning produces instead a set of guidelines— goals that give indications of the possible, the desirable. During the 1920s, the Soviets published many indicative figures, but from the end of that decade to the present day, their formal plans have been obligatory for all the units in the planning structure. This is even true, in this age of Gorbachev, of the latest Five-Year Plan (for 1991 to 1995) issued during December 1989.

Central planners may use either administrative or economic methods to achieve the plan's goals; that is, the planners may use administrative orders to achieve something or use prices for the same end. For example, if the planners want farmers to produce more wheat next year, they could issue directives ordering them to do so, or they could raise the procurement price of wheat purchases by the government. As another example, a decision to limit migration into cities could be carried out either administratively or perhaps by imposing a tax on such entries. The economic method could use prices determined in a more-or-less free market to attain some specific aim. Much of Soviet planning has leaned toward the administrative method, although some planners' decisions have been shaped by market or economic forces as well.

Another choice for planners is between a vertical and a horizontal planning structure—that is, planning by economic *function* versus planning by economic *area*. A vertical structure is composed of economic ministries organized by type of industry or commerce. A planning unit extends, for example, along the entire scope of metallurgical industries, from large national firms to small local ones. A horizontal structure is established by regions, and all economic activity within each region comprises a planning unit. Most of the time, the Soviets have set up a vertical structure, the chief exception being Khrushchev's reorganization to a horizontal one from 1957 to 1964.

Beyond these basic forms, central plans may be long-term, generally five years for the Soviets, or short-term, one year being typical. Central plans can also be divided into the various sectors of the economy, giving us production, financial, trade, and many other sectoral plans. Central plans can be optimal, based on optimistic assumptions, or minimal, based on more modest expectations. The directives of the plans may be expressed in physical quantities or in value terms.

During the 1920s, some Soviet experts debated the merits of yet another pair of options: genetic versus teleological. In genetic planning, the target figures in the plan would be extrapolations of existing trends. In the teleological approach, planners would strive to set new trends, take a few leaps, suggest departures from existing movements. The teleological position won out for the First Five-Year Plan and was a major component of later plans during the 1930s. In more recent years, however, modest extrapolations have mostly ruled the day.

Ever since the writings of Marx and Engels, Marxists have considered central planning to be an integral part of a socialist society. Because of this, some elements of central planning were established in Russia even before the civil war had completely cooled. An early move was the creation of the State Commission for Electrification (Goelro) in 1920 to devise a plan to bring electricity to all of the country. Lenin backed this wholeheartedly, formulating a catch phrase for the project: "Communism is Soviet power plus electrification of the whole country." This slogan suggested that the productive forces, or more widely the economic base, would have to expand mightily if socialism were to succeed. The State Economic Planning Commission (Gosplan) was set up in the following year, and Goelro became a part of it. Lenin at first was lukewarm toward comprehensive planning, but toward the end of 1922 he began to give it more support. Planning for the economy as a whole did not stand much chance in the early 1920s, not only because it had never been done before in the world and so required years of theoretical work and practical experience, but also because the NEP was market-oriented, the antithesis of planning by orders from the top.

Nevertheless, a five-year plan for the metal industry was put together in 1922–23, followed by the first general industrial plan of 1923. Work started in 1923 on a five-year plan for agriculture, which was completed two years later. At that time, plans for internal trade were made. Regional and local plans were also in the making around this time. These partial and tentative steps finally culminated in a set of "control figures" from Gosplan for the economic year 1925–26, which covered the overall economy for the first time. These were the figures that were music to Trotsky's ears. None of the above efforts, however, proved operationally practical, except the electrification plans.

Despite the presence of the NEP, central planning gained increasing credence as the decade went on. This was owing to the realization that the NEP was not destined to last much longer and that a drive for industrialization, which would demand central planning, was the next logical step beyond the NEP. Control figures for each of the next three economic years were produced, each set containing more detail and fuller coverage than the preceding one. Finally, based largely on the latest control figures, the First Five-Year Plan for 1927–28 to 1932–33 was issued, initially as a minimal version and then as an optimal one. The Communist Party adopted the latter, but this was amended a short time later with even more optimistic figures. A few of these numbers, along with some actual results in this period, relating to industry only, are shown in Table 2.

I have chosen five industrial products to illustrate the planning process during the initial plan, which was originally intended to span five years but was actually terminated at the close of 1932, a little more than four years after its beginning. The table shows actual figures in the economic year 1927–28 (the economic and calendar years were made the same in 1930), the initial or minimal targets, the optimal ones, the even more optimistic (amended) goals, and the actual results. The

TABLE 2

THE FIRST FIVE-YEAR PLAN, 1927-28 to 1932-33:
PLANS AND RESULTS FOR FIVE INDUSTRIAL PRODUCTS

	Actual 1927–28	Planned for 1932–33			Actual 1932	Annual Growth Rate
		Initial	Optimal	Amended		
Electricity (bils. of kwhrs.)	5	17	22		13	25%
Oil (mils. of tons)	12	19	22	40–55	22	14
Steel (mils. of tons)	4	8	10		6	10
Coal (mils. of tons)	35	68	75	95–105	64	15
Cement (mils. of tons)	2				4	17

Soviets were carried away early in the period when they envisioned a bigger leap forward than they were capable of producing. But the country did make huge percentage gains in industry, as the last column indicates, at least for the few items shown here. If we were to look at the plan as a whole—including agriculture, services, and transportation—we would still find many valuable accomplishments, but it would be clear that the overall actual results not only failed to meet the optimal expectations but did not, in many instances, come up to the minimal ones, either.

The Second and Third Five-Year Plans were set for 1933–37 and 1938–42, although the third was cut short in June 1941 by Hitler's armed forces. Table 3 covers performance during these years, focusing on the same industrial items shown in Table 2. It indicates the planned targets during the second plan, the actual results of this plan, and the

TABLE 3
THE SECOND AND THIRD FIVE-YEAR PLANS, 1932-1940:
PLANS AND RESULTS FOR FIVE INDUSTRIAL PRODUCTS

	Actual 1932	Plan 1937	Actual 1937	Actual 1940	Annual Growth Rate	
					1932–40	1927–28 to '40
Electricity (bils. of kwhs)	13	38	36	48	18%	20%
Oil (mils. of tons)	22	47	29	31	4	8
Steel (mils. of tons)	6	17	18	18	15	13
Coal (mils. of tons)	64	153	128	166	13	13
Cement (mils. of tons)	4	8	6	6	6	9

results of the third plan up to the end of 1940. For many specific products, the actual results of the second plan fell short of the targets, but the gains were nevertheless fairly good. Further progress was made in the abbreviated third plan. The table records annual rates of growth for 1932–40 and for the full period from 1927–28 to 1940. The average of the annual growth rates for the five products over the entire period is around 12 percent. That, or probably a few percentage points less, can be taken as roughly typical for industrial production over this period. There is no way that these results, in and of themselves, can be judged as anything but really good.

★

ACCOUNTING FOR THE SUCCESS OF INDUSTRIALIZATION

The industrial gains in the 1930s were based on unusually high investment rates, which squeezed consumption; large pools of cheap labor, which kept wages and consumer demands low; the reorganization of rural labor into collective and state farms, which eventually provided food surpluses for industrialization; a successful planning structure that set priorities and organized all of the country around these goals; and, despite the harsh repression visited on dissidents, an enthusiasm for building the first socialist society that stimulated long and hard work by enough of the labor force to make a difference.

During the 1930s, capital formation in new industrial plants, dams, canals, transportation facilities, and other structures and durable equipment rose, as a percentage of GNP, far above the norms of the day for a relatively underdeveloped economy. The investment boom—although it slowed down after 1937—was one of the principal factors accounting for Soviet growth in this decade, when most of the rest of the world was in a depression. The expanding industrial machine raised the productivity of labor and attracted idle and barely productive workers into these more vigorous sectors. As the economy used its real resources to produce more and more capital goods—and, later in the decade, increasing volumes of military goods—there were fewer resources left over to produce consumer goods and services. The squeeze on consumption was part of the price paid for growth.

Soviet industrialization could not have been achieved so rapidly without the mobilization of the peasants into collective state farms. At first, the countryside was a scene of turmoil and upheaval. Stalin believed that the poorest peasants and their families, perhaps numbering 25–30 million, would gladly give up what little they had to join the more secure and wealthier collective farms. He gave orders "to liquidate as a class" the 8–10 million *kulaks* and their families. The remaining peasants, around 80 million altogether, were to be driven into the collectives. The great majority of the peasants passionately resisted collectivization but were nevertheless forced, in what amounted to a civil war, to submit. *Kulaks* by the millions were rounded up and deported to remote areas of the country. Great masses of peasants slaughtered their animals and destroyed other assets to prevent the state from claiming them (not understanding that the collective members themselves would actually have owned the animals, implements, and other resources).

Against all resistance, the collective farms were established—at first with a rush and then at a much slower pace—and before too long began producing surpluses for the cities and the industrial work force. These large rural units required an infusion of agricultural machinery to be efficient, and so industry was stimulated by the countryside development. Collectivization demanded industrialization. The industrialization needed to support the agricultural revolution was not confined to tractors, combines, and other machinery, but included oil, coal, steel, power stations for the spread of electricity—and ultimately the whole works. Industry in turn received not only the agricultural surpluses necessary to sustain the urban population but excess rural labor as well.

This last point reveals one of the secrets of Stalin's success in industrializing Russia in so short a time—his widespread use of cheap labor by the millions. The new industries obtained such labor from the collective farms, in much the same way that early capitalist industries drew on impoverished peasants who were cut off from any decent living on the land. Under capitalism, the peasants "freely" found their way into the new urban centers; in Stalin's scheme, they were sent in by their collective farms according to written agreements. Much cheap labor was also supplied by prisoners in felling timber and building canals, railways, and roads. Millions of former *kulaks*, political opponents of the regime, and common criminals were arrested and sent to the labor camps, where they were organized into huge work battalions throughout a vast "gulag archipelago," as described by Solzhenitsyn in his mammoth work on this topic.

In addition, the industrial growth of the country was accomplished by the hard work of tens of millions of peasants who literally fed the process while they themselves were half starving.

People labored cheaply as free peasants on the land, as forced peasant labor in industries, and as convict labor on public works to build the industrial base of the new society and to support the higher living standards of the industrial elite and the new intelligentsia. "A wide gulf came to separate the vast mass of unskilled and underpaid workmen from the privileged 'labor aristocracy' and bureaucracy. . . ."

Under such a relentless, even oppressive, drive to industrialization, how did Soviet workers during the 1930s maintain their enthusiasm—or did they? One might well be skeptical of the glowing accounts by Soviet novelists, celebrating the energy and dedication of the workers during these years. Nevertheless, quite a few signs point to the presence of those qualities as well as to a pride of workmanship. Soviet workers accomplished more than seemed possible.

★

KATAEV: GLORIFYING THE WORKER'S SPIRIT

One well-known story illustrates the intense competitive spirit of the workers during the early years of the initial plan. This novel by Valentin Kataev, *Time, Forward!*, is a classic example of socialist realism.

Time, Forward! describes the building of the huge industrial complex at Magnitogorsk in the Ural mountains. The city itself was built from scratch in 1929–31 and quickly became a center for the production of steel, chemicals, coke, machinery, and many other industrial goods. The novel is set in the concrete-making section of this industrial complex. Margulies, the engineer in charge of this section, accedes to popular demand to try to beat the record set by a brigade in Kharkov (1,000 miles to the west): 306 batches of concrete in one shift of eight hours. His boss, the assistant chief of construction, is against this project. "This is construction, not a stunt," is his warning. According to the boss, each batch would be made too quickly and hence would lack strength. Further, the cement mixer would be damaged by such continuous, rapid operation. Besides, it is against the rules to produce cement so rapidly, against industry instruction. "I am calling your attention to the fact," he tells Margulies, "that you are contributing to the exceedingly rapid amortization of imported machinery which has been paid for in [dollars], and we do not happen to have dollars scattered on the ground." Margulies replies that his plan is based on other elements—the more efficient use of the inputs (gravel, cement, sand, water), a more rational employment of the brigade's workers, and the heightened enthusiasm of the workers for the project. On this last point, the novel reveals why labor productivity was so high in this industrial project (and, presumably, throughout the Soviet Union): The workers had pride in their work; there was genuine enthusiasm for "building socialism"; internal competition among brigades kept everyone alert; external competition (for example, with the brigade in Kharkov) brought forth demands to prove local superiority; and there were medals, awards, and public acclaim for outstanding workers, and opprobrium for shirkers.

Despite the few shirkers who care more about drinking and lolling around than working—but who in the end do shape up to contribute something—and despite some glitches in the operation, Margulies's brigade beats Kharkov's record rather easily. However, just as they best Kharkov, with 2 hours and 53 minutes still to go, they learn that a group in Kuznetsk (1,000 miles east) has poured out 402 batches in one shift! Back to work!

But now the water is mysteriously turned off. Why? It develops that the shutdown has been made so that a water meter can be installed to audit the water during the record-breaking attempt. The person responsible for this disaster, Semechkin, tells Margulies: "'I arranged to have the meter put in. In an hour and a half, it will be working. How else can you maintain cost accounting? . . . We have to audit with the ruble.' Margulies was choking. 'Immediately connect the pipes and give us water!' he cried piercingly, screaming." The damage is quickly repaired, Semechkin is arrested, and work recommences. (We are not told whether poor Semechkin is liquidated.)

The brigade works feverishly but at the zero hour they are one batch short—just one!—of tying the record set at Kuznetsk. Now for a little cheating. Margulies calculates that they had started the shift at eight minutes past the hour, the water had been turned off for another eight minutes, and a couple of other snafus add up to seventeen minutes—meaning that the brigade, which thought it had run out of time, actually has 33 more minutes. Needless to say, with that extra time, they handily whip Kuznetsk—429 to 402. Alas, the very next day a group at the Chelyaba tractor plant surpasses their effort, with 504. Fleeting fame for the individual brigade but lasting glory for the entire industrial campaign!

The novel has some interesting sidelights. Also working in this plant is an American engineer, Thomas George Bixby, who has been in Russia for five years, not to "build socialism" but to make money. He wants to accumulate $20,000 so that he can open a business of his own when he returns to his family in Chicago. To this end, he lives frugally, saving most of his pay, half of which he sends to his family and the other half to his Chicago bank, where he now has $18,427.40. Almost immediately after the brigade sets the records, Bixby reads, to his horror, a newspaper article about the financial crash in the United States—in particular, about the bank failures in Chicago. He cannot believe that all of his savings have disappeared, just like that, but it is apparently true. (Deposit insurance was introduced a short time later, in January 1934.) He goes berserk. In this episode, the author has provided an interesting contrast between a country with energy to spare, on the move economically, and another country that was financially on the rocks: triumphant socialism, deflated capitalism.

The socialist economy portrayed by Kataev, like the one in Gladkov's *Cement*, not only makes products but produces music as well—the music of humming machines. Moreover, the machines seem to talk: "Ten times the scoop [of a steam shovel] opened over each flat car. Then the excavator blew a siren. Immediately it was echoed by the thin whistle of the donkey engine of the train. The machines were talking to each other. The excavator demanded that the next flat car be brought up. The little steam engine replied: 'Good! Wait! Right away!' The train jerked. The buffer plates knocked noisily, tapping signals to each other. The train moved up one flat car. 'Stop!' cried the excavator. 'Here!' replied the little steam engine."

The machines have rhythm, too; they have a tempo, a beat. Margulies's boss believes that "tempos, in the epoch of Reconstruction, decide everything." Another worker sees infinite links among the tempos of machines throughout the country: " . . . increase of the productivity of one machine automatically entails the increase of the productivity of others indirectly connected with it. And since all machines in the Soviet Union are connected with each other to a greater or lesser degree, and together represent a complex interlocking system, the raising of tempos at any given point in this system inevitably carries with it the unavoidable—however minute—raising of tempos of the entire system as a whole, thus, to a certain extent, bringing the time of socialism closer."

So socialism was being constructed to the accompaniment of the music, the conversations, and the tempos of innumerable machines.

Gladkov's and Kataev's novels, both involving the production of cement, suggest that whatever successes the Soviet industrial machine might have achieved subsequently, cement could well have represented one of them. And sure enough, we can readily find in the comparative statistics that the Soviet Union today far outproduces the United States in this important construction material. Just like the brigade at Magnitogorsk, the Soviet Union is the new champion!

★

UNDERMINING THE WORKER'S SPIRIT

During the 1930s, as glitches in the economic system began to show up, planners were quick to find scapegoats rather than consider that something might be wrong with the system itself. The excess demands over supplies of commodities and the consequent black markets were blamed, not on prices set below equilibrium levels, but on a bunch of evil-doers. The "shortages" were seen as the work of speculators, who raised demands far above the supplies.

They were also blamed on those who reduced the supplies: saboteurs, wreckers, spies, shirkers, minimalists (those who favored going slow, thereby ensuring insufficiency of supplies), diversionists, malingerers, and others. The entire, traitorous crew were often simply called wreckers. Many of these class enemies were arrested, tried, and sent into labor camps, if not executed. (In Kataev's novel, the repair boss who turned off the water supply might have been charged with "wrecking.") Ironically, many of the industrial and engineering successes during these years could be attributed to the forced labor of these wreckers and other saboteurs, along with millions of others who were found guilty of one thing or another.

At the very time when Magnitogorsk was being constructed, a famous trial was held in which eight engineers were accused of "wrecking." The more precise charges, Solzhenitsyn tells us in *The Gulag Archipelago*, were that "they planned to reduce the tempo of development, as, for instance, to an over-all annual increase in production of *only* 20 to 22 percent, whereas the workers were prepared to increase it by 40 to 50 percent. They slowed down the rate of mining local fuels. They were too slow in developing the Kuznetsk Basin. . . . They tied up capital funds, for example, by using them for costly and lengthy construction projects. . . . They created an imbalance between the departments of a plant and between the supply of raw materials and the capacity for processing them industrially. . . . Then they leaped from minimal to maximal plans. And obvious wrecking began through the accelerated development of [the] textile industry."

No matter what the defendants had done, it was interpreted as purposeful action to sabotage the Plan. As Solzhenitsyn puts it: "They were damned if they did and damned if they didn't. If they went forward, it was wrong, and if they went backward, it was wrong too. If they hurried, they were hurrying for the purpose of wrecking. If they moved methodically, it meant wrecking by slowing down tempos. If they were painstaking in developing some branch of industry, it was intentional delay, sabotage. And if they indulged in capricious leaps, their intention was to produce an imbalance for the purpose of wrecking. Using capital for repairs, improvements, or capital readiness was tying up capital funds."

Such abuses of human dignity by the Stalin regime, self-serving in the short run, undermined the people's spirit in a way that would prove devastating to the growth of the socialist society.

★

TROUBLES OF THE
POSTWAR ECONOMY

At the time of the German invasion in 1941, the Soviet Union had achieved large gains in iron and steel, in engineering, coal, oil, electric power, chemicals, and agricultural machinery. Industrialization also brought forth brand new industries such as synthetic rubber, plastics, aircraft, and heavy chemicals. We can add to this list of accomplishments huge dams and power stations, canals, and a massive defense establishment.

During the war years 1941–45, economic progress was generally halted and much was destroyed. Afterwards, the immediate task was reconstruction, just as it was after 1920. Once the damage was repaired, industrialization took off from where it was interrupted in 1941, with about the same Stalinist priorities as before: heavy industry, then light industry, and agriculture bringing up the rear. Investment and defense expenditures once more left only a narrow space for the production of consumer goods and services. These patterns persisted until shortly after Stalin's death in early 1953. After that, activities that had been low on the totem pole under Stalin received somewhat more favorable treatment, especially agriculture and the living standards of the peasants. Even with resources diverted in those directions, industrial production continued to rise for many years, even more rapidly than GNP. Then, around the middle of the 1970s, the wind began to go out of the red sails and almost everything started slowing down. The economy soon became a nightmare for the central planners—in fact, for just about everyone.

In Table 4, which covers the sixty-year period extending from the First Five-Year Plan to the present day, we can compare prewar with postwar performances, though the figures for the former are far from certain and those for the latter have been disputed, too. Still, these data are the best estimates we have. They reveal what all other sets of figures point to: namely, that annual growth rates of GNP and industrial

TABLE 4
INDICATORS OF SOVIET ECONOMIC PERFORMANCE: 1928-1989
(Average annual rates of growth)

	Real GNP	Industrial Production	Agricultural Production
1928–1941	7.2%	8.4%	1.5–2.0%
1950–1975	5.1	7.7	2.8
1976–1985	2.1	2.2	1.4
1986–1989	2.3	2.7	1.1

production were quite high during the prewar period and somewhat lower during 1950–75 (but still high by international standards—or "respectable," as almost all U.S. experts on the Soviet economy say). Then in the next ten years, 1976–85, both GNP and industrial production grew much less rapidly, and the trend turned decidedly downward. Soviet agriculture has also been on a downward slide during the postwar period. The prewar estimates for agriculture largely reflect Stalin's low priority for this sector; the figure for 1950–75 was raised by special programs to beef up the rural areas and to expand crop acreage; and the estimate for 1976–85 indicates continuing, and worsening, difficulties in this sector. Unlike GNP and industrial production, agriculture has not turned around during Gorbachev's tenure. None of the figures for 1986–89 are anything to cheer wildly about.

★

BEHIND THE
RECENT SLOWDOWN

Щ hat accounts for the decline of the Soviet economy? The easy and approximately correct answer is that the same five factors that fed its successes during the earlier decades went into reverse during recent years. Before we examine these factors, I want to state what I consider the principal cause of the economy's difficulties: namely, the moral corruption of Soviet society that originally set in during Stalin's rule and then spread throughout the leadership, the bureaucracies, and the Communist Party until it numbed the working class and debased just about every relationship in the society. The moral corruption began with the arrests, internal deportations, and labor camp sentences inflicted on millions upon millions of ordinary citizens. According to the KGB (the Soviet intelligence agency), during Stalin's reign almost four million people were sentenced for counterrevolutionary activity and crimes against the state, and, of these, 786,000 were shot to death. (*New York Times,* 2/14/90) While much of this was long hidden from the view of those above ground, the rot nevertheless was there and slowly did its damage. Any economy would decay when the society of which it is a part falls into spiritual decline.

The decay was evidenced by a fading interest in work among much of the labor force, a loss of faith in the Party, a growing distrust of bureaucrats and their pronouncements, and disillusion with the type of society that Bolshevism had fashioned. When did the great majority realize that they were never going to attain the beautiful socialism promised by Marx and Lenin? It could not have been in the 1930s, for the Revolution was still too fresh; Lenin's inspiration was still in the air. It did not likely occur in the late 1940s, for great Soviet war victories must have stirred the imagination to suppose even grander economic triumphs ahead. But probably by the late 1950s and early '60s, and without any doubt by the 1970s, the truth was seen: Socialism, Soviet style, was in hot water; it was struggling and really going nowhere. Social classes would not disappear, socialist affluence would not be attained, the exalted communist society was but a mirage, and the Party could no longer be trusted. These revelations, on a societal level, have an analogy on a personal plane—the point when we suddenly realize that our youthful dreams are never going to be fulfilled, and that we must adjust downward to a more humdrum existence. At that point, one might lose heart and simply accept the inevitable. Would not the same be true of people's dreams and ambitions for their own society? The awful truth sneaks into their consciousness, and the moral decay spreads.

When Yuri Trifonov, one of the Soviet Union's best fiction writers of recent years, wrote his novel *Students* (1950), he pictured a group of happy and optimistic young people. Many were back from war after serving as soldiers, sailors, nurses, and factory workers, and they were looking forward to all the good things of life in an ever-abundant and exciting socialist society.

Just a quarter of a century later, Trifonov wrote a novella, *The House on the Embankment* (1976), that depicted bitter arguments, sharp class differences, political witch-hunts, unethical and atrocious behavior, and not one word about the coming communist society. Did something dreadful happen between 1950 and 1976 to alter Trifonov's assessment of Soviet life? I believe it did. And what happened adversely affected work attitudes, work habits, and whatever enthusiasm was still left for building a new, better society along socialist lines. Incidentally, Trifonov received the Stalin Prize for prose for the early work. No prizes, no official tributes of any kind followed the later one.

Aside from the spiritual decline—which Gorbachev has more than once referred to—the retardation of economic growth in the last fifteen years can be traced to the critical disappearance of continuing supplies of cheap labor, the growing ineffectiveness of investment expenditures, the deadening impact of central planning, and stagnating and wasteful conditions in agriculture.

Everyone agrees that Soviet economic growth has been distinguished by the expansion of basic inputs into the system—that is, inputs of labor, capital goods, and land. Soviet growth has not been much aided by increases in the productivity (or efficiency) of these inputs. The Soviets have had to rely on the quantity dimension, quality being out of reach. To use the jargon of today, Soviet growth has been extensive, not intensive. In the phrases of yesterday, we would say that economic growth has been characterized by widening rather than deepening—that is, by adding structures and capital equipment that are more or less the same as those on hand, just duplicating the old rather than grasping the new.

The problem is that one element of widening has virtually disappeared and another element, while not abating, has become decreasingly effective. Labor supplies are no longer feeding the economic machine as they once did, and they are no longer cheap. During the 1960s, the annual percentage increase of manhours of work was over 2 percent, in the 1970s about 1.5 percent, and in the 1980s less than 1 percent. This steady decline accounts for some of the retardation of output growth. The fact that labor is no longer as cheap as it once was is important because expensive labor means larger consumer demands, which, if met, draw real resources away from capital formation. If rising consumer demands are not met, then families' excess incomes pile up as undesired savings—money that threatens price stability and is available for black markets. Either way, the economy has problems.

During much of the postwar period, the central planners have had to seek economic growth through ever-larger investment expenditures. In the 1950s, these were less than 20 percent of GNP. In the next two decades, they rose to about 25 percent and then to almost 30 percent of GNP, and in the 1980s the ratio shot significantly past 30 percent. This rising capital formation has required increasing amounts of labor, raw materials, and machinery, which means that less were available for the production of consumer goods and services. Capital formation, for reasons noted above, has not been highly effective in raising the rate of growth, and, since labor additions have become scant and productivity gains niggardly, the only "out" has been even further increases in investment. This was an "out," that is, until consumers began grumbling and then screaming, at which point (in the late 1970s and early '80s) the investment programs were temporarily cut back.

Central planning and agriculture are two other areas that have contributed to the braking of the Soviet economy. I discussed the problems of central planning in Chapter 3, and the difficulties of agriculture in Chapter 4. The movers and shakers behind *perestroika* know that both these areas require streamlining and reconstruction if the Soviet economy is to have a new lease on life.

One of the main conclusions of this chapter is that loss of spirit is primarily what ails the big red machine, even though the strictly economic factors are important, too. If this is correct, *glasnost* becomes every bit as important as *perestroika* as a cure. It will be necessary to air fully the political terror of the past if current leaders are to restore the confidence of the public in the aims of the founders of socialism and in their successors' continuing efforts to achieve the dreams of a few generations ago. If such confidence cannot be restored, then economic reforms can be made from now to kingdom come and they will not turn the economy around in a socialist direction. If the ideals of socialism cannot restore people's pride in their work, if they cannot re-establish the social goals that provide meaning and hope in people's lives, then the capitalist engine of self-interest will have to be wheeled in—or back to a reformed Stalinism, which seems more likely.

★

WANTED:
PRIDE OF WORKMANSHIP

I have just suggested that pride in one's work can be translated into high labor productivity. In Kataev's novel, the members of the concrete-producing brigade that set out to break records had that pride. Often it is difficult to account for the existence of this precious trait—the self-respect for, or delight in, what one does well. It was once there and now it is gone. I can think of no better—nor more startling—description of this quality of character than the one penned by Solzhenitsyn in his short novel, *One Day in the Life of Ivan Denisovich* (first published in the Soviet Union in November 1962, during the so-called Khrushchev Thaw). It is startling because of the conditions under which it appears.

In this story, Ivan Denisovich Shukhov has been in labor camps for eight years, serving out a highly questionable ten-year sentence for treason. The day in the title is a January day in 1951, in Siberia. The story begins at 5 A.M. (reveille) and ends at 10 P.M. (lights out). The prisoners live under miserable conditions—freezing cold, poor and inadequate food, strict discipline, innumerable indignities, beatings, and so on. Shukhov, just an ordinary Soviet worker, employs all the craftiness, the trickery, and the bits of crucial information at his command simply to get through the day unscathed and with enough to eat to survive into the next day.

Within this hell that provides only minimum room to maneuver for better positions, Shukhov, at the end of the day, thinks to himself what a really good day it has been! "He didn't even feel like sleeping, he felt so great." He lies back on his bunk and counts his blessings. "They hadn't put him in the cooler. The gang hadn't been chased out to work in the Socialist Community Development. He'd finagled an extra bowl of mush at noon. The boss had gotten them good rates for their work. He'd felt good making that wall. They hadn't found that piece of steel in the frisk [of his body]. Caesar had paid him off in the evening. He'd bought some tobacco. And he'd gotten over that sickness."

He goes to sleep. "He'd had a lot of luck today . . . Nothing had spoiled the day and it had been almost happy." Luck was indeed part of it. But the outcomes are also the results of dozens of quick decisions that he has made throughout the entire day; and they owe something to favors granted him for past good deeds. All in all, more than OK.

Solzhenitsyn has several closely related themes here. Happiness, or something close to it, comes from knowing one has beaten the system, no matter how barbarous that system is. A satisfying creativity is possible only within imposed limits. Happiness has no meaning in the absence of its opposite. Can these themes explain the nostalgia that some old-timers have for the "good old days" under Stalin, when order prevailed, everyone knew the rules, and one had to create either within these rules or around them? I am reminded, too, that Igor Stravinsky once said that creativity in music was impossible without definite boundaries beyond which one could not go. If happiness comes from creativity, then it comes from boundaries.

"He felt good about making that wall." Here Shukhov is thinking about the afternoon's work of constructing a brick wall for a second story in freezing weather.

The mortar was steaming in the freezing cold, though there wasn't much warmth in it. When you slapped it on the wall with your trowel you had to work quick so it wouldn't freeze. It if did, you couldn't get it off again, either with your trowel or the back of your gavel, and if you laid a brick a little out of place it froze to the spot and stuck there. Then the only thing to do was pry it off with the back of the pick and hack the mortar away again.

But Shukhov never made a mistake. His bricks were always right in line. If one of them was broken or had a fault, Shukhov spotted it right off the bat and found the place on the wall where it would fit.

He'd scoop up some steaming mortar with his trowel, throw it on, and remember how the groove of the brick ran so he'd get the next one on dead center. He always put on just enough mortar for each brick . . . he'd level off the mortar with a trowel and drop the [next] brick on top. He had to even it out fast and tap it in place with his trowel if it wasn't right, so the outside wall would be straight as a die and the bricks level both crossways and lengthways. . . .

The work continued at a furious pace right up to quitting time. Other gangs were turning in their tools and, since the entire group had to march back to the barracks together, they were anxious that everyone should finish up on time, so no one would have to wait around, half-frozen. But Shukhov and some of his buddies were determined to finish the job. The boss told them to quit and toss the extra mortar over the wall.

But Shukhov was kind of funny about these things. And he couldn't help it even after eight years of camps. He still worried about every little thing and about all kinds of work. He couldn't stand seeing things wasted. Mortar, brick, mortar, brick. . . . "That does it!" Senka shouted. "Let's get the hell out of here."

He grabbed the hod and went down the ladder. But Shukhov—the guards could set the dogs on him for all he cared now—ran back to have a last look. Not bad. He went up and looked over the wall from left to right. His eye was true as a level. The wall was straight as a die. His hands were still good for something!

Why would a prisoner in a Siberian labor camp work like that with such loving care? Part of the answer might be that Shukhov and others had always done their best their entire lives on any job they were given—so it was just an automatic, unthinking response. Another part, perhaps, is that under the circumstances, it was the only way to maintain one's sanity—one's humanity—and not simply let oneself go to the dogs. Fear of the boss and of what other gang members would say about slovenly work may have spurred him on. But in this case, Shukov's action defied the boss's orders and ran against the wishes of his comrades, who were freezing while waiting for him. Thus, pride of workmanship was surely there, too—undoubtedly it was written all over Shukhov's face when he went back for a last look and found the result good.

Where does such pride of workmanship come from? And when it has disappeared, how can it be restored?

★

RESTORING THE SOCIALIST SPIRIT

Let's take an easier question: What can Gorbachev learn from all this fact and fiction about what has happened to the working class since the Revolution? Probably the most important lesson is that, when workers wholeheartedly believe in what they are doing, when they are willing to go all out to achieve worthy, even noble, goals, many marvelous economic results are possible.

It may be that such enthusiasm and solidarity among Soviet workers belong only to the past and are no part of the future. It may be that the glorious task of building the world's first socialist society and the patriotic duty of defending it against fascist and imperialist foes—both of which sparked the energy and ingenuity of the working class earlier in this century—have no modern equivalents. Are there any? Not the threat of outside enemies, for Gorbachev is making friends right and left. Not the distant goal of a classless communist society, for that dream was shattered long ago by nationalist strife and ethnic and religious intolerance, multiplied so many times that brotherhood on any basis seems a laugh. And who has any faith these days in the dream of attaining unity among the workers of the world?

What remains, if Gorbachev's stated aims are taken seriously, is the more modest goal of achieving a better socialist society—one that is democratic, contains no major exploitive relationships, encourages and rewards cooperative and generous behavior, distributes its wealth in equitable ways, and is guided by the workers and farmers. This is my list, not necessarily Gorbachev's. The Soviet leader has said many times that he wants not only a more dynamic socialism, but also to restore the spirit of socialism to his country. While my list does not contain all the economic ingredients for a more dynamic socialism, it does include those aims that might conceivably arouse the enthusiasm of the masses. "Sharing" is more worthy of one's dedication than "freeing the exchange rate."

Marxian ideals have been buried so deeply beneath the grim horrors of Stalinism that it will require a superhuman effort by Gorbachev and his colleagues to disinter them. Cynicism and alienation are now the marks of the working class. It is possible but not likely that they can be overcome with promises and talk of returning to the original Marxian dream. As the periodical W would say, capitalism is in, Marxism is out. This means that hard work and dedication are forthcoming not for any general social good but only for each individual's own material welfare—personal greed, not social need. If so, then so much for what Gorbachev says he wants. And so much for Gorbachev himself. Is that too extreme a picture? We'll weigh these issues in the two final chapters.

"Who lives in this castle?
Bribery. Extortion. Racketeering. Speculation. Embezzlement."

THE POWER
AND PERILS OF
PERESTROIKA

In our appraisal of *perestroika*, four important questions keep popping up. First, exactly what is the Soviet economy? At one extreme, it has been called empty and idle; at the other, it is deemed the second most powerful economy in the world. If the latter is true, then the Soviets, despite their mistakes, must have done some things right.

What is really wrong with the economy? That is the second question. Is there enough wrong to justify restructuring the whole thing? In fact, there are problems both on the production end and on the consumers' side. Apparently an economy can be the second most powerful in the world and still have feet of clay.

Third, what are the options for correcting whatever ails this economy? What are the likely cures? The current program of *perestroika* has its own set of answers for this.

Big question number four: Is *perestroika* likely to succeed? Success depends on correctly resolving some major dilemmas—on placating the Furies, if you will, unleased by *glasnost* and *perestroika*. These Furies have not only an economic mien but social, ethnic, and nationalist ones as well. And therein lie a few tales.

Let's consider these four questions singly as we explore further the challenges facing Gorbachev.

★

WILL THE REAL SOVIET ECONOMY PLEASE STAND UP?

It is tempting to ask the real Soviet economy to please stand up. What we see before us are several candidates, and all but one are imposters. Is the real one that little weakling near the middle, or that small muscleman at the end, or the ungainly giant next to him?

The weakling is the answer if we heed *The Economist*, the weekly magazine from London with a decided capitalist bent. One can excuse any reader who gains the impression from *The Economist* that the Russian economy is empty and idle. No one really works and nothing is produced. "We pretend to work and they pretend to pay us" is the oft-repeated expression for the charade presumably going on in every factory. Since nothing is produced, *The Economist* is consistent in informing us that there is nothing to buy in the stores. The shelves are empty. The picture we get is one of workers going to work, fooling around the whole day, and getting paid in paper rubles each week. These rubles are not good for anything because there is nothing to buy. So they are saved, as either additional currency or bank deposits. *The Economist* sees in these monetary accumulations an overhang of savings or rubles that threatens to explode onto markets and send prices skyrocketing. (Prices of what, one is tempted to ask sardonically.)

We can elaborate on this fantasy by having the Soviet government borrow rubles from the banks (equal to the new savings deposits) and create new rubles (equal to the additional currency holdings). With these rubles, the government pays subsidies to the enterprises, which are earning nothing, so that they can pay their workers in the following week. Thus, the government's debt rises every week, the subsidies are large and continuous, workers are paid (in worthless paper) for not working, nothing is produced, savings pile up threateningly. To account for the queues in front of retail stores, we have to suppose that there are occasional rumors that certain items have suddenly appeared in this store or that. People, curious as always, check them out.

The Economist's answer to these problems is, naturally, capitalism. In the short run, the Soviets are told, import consumer goods by international borrowing. In the longer run, forget planning and change over to markets. Bring in foreign capitalist firms to give the economy a shot in the arm and to demonstrate how it should be done.[1]

As *The Economist*'s readers were trying to absorb these messages, this very same magazine published the average annual growth rates of 24 leading countries from 1900 to 1987, measured in real gross domestic product per capita. Over this long span, the Soviet Union (it was Russia for 20 percent of the time) was in fourth place behind Japan, Taiwan, and Brazil; it was tied for fourth with Sweden, South Korea, and Canada, and ahead of Italy, France, Switzerland, the United States, Britain, India, and several others. This information must have come as a shock to many readers of *The Economist*, if they had relied exclusively on this publication for their information on the USSR's economic situation. *The Economist* (10/21/89) felt obliged to note that "even western economists tend to agree that the Soviet Union had the fourth-highest increase, averaging 2.3% a year." The Soviet Union has outperformed most countries of the world during this century, even (according to *The Economist*) with empty shelves over the past several years, one of the most wasteful and inefficient economies in the world, and a badly flawed planning system.

"Empty shelves" and "no production" are not phrases that apply to the Soviet Union in the view of the U.S. Central Intelligence Agency (CIA). Scholars of the Soviet economy assembled in this agency, aided by experts in research institutes and universities, have accorded the Soviet economy the rank of number two in the world, measured by absolute production of goods and services. The CIA places the GNP of the USSR at roughly 50–55 percent of that of the United States, which sets it ahead of Japan, West Germany, Britain, and all other

---

[1] Many Americans undoubtedly considered the opening of a McDonald's franchise in Moscow in early 1990 to be no less a triumph for capitalism than if the New York stock exchange had opened a branch bordering on Red Square. Still, the real capitalist spirit was shown by those Muscovites who, after standing in long lines for over half an hour, ordered extra quantities of Big Macs to sell at a profit to those far back in the pack. Stalin's ghost returned, though, in the form of the fast-food franchise's quickly imposed rule to limit the number of burgers per customer. The many years that it took to bring this deal to fruition attest to a bureaucratic mess and to an economy in tatters— for McDonald's had to construct all of its own sources of supplies, including the world's largest food-processing plant, if it were ever going to open. Fast food in Russia was a slow business.

countries of the world—except, of course, the United States. The CIA estimates that the Soviets produce more than $2.5 trillion in current output of goods and services (although other estimates range as much as 30 percent lower).

It is true, however, that the Soviet population exceeds that of the United States and is far higher than the populations of Japan, Britain, and other close economic competitors. Hence, in terms of GNP per capita, the USSR is not number two but far down the list. In per capita production, it is about on a par with Israel, South Korea, Hong Kong, Hungary, and other countries much smaller in size than it is. So it is an economic giant absolutely, but mainly because it is huge geographically and has a large number of people.

While the Soviet GNP is about half that of the United States, its production of consumer goods and services is significantly less than half of the U.S. level, while its production of capital goods and military supplies is substantially higher than half. Compared to the United States, the USSR has a much larger proportion of its workers in agriculture (25 percent versus 3 percent) and a much smaller proportion in services (roughly 30 percent compared to 60 percent). If the U.S. economy is used as a standard, the Soviets produce too few consumer goods, are poor in basic services, waste many resources in growing food, and are overburdened in defense production.

According the the CIA's view, the Soviets are the world's leading producer (which means, in general, that they beat the United States) of crude oil, natural gas, iron ore, crude steel, tractors, synthetic rubber, granulated sugar, mineral fertilizers, lumber, shoes, textiles, and a large number of other industrial and consumer products. They also rank near the top in the production of coal, cement, and electricity.

While the growth rate of the USSR has been declining recently, the CIA's estimates reveal that on the average, from 1950 to 1988, Soviet economic growth was quite a bit higher than that of the United States. Precisely, Soviet real GNP in that period rose by 3.9 percent per year vs. 3.1 percent for the United States. Even more surprising, the CIA data indicate faster growth by the Soviets in consumer goods and services. And the Soviets' agricultural gains have been at least comparable to those of the United States. Remember, too, that *The Economist* reported that the Soviet Union was near the top of the growth-rate parade, ahead of the United States, over the longer period from 1900 to 1987.

Almost all analysts agree that the growth record of the Soviet Union, while "respectable," is not nearly as good as the Soviet government has claimed. For example, the official growth rate of national output from 1950 to 1987 is 6.7 percent, while the CIA puts it at 3.9 percent; likewise for industrial production, where the two figures are 7.8 percent and 5.4 percent. An economist close to Gorbachev, Abel Aganbegyan, has challenged his own government's estimates of growth over the shorter period from 1966 to 1987. Similar challenges have come from two other Soviet investigators, economist Grigory Khanin and journalist Vasily Selyunin, who have worked together on long-term Soviet performance. This pair finds, for example, that the growth rate from 1950 to 1985 was 3.4 percent, barely lower than the CIA's estimate but only about half the Soviet government's figure. Khanin and Selyunin also assert that from 1928 to 1985, Soviet output rose by only 3.5 percent per year; the official estimate is 8.2 percent. Western economists have been making similar claims for years, long before the Soviet investigators were permitted to speak up.

The CIA's estimates of Soviet growth during the postwar period have also been challenged by some critics as being on the high side, but so far these figures have stood up fairly well, though certain components have been substantially revised in response to the criticisms. The upshot is that current scholarship shows good economic growth in the Soviet Union since 1950, although the forward pace has slowed in the last decades. In any case, such scholarship indicates strongly that the correct view of the Soviet economic record is much closer to the CIA's than to the impression one gains from *The Economist* and other sources that invoke the "no work–no goods–nothing" formula for what is going on—or, rather, not going on.

★

LACKADAISICAL LABOR PLUS CREAKING CAPITAL EQUALS LONG LINES

I f the CIA's account of the strengths of the Soviet economy is close to correct, what, then, is so wrong with that system? The CIA and other analysts have paid much attention to the negative side of the story, which is more familiar to Americans than the happier faces.

From the production standpoint, the economy seems to be running almost solely on past momentum; now it is running down. Production growth rates have been declining for fifteen years. Most workers lost their taste for setting records long before that. Net additions to the labor force have been dwindling, and many workers have inadequate training for modern production. The capital stock (structures, machinery, other equipment) is old and sick, and additions to the capital stock generally duplicate the old technology.

The Soviets hang on to their plants and equipment for much longer than American entrepreneurs do. They repair and patch more frequently, in response to frequent breakdowns. Soviet industry lags badly in the use of advanced technology, in electronics, in steel making, and in machine tools. The Soviets are 8–10 years behind in supercomputers, 4–6 years behind in robots. Research and development expenditures have garnered poor returns. The Soviets produce industrial goods that are less reliable and less durable than comparable U.S. products. Gorbachev estimated that less than a third of Soviet-produced machinery meets world standards.

A lackadaisical and poorly trained work force plus old and sick capital add up to low productivity. Soviet output per worker is only half that of the United States. At a time when the industrial work force in the United States has been declining, Soviet industry has had to add millions of workers to raise output. The United States has done it with improved technology and heightened productivity. Nevertheless, Soviet industrial gains since 1970, even with these old-fashioned methods, have exceeded those in the United States—and they have been steadier. GNP measures production, whatever happens to the products after that. The Soviet economy wastes a significant share of what is produced, particularly in agriculture. Some of the production, moreover, is unwanted and so shows up as involuntary additions to inventories. Another portion of the production goes into voluntary inventories of enterprises, which are unusually large owing to the uncertainties of supplies. Still another share is purchased by families for additions to their larder-stocks—again because of supply uncertainties. Finally, some production finds its way into black markets. All the "leakages" together suggest inefficiency in the operation of the economy, even though GNP—that is, production—registers success.

Some of these failings, as well as others, have been widely publicized when the focus is on the consumer sector. To begin with, the Soviets produce fewer consumer goods and services, relative to their GNP, than most industrial countries do. Their effort has disproportionately been centered on investment and military goods. Soviet workers earn incomes in all of these sectors, but these incomes do not find a commensurate volume of consumer items for sale. One result has been a large accumulation of ruble savings, which many experts believe would threaten the economy with open inflation if prices were free to move.

Second, consumer services—repair shops, restaurants, taxis, sales clerks in most stores, maintenance workers, beauty shops—have been in especially short supply. Third, consumer goods are often shoddily made. Once produced, they are added to the GNP whether anyone wants them or not. The Soviet Union, for example, produces far more shoes than any other country, but many shoes go unsold as Soviet people await more attractive models. Many women are better dressed than would appear possible from department-store merchandise—but only because they purchase their own fabrics and either make the dresses and suits themselves or have them made. A Soviet cartoon suggested that the most exciting thing about television (before *glasnost*) was that the set was likely to blow up at any moment.

Finally, there are always lines in front of shops. Why? Mainly because many essentials are priced below their equilibrium levels, so that the amounts demanded exceed the amounts supplied. If the state gave away soap, bread, and sugar, people would certainly have to stand in lines to obtain them. When prices are set somewhat higher, but still below the point where demand and supply meet, the lines will be shorter—but lines there will be. Other reasons for the lines are slow service; the acceptance by consumers of only certain brands, which leads to ganging up on these items; and a poor distribution system, which leaves surpluses here and creates deficits there, provides too few retail outlets, and delivers supplies of goods in spurts—none for two weeks and then a sudden cornucopian flow.

The Soviet economy has serious failings in production, consumption, and the distribution of goods. It is also considered, by many Soviet citizens, an economy of privileges, inequities, and corruption. In the previous chapter, I noted the growing inequalities among the republics, mainly between the European and the Asian ones. High Party and government officials, military brass, the elite in entertainment and the arts, and other notables have access to better medical care, better schools, more travel opportunities, and fancier goods than the general run of the population. A secondary or black economy thrives below the legitimate surface of economic life. Social property is neglected, ill treated.

Boris Yeltsin, former head of the Moscow Communist Party and now Gorbachev's influential opponent, has charged in his autobiography that the Moscow administration was throughly corrupt—that a mafia-like network was profiting from extortion, black-market activities, and other crimes. When the Congress of Soviet Deputies met in March 1990, speaker after speaker rose to denounce crime waves and mass disorders throughout the country. (*The Economist*, 3/7/90)

Payoffs are often required to get anything done well, on time, or at all. Directors of La Scala opera company (Milan, Italy), upon their return in November 1989 from a month at the Bolshoi Theater in Moscow, complained of the bribes they had to pay to assure that their performances would go on. An assistant manager reported that "every day we had to slip money to bureaucrats so that the curtain could rise. While we were unloading scenery from our trucks, the trucks would disappear." The performances went on "only through daily payoffs and gifts to corrupt officials . . . we were in the hands of a criminal organization." Another official said that they were caught up in a pro-Gorbachev and anti-Gorbachev feud within show business and in "the upper echelons of politics." (*The Economist*, 11/18/89; *San Francisco Chronicle*, 11/9/89)

★

WHAT IS TO BE DONE?

The overall goals of reform. The particular cure chosen for these economic ills depends largely on the ultimate goal. I see three broad possibilities: a reformed Stalinist economy, market socialism, or some type of capitalism.

There continue to be believers in the Stalinist system. This system relied on strong central planning in which administrative orders from the top on down established outputs and allocated materials among enterprises and farms, with only minimal help from markets. Many production units were told what to produce, how to produce it, and where to obtain their inputs for production. Stalinism also minimized private ownership of productive assets; set high priorities for industrial development, especially in heavy industry; and closed the economy to all but some necessary exchanges with foreign countries. Although we have already discussed the rigidity of this system and the reasons for its increasing failures, a good number of Soviets feel not only that it can be reformed to work well, but that it is the system most consistent with socialism.

Market socialism for the Stalinist group is an oxymoron. For them, any system relying heavily on market activity is not a socialist one. This, of course, is a matter of definition. If the reliance on markets ruled out all central planning, I would agree that socialism, as it has come down from Marx and Lenin, would not prevail. However, some Marxists have believed that market activities would not only be consistent with central planning, but would actually increase its efficiency.

Over fifty years ago, Oskar Lange ("On the Economic Theory of Socialism") showed the consistency and the desirability of the two together—markets and planning. Fred M. Taylor, a decade before that, had outlined a cruder model of the same thing. Lange postulated an economy in which consumers have freedom of choice in their purchases and workers have freedom to choose their occupations. The principal means of production are socially owned, the working class has political power, and a Central Planning Board (CPB) guides much of the economic activity. While small firms and all farms continue to be privately owned, large enterprises and the banking system are socialized, with managers appointed by the workers. These managers are instructed by the CPB to minimize costs and to produce where marginal cost (i.e., the additional cost of the last unit produced) is equal to price. This rule insures that production is efficient.

In Lange's model, the prices of consumer goods and services are established on free markets, not by the central planners. The same is true for the prices of labor services—that is, wage rates. Consumers and workers are free to choose, and prices reflect their choices and the availability of goods and jobs. However, capital goods and productive natural resources do not trade on free markets, inasmuch as they are socially owned and not for private sale. Hence, market prices for them do not exist; instead, central planners assign them "accounting prices," which managers of socialist enterprises use in deciding how much of such products to purchase. These accounting prices are changed from time to time according to whether excess demands or excess supplies develop. If the former, then the current price is too low and should be raised; if the latter, the opposite is true. Thus, equilibrium prices for capital goods and productive resources, characterized by the equality between demand and supply, can be achieved or at least closely approached by the central planners.

Looking at the macro-dimensions of this system, Lange notes that households' incomes are equal to their wages or earnings plus their share of the "social dividend"—this being the surplus of socialist enterprises. The social dividend can also be thought of as the income society derives from its ownership of enterprises. The social dividend can be either distributed to households or set aside to provide investment funds for socialist enterprises. In the first case, households then decide how much to save—that is, how much saving will be available for investment. In the second case, the central planners make the saving-investment decision. In a socialist society, the presumption is that central planners rather than households should control the time-shape of the income stream—that is, the planners should decide whether society should consume more now, by saving little, or consume more later, by saving and investing much right now.

Managers of each industry—as contrasted to managers of each firm—decide whether new firms are required or old ones should be shut down. Such decisions are based on whether demand for the industry output, at the current price, exceeds or falls short of the amount being produced when the industry is producing where its marginal cost is equal to that price.

The Lange model is one of market socialism. It is "market" because there are free markets for consumer goods and services and for labor services. It is "market," too, because prices of capital goods and productive resources are set by central planners, based on excess demands and supplies in simulated markets. It is "socialism" because the working class has the political power, the main industries and financial institutions are socialized, and central planning plays key roles in setting some prices, establishing saving rates, allocating saving for investment, and programming social goods and defense needs.

At the least, the Lange model demonstrates that central planning and a market economy are not entirely incompatible—that a market socialism is possible. However, critics have pointed out that this model assumes that enterprise managers and planners have already solved the crucial problems of what to produce and how to produce it, and that the model assumes away technical advances and other dynamic changes. All that remains for the planners is to equate the marginal costs of production to the prices. The crucial problems assumed away, the critics say, are in fact solved efficiently only in an economy of private-property rights, in which rivalry exists among enterprises in their quest for profits. It is the competitive clash among entrepreneurs that informs them about new products, new techniques, and the most efficient production methods. Managers of state enterprises, it is contended, cannot generate and do not have the incentive to obtain the information required to produce efficiently in an ever-changing world. Thus, the critics conclude, when the major means of production are socially instead of privately owned, central planning plus markets do not begin to do the job that is accomplished by private property plus markets.

Even-sterner capitalist critics—in ironic accord with Stalinists—contend that there is nothing viable at all between Stalinism and capitalism, that there is no "middle way." This view rules out combinations of markets and planning, that is, any economic convergence of the two systems. One must choose either evil or good, for there is nothing in between. Gorbachev, nevertheless, is seeking the middle way, proposing to combine socialist principles and the most progressive ideas and institutions of capitalism.

Some form of capitalism is the third alternative for restructuring the Soviet economy. A capitalist system requires that political power be held by the capitalist class—the industrial, commercial, and financial entrepreneurs and owners of the principal means of production. It requires, as this suggests, private ownership of capital goods. Capitalism also means chief reliance on free markets for the allocation of resources, such markets existing not only for consumer goods but also for privately owned capital goods and natural resources. A capitalist system can have much or little state involvement. The state could own some industries, interfere in some markets, and conduct indirect planning through monetary and fiscal policies. All these interventions are consistent with the political dominance of a capitalist class, the economic dominance of free markets, and the legal dominance of private ownership.

Were a socialist society to embrace capitalism, political parties that represent business and financial interests would be allowed. Additionally, the state would no longer represent the working class (or a bureaucracy, as it does in a deformed socialism, like that of the Soviet Union), but would reflect the means and aims of the entrepreneurial class. The first order of business would have to be the development of that class, which could be achieved by opening up industry, agriculture, and commerce to private ownership and management.

How does an economy that is essentially Stalinist, even though it has been reformed several times, get from here to there—whatever "there" is? Recall the four principal ways of restructuring the economy, discussed in Chapter 3: reorganization, decentralization, decontrol, and desocialization. Reorganization would reshuffle economic ministries, streamline them, or otherwise change them to gain greater efficiency; it would alter the structure of central planning or change the rules of the game; but it would retain the essential administrative, top-to-bottom system.

Decentralization would retain the planning system, but the lower rungs of the hierarchy would become less passive, more involved in the planning process. Khrushchev used a reform of this type in the late 1950s, when he junked the vertical hierarchical system emanating from Moscow and substituted a horizontal, geographical structure, in which more decisions were made regionally.

Decontrol would move some of the burden of decision making out of central planning and into socialist enterprises and collective and state farms, while retaining socialism. If these socialist enterprises are to make wise choices, prices must be free to move and reflect relative scarcities in the economy; thus, decontrol measures would have to be accompanied by price reforms.

Desocialization would turn socialist enterprises into privately owned and privately operated firms, or perhaps into collectives, a lower form of socialism; state farms could become collective farms; some collective farms might be broken up into family farming or leaseholds; and personal enterprises could be greatly expanded. Once again, these measures would have to be accompanied by the activation of markets and price reform, for central planning would be scrapped.

To summarize, our starting point is a Stalinist economy. The broad reforms possible are of four types, and the economy's aim could be any of three ultimate goals. If the goal is market socialism, all four types of reform would be consistent with that ultimate aim; the decontrol measures, however, would be predominant. Only two types of reform are compatible with the ultimate goal of a reformed Stalinist (bureaucratic) economy—reorganization and decentralization. Only one reform—desocialization—would lead to capitalism; the others would be superfluous.

Gorbachev has said repeatedly that *perestroika* aims for a more vibrant socialism, for some form of market socialism. Thus far, *perestroika* has traversed along all four avenues of reform. This does not mean, of course, that the final aim is inviolable. Market socialism may turn out to be a way station on the road to capitalism. Or, somewhere along the road, a reactionary group could stage a coup and restore the old bureaucracies. Nonetheless, Gorbachev's stated goal is clear.

★

The particulars of the cure. There are different general routes, then, depending on where one wants to end up. That is the broad picture. But exactly how does one proceed? Some Soviet economists and many Western ones believe that the first problem that must be confronted, whether the ultimate aim is capitalism or market socialism, is that of irrational prices, many too low, others too high. Such prices distort decision making by both consumers and enterprises, lowering allocative efficiency throughout the economy.

Suppose, for example, that central planners fix the price of bread below the equilibrium of supply and demand, and that the government produces bread until demand for it is entirely satisfied at that low price. At this level of production, the marginal (extra) cost of producing the last unit of bread will exceed the value that consumers place on it. In fact, at such a low price, consumers will demand bread not only to eat but to feed to animals, to use for footballs, and for other trivial purposes. Economic resources are wasted. If, alternatively, the government produces bread short of total demand, then queues will form, introducting another type of inefficiency.

Consider the opposite case, in which central planners fix the price too high, for, say, athletic shoes. Suppose that the government produces these shoes only up to the demand for them at the high price. At this level of production, the marginal cost of producing the last pair of shoes is less than the value that consumers place on them. Therefore, from this standpoint, more economic resources should be put into the production of more athletic shoes, until the marginal cost of producing the last pair is equal to the high fixed price. But the artificially high price is the culprit here, for at such a price, the extra production of shoes cannot be sold. They will simply pile up in retail stores as unsold inventories. Whatever amount of these shoes is produced, the artificially high price for them guarantees that some type of waste will appear in the system.

Similar inefficiencies occur within enterprises, where the irrational prices assigned to the production inputs lead producers to use inefficient input combinations—inefficient, that is, from the viewpoint of the economy. Relative scarcities of labor, capital, and land are not reflected accurately in their relative prices.

The economy suffers even more when interest rates are fixed at artificially low levels that simultaneously discourage saving and sacrifice an efficient mechanism for allocating saving to investment. If the currency is overvalued in international transactions, export industries are damaged and superfluous imports crowd in. Artificially low pay for teachers, doctors, and researchers; penalty tax rates on entrepreneurial success; free rights to pollute rivers, air, and land; and unreasonably low charges for depleting natural resources—all of these errant pricing policies either destroy wealth outright or prevent its augmentation.

Soviet economists know the wastefulness of their price structure, and they know, therefore, that a more rational system should be established, probably by raising the controlled prices of many necessities, lowering others, and freeing some prices from any controls at all. The real social and political problem concerns the necessities—food, clothing, rents, utilities, medical care—many of which have been heavily subsidized by the government at artificially low prices for decades and decades. Can these prices be raised? Not now, absolutely not now, many Soviet observers answer; not next year either, but sometime!

Listen to this recent conversation between Ed Hewett, a Brookings Institution economist who specializes in the Soviet Union, and Nikolai Shmelev, a leading Soviet economist:

SHMELEV *(referring to a general price increase):* That's impossible just now, impossible. It would be a very effective step purely from an economic point of view, but it is unthinkable just now because of our social problems, social tensions. People are grappling with increasing shortages in all our shops. To raise prices in this situation would undermine any faith, any belief in our *perestroika.*

HEWETT *(a little later):* Let's talk for a minute about price increases. You and I know that in the long run if you're going to have a successful reform, you will have to increase prices, and the sooner the better.

SHMELEV: No, no, the later the better.

HEWETT: You are talking politics. I am talking economics.

SHMELEV: In economics we should do it tomorrow.

HEWETT: And I don't understand, as an aside, why Soviet economists have started being more political than some of the politicians. Economists are terrible politicians.

SHMELEV: Maybe they have a little more imagination than our politicians. . . . All of us are frightened of social problems if prices are raised.

Hewett pointed out that if prices are not raised and shortages overcome, the social problems will just get worse. But Shmelev was unmoved.

A potentially serious problem, according to many experts, is that an inflationary spiral might be set off by an initial increase in the prices of necessities. For one thing, such price increases would probably have to be accompanied by general wage increases to prevent real incomes of families, especially the poorer ones, from falling sharply. But wage increases would add to purchasing power, which could fuel the inflationary fires. For another thing, these experts say, Soviet families now have hundreds of billions of rubles in liquid savings and cash, which could be thrown onto consumer markets if inflationary fears were generated.

These are undoubtedly potential threats, but it is easy to exaggerate them. Wage increases could be limited so that real incomes were no higher than before the price reform. If most of the raised prices are controlled prices, and if they continue to be controlled, it is not clear why consumers should expect further inflation. Moreover, the overhang of liquid savings is only about a third of the value of all consumer goods and services produced in a year, which is below similar ratios in other countries. In the United States, for example, liquid assets of consumers are at least twice as high relative to the value of consumption goods and services as the Soviet ratio. Soviet liquid savings would become a threat only if inflationary expectations rose sharply; otherwise, it is not likely that these rubles would suddenly be dumped onto consumer markets.

Nevertheless, some Soviet economists believe that this ruble overhang must be reduced before anything else can be done—whether the aim is capitalism or market socialism. There are several ways to do this. First, in a monetary reform, old currency could be called in and new notes be issued in exchange, in a ratio, say, of two to one. At the same time, bank deposits could be reduced commensurately. Alternatively, prices of consumer goods and services could be, say, doubled, which would halve the real value of liquid savings. Another method, preferred by several Soviet economists, is for the government to sell some of its own real assets—such as houses, apartments, land, businesses, gold—to private individuals for their rubles. Financial assets, such as government bonds paying an attractive interest rate, could also be sold. Rubles would be mopped up and, in the case of real assets, individuals would be given a stake in private ownership. Finally, the government could import large quantities of consumer goods from the West and set the prices high for the purpose of reducing the excess liquid savings. This last measure is favored by many Soviet economists. Thus far, *perestroika* has made no dent in this problem.

It is generally agreed that, from an economics standpoint, price reforms (accompanied perhaps by other measures to alleviate the ruble overhang) should come early, as part of a decontrol package that would also include shifting most of the daily decisions from the central planners down to the managers of enterprises. Once this is done and prices are rationalized, net profits would become the main test of enterprises' performances. The movers of *perestroika* are hardly halfway along this run—for reasons expressed above so dramatically by the Soviet economist Shmelev—although Gorbachev has recently considered accelerating the pace.

Some desocialization of the economy should also occur at an early date in the *perestroika* program—and it has. The easiest early move is to open the gates wide for personal enterprises. These activities would help to fill many of the gaps in retailing, services, and small-scale production. Team or family farming, under contracts to the collective and state farms, would also qualify as personal enterprise. Small-scale private enterprises, along capitalist lines, need to be encouraged. The *perestroika* programmers have been cautious in opening these gates, but a start has been made in both the urban and rural areas.

The next step in desocialization should be the encouragement of cooperative enterprises throughout the economy in order to alleviate the shortage of small and medium-sized firms in manufacturing, processing, and other sectors. Later steps might involve the breaking up of some state enterprises into cooperatives, the transformation of some state farms into collective farms, and the like. The way should also be opened for foreign private firms to operate in selected areas of the economy and for much freer foreign trade, both of which require a convertible currency. I have not mentioned large-scale private domestic enterprises because *perestroika* at the present time considers these to be too blatantly capitalistic.

Price reforms cannot be successful unless competitive conditions prevail in most markets. Competition would be increased with a proliferation of personal enterprises, small-scale private firms, cooperatives, leaseholds, and foreign firms. In addition, more competition can be gained by breaking up some of the huge monopolistic enterprises. If the latter is not done, free markets will be manipulated by the few powerful firms in them.

Many other important measures under the rubrics of reorganization and decentralization, as well as lesser measures under decontrol and desocialization, belong in any package of reforms aiming for a more vibrant socialism, but the ones covered here convey the general thrust of what must be done.

A gradualist approach may be proper if the ultimate aim is a reformed Stalinist system or even market socialism. In the latter case, new elements like free markets have to be meshed with old elements like state enterprises. Central planners would continue with their duties, albeit much lessened, as they incorporate market prices into their calculations. The new and the old would have to get used to each other, and that might take a little time. Even so, the drive to market socialism cannot be allowed to drag—as the Soviet one now is doing—because its elements are so interrelated that success of any one of them depends on the ready availability of the others. Much of the decision making, for instance, may be decentralized from central planners to enterprise managers, but the success of that hangs on whether rational market prices prevail—and those depend on whether competitive conditions have been established in the relevant markets.

The need to do everything at once, and fast, is even more urgent if the ultimate aim is capitalism, because in this scenario new and old elements are no longer compatible; the old have to be swept away, and new ones introduced to plug the holes. Piecemeal solutions cannot work, for the reform package makes sense only as a package; each piece is necessary for the whole to work. Prices must be freed of controls; private enterprise must be allowed to operate, without undue hindrance, just about anywhere; state enterprises must be privatized; central planning must be dismantled and macroeconomic controls tuned up; the economy must be opened wide to foreign trade and investment, with a convertible currency; and new political parties representing capitalist interests must be allowed to reorganize. To get from here to there, across the chasm, one giant step is essential, not two or a dozen. (Jeffrey Sachs in *The Economist*, 1/12/90)

★
IS PERESTROIKA
LIKELY TO SUCCEED?

Given the situation in the Soviet Union, does *perestroika* stand much of a chance? This is such a whopper of a question that only history can provide the answer. In assessing the odds, however, we uncover two serious dilemmas that these revolutionary reforms must solve if they are to succeed.

First of all, *perestroika* must overcome an entrenched and conservative bureaucracy. If it does not, reform measures will be subverted as they move down the line for implementation, just as they have been in the past. To weaken the bureaucracy, *perestroika* requires *glasnost*, a full discussion by the public of means and ends; this will lead, it is hoped, to public support of the economic measures. Only with such grass-roots backing for *perestroika* can the Soviet reformers hope to overcome the standpatters within the ministries and in other key economic and political agencies. *Glasnost* is needed to get as many people into the *perestroika* act as possible, to surround the old bureaucracies with new political forums and new social alliances. In an authoritarian, highly censored system, the *perestroika* reforms would be issued from the top, unsullied by the masses' dirty hands, into the maws of reaction, never to be heard of again.

Glasnost has an even more important role in the *perestroika* reforms. The Soviet economy, as we know, is in serious trouble mostly because it is not producing the consumer goods and services demanded by its citizens. Without digging deeply into the underlying causes, this failure can be traced to two sources: extraordinarily large defense expenditures and even-larger, but ineffective, investment outlays. Defense preparation and capital formation together make up around 45 percent of Soviet GNP, which is far above the levels of most other countries. This accounts for the squeeze on consumer products and services.

Gorbachev's plan is to cut defense expenditures substantially over the next several years. He also is aware of the need to raise the productivity of capital goods far above the present unsatisfactory levels, so that, in time, real output growth can be achieved with reduced rates of capital formation.

Glasnost is an important part of Gorbachev's answer to both the defense and investment problems. By helping to create a less-threatening world, *glasnost* can reduce defense expenditures. A more democratic Soviet Union would reduce fears in the West of hostile communist behavior—of imminent attack. On many occasions, the Soviet leader has expressed a desire for a united, peaceful Europe. *Glasnost*, by extension from the Soviet Union, has enabled the peoples of Eastern Europe to move toward democracy and to make progress toward "a common European house"—and so it has begun to pave the way for reductions in defense expenditures by the Soviets, the Americans, and others. In these ways, both at home and abroad, *glasnost* has held out the possibility of releasing resources from the production of guns and making them available for more goulash.

Is it possible for *glasnost* to aid in raising the productivity of capital goods (structures and equipment) in the Soviet Union? Maybe so. For one thing, it could help to create a friendlier world in which Western technology would become more freely available to the Soviet Union. If the leading industrial countries increased their trust in the Soviets' good intentions, state-of-the-art technology would flow more abundantly to them. *Glasnost*, as we have already seen, can also help in a more domestic way—that is, by contributing to the undermining of the Soviet bureaucracy, which has often stood in the way of new ideas, new ways of doing things, and innovations in general. *Glasnost* is needed to apply public pressure to these citadels of reaction.

Glasnost is an integral part of Gorbachev's foreign policy, and the latter is a powerful weapon in furthering his domestic policy. The Soviet leader has pointed out, many times, the relation of his foreign policy to his domestic economic efforts: "Our extensive plans for social and economic development are inseparably linked with a foreign policy which is aimed at promoting peace [i.e., reducing defense expenditures] and all-around international economic cooperation [i.e., importing advanced Western technology]."

Gorbachev believes that the *perestroika* and *glasnost* reforms in the Soviet Union have sparked not only the upheavals in Eastern Europe, but many changes elsewhere as well. He has grandiloquently called these reforms "the central point of all changes that are now taking place in the world." These worldwide changes promise, Gorbachev tells us, to place "the entire human civilization" onto a new stage—presumably a higher stage—of human accomplishment. (*New York Times*, 1/15/90) The gradual integration of the Soviet Union and Eastern Europe into that "new stage of human accomplishment" is bound to aid Gorbachev's purposes.

But *glasnost* is a dangerous business; it entails huge risks. There are obvious dangers in permitting people to speak up, especially if they have had to suffer silently for many years with their painful memories of deportation; of attempted suppression of their culture, language, and religion; of imperialistic incursion by the Russians into their lives; of intertribal atrocities; and of the miserable conditions of their labor. Pent-up and bitter grievances, released by *glasnost*, fly around as furiously as the Furies, three avenging deities in Greek mythology who harassed and inflicted stinging punishment on those who had committed terrible crimes. In the modern setting, there are also three Furies, representing fervent nationalism, ethnic and religious grievances, and the wrath of the working class. These three Furies are buzzing around and tormenting Gorbachev—to avenge what crime? His "murder" of Stalinism, his death blow to the patriarchal system. In their fervor, these Furies threaten nothing less than to bring about the dismemberment of the Soviet Union.

So while *perestroika* without *glasnost* may have little chance of success, *perestroika* with *glasnost* carries frightful dangers. That is the first dilemma.

There is another. *Perestroika* without markets (that is, without price reforms and the establishment of competitive markets) is not likely to get anywhere. If the *perestroika* reforms fail to establish a working market-oriented socialism, many prices will continue to misrepresent what is scarce and what is surplus; therefore, profits of enterprises and farms will be poor indicators of where resources should be added or subtracted. Under these conditions, the planners would have to return to commands, to administrative orders, because if consumer preferences cannot be registered properly, planners' preferences would have to take over.

But *perestroika* with markets could unleash its own set of Furies—those of inflation, inequalities, and unemployment. Under the command economy, the prices of many basic commodities and services have been controlled at levels far below equilibrium for many years. If this command regime is switched to a market system, the prices of these items—rents, bus fares, bread, utilities, meats, children's clothes—would be allowed to rise, which means inflation and, unless there is compensation, lower living standards for the masses. Politically, then, such price increases would have to be accompanied by widespread wage increases, if a sharp and sudden deterioration in living standards is to be avoided. A wage-price spiral is then a possibility, the one chasing the other until inflation becomes too high a price to pay for free markets. An open inflation like that is not inevitable, but it is more likely with open markets, especially if families with large holdings of liquid assets throw them onto uncontrolled markets in fear of worsening inflation, as many Soviet economists anticipate. Of course, even in a command economy with controlled prices, there may be inflation, but it shows up in a suppressed form, reflected in long queues, wasted time in hunting for commodities, bribes, and rationing coupons. Nonetheless, as we shall see in the final chapter, many Soviet citizens seem to consider open inflation worse than the rough justice dispensed by the command system.

A market-oriented economy also means that prices frequently change, some rising and others falling. Thus, large gains accrue to some people, and large losses are suffered by others. In an economy of market opportunities, these gains and losses are not likely to cancel out, especially in the short run, for each person. They are most likely to produce growing disparities of income as some people get into more advantageous positions or build on lucky gains, while others fall ever deeper in the hole. Income inequalities are the bane of socialist societies, but they may be another necessary cost of developing a more efficient economy through market activities. The question is whether the Soviet people are willing to pay that cost.

Finally, in a market-oriented economy, even a socialist government would have to close down those state enterprises that are mired in losses. Many small cooperatives, too, might have to go out of business, and personal enterprises could come and go. Thus, unemployment could become a serious problem for a socialist government that is seeking efficiency through markets. Of course, a command economy might have a large amount of hidden unemployment in the form of excess workers with little to do and underemployed skilled workers. Even so, those arrangements offer a certain level of job security to everyone, which many might prefer to the uncertainties associated with volatile markets.

Perestroika would have a difficult time without help from well-functioning markets. But *perestroika* with such markets attracts a second set of Furies, and these may in time drive *perestroika* to an early death. That is the second dilemma.

The two dilemmas facing the Soviet reformers are formidable. Gorbachev has chosen his horns—*perestroika* with *glasnost* and with markets—and so the Furies are after him. Can he placate them? Let's first look at the Furies a little more closely.

★

WHAT HAVOC
DO THE FURIES WREAK?

Consider the second set of Furies: inflation, inequalities, and unemployment. Inflation is a touchy subject in the Soviet Union, though perhaps not quite so sensitive an issue as it is for the Chinese communists. Both countries have had hyperinflations during their civil wars—the one in China coming before, and helping to prepare the ground for, the communists' victory; and the Soviet one coming after, and almost undoing, the Bolsheviks' assumption of power. Inflation redistributes incomes, often in unwanted ways, and it disrupts the balance among social classes. It also plays havoc with central planning. Moreover, it is part of communist lore that inflation has toppled many a capitalist government. To show how far Soviet socialism was removed from this malady, Stalin made it a dramatic point to lower consumer prices whenever the circumstances allowed.

The Soviet reformers are hesitant to carry out a price reform—that is to free many of the prices now controlled—precisely because they fear that consumers will send prices skyrocketing with their accumulated savings and higher wages. For example, Stanislav Menshikov, a Soviet economist, "contends that in the current situation of acute shortages and excess demands, freeing prices would cause runaway inflation, popular disillusion with economic reforms and increased social and ethnic unrest." (*New York Times*, 9/22/89) There have been many reports that the government fears, if it goes through with price reforms, a political upheaval stemming from the social fissures produced by inflation. We saw earlier these same attitudes expressed by the economist Shmelev. In October 1989, the Supreme Soviet turned down a government proposal to increase the prices of cigarettes, beer, caviar, crab, and smoked fish. The proposal was designed to increase government revenues by three billion rubles in 1990, for the purpose of covering some extraordinary budget expenditures connected to the miners' strikes earlier in the year. Delegates shied away from this because the proposed price rises looked like the start of inflation that would ultimately hurt the masses. "The Parliament directed the government and parliamentary committees to find additional revenues without raising prices of mass consumer goods." It also noted that Gorbachev had promised to shield consumers from a price reform until 1991. (*New York Times*, 11/1/89) The Soviet reformers are acutely aware of the large number of retired people, living on very small pensions, who would go under with upward price spirals.

The Fury we call inequalities or inequities is closely associated with her partner, inflation. That is, inflation often produces inequities. Socialists have prided themselves over the years in favoring a social system that excludes the exploitation, unequal incomes, and social inequities that are integral parts of capitalism. Although Marxists do not aspire to absolute income equality in socialism (as distinct from communism)—and certainly Stalin did not—they do point out that the absence of property incomes in socialism is bound to make income distribution more even than it is in a capitalist society. Socialism has the tradition within itself of caring more for "the masses" and of rooting out all social inequities. For those reasons, the Soviets are particularly tuned in to these concerns. In addition, the Russians themselves have long had the reputation of being disdainful toward those who move far ahead of the traditional economic line-up. As one observer put it: "The Russians traditionally have had a hang-up about any material gain not justified by some higher, nobler cause." Another referred to the Russian "distaste for individual ambition," and still another called this attitude a "sullen egalitarianism." A Siberian journalist, with understandable exaggeration, claimed that "the ideal of social justice here is that everybody should have nothing." (*New York Times*, 2/19/90)

In late 1989, many deputies in the Supreme Soviet expressed outrage over the high prices charged by the recently opened cooperatives and over the large incomes accruing to their owners. Gorbachev noted that he had received many complaints about the pricing policies of cooperatives, and he promised to tighten regulations on these practices and on economic speculation and corruption generally. Earlier in the year, Aleksandra P. Biryukova, a non-voting member of the Politburo and the highest-ranking woman in government, said that she fully sympathized with citizens "who resent the new entrepreneurs who are getting rich running private restaurants and clothing shops." She added that "unjustified income is a social injustice." (*New York Times*, 1/24/89) At about this same time, it was reported that irate farmers and officials attacked some neighbors who were getting too rich. For instance, "Soviet newspapers have reported cases of leased machinery being sabotaged and farmers being hassled by local authorities. Pig sheds at one profitable cooperative farm were burned down three times. . . ." (*Wall Street Journal*, 12/2/88)

Alarm about inflation and inequities has prevented Soviet reformers from undertaking an early overhaul of the price structure and has made them extremely cautious about promoting cooperatives and personal enterprises—necessary as these tasks are to the success of *perestroika*. These two Furies have been after Gorbachev almost from the beginning of the reform movement.

The third Fury is the specter of unemployment. This is another bugbear for socialists, for it has long been their contention that, when central planning replaces chaotic markets, the business cycles that haunt capitalist economies will disappear—and with them, the mass unemployment that capitalism periodically produces. Moreover, socialists allege that capitalists dominate workers and can fire them at will. In socialist societies, on the other hand, the working class has the power and so is protected from arbitrary dismissals. The Soviets have long claimed that unemployment did not exist in their economy. This claim seemed reasonable during the 1930s when most of the world thrashed about in depression and only the USSR (and a few other countries) moved rapidly ahead, seemingly with everyone employed.

In recent years, however, there has been evidence of serious unemployment in certain areas of the Soviet economy. *Pravda*, the Party's newspaper, has reported unbelievably high rates of unemployment in many of the non-Russian republics: for instance, over 25 percent in Azerbaijan and almost 20 percent in Armenia—which may, if true, partly account for the ethnic violence between these two peoples. Some of the unemployment throughout the country is a direct result of *perestroika* programs, which have cut back or terminated activities of those enterprises that continue to chalk up losses. Payrolls have been trimmed for some, and shops closed down for others. In both cases, workers have been laid off—by *Pravda's* estimate, around three million as of the end of 1989. *Pravda's* prediction, which strikes me as extreme, is that fifteen million will be similarly unemployed by 2005.

Turning now to the other dilemma, we encounter the three Furies of nationalism, ethnic and religious grievances, and workers' anger—all raised by the combination of *perestroika* and *glasnost*. Marxism assumed that, as the working classes around the world formed socialist societies, nationalism would give way to the international solidarity of workers. Marx noted how capitalism itself was tending to break down national borders. They would vanish even faster, he thought, as the proletariat gained world supremacy. Marxists saw nationalism as a necessary phase in the march to internationalism: The working classes would first come to national power; then, on the basis of this advance, a true international unity of workers would be established.

The Bolsheviks inherited the tsarist empire, which included many non-Russian peoples. Early Bolsheviks (led by Lenin, but including Stalin, too) believed that the backward areas and nationalities could be brought into equality with the more-advanced ones only by a long process of industrialization in those areas, in developing an industrial proletariat that would eventually overcome nationalist divisions. In the meantime, the early Bolsheviks promised these territories the right to national self-determination, the right to secede and to form independent states. True, socialism could not be built on such fragmentation, but voluntary national states were deemed the stepping stones to an eventual unity of working people. However, Lenin added, reverting to a marriage analogy: "We hardly mean to urge women to divorce their husbands, though we want them to be free to do so." In practice, the Bolsheviks' lofty principle was understandably revised during the civil war, and it was violated outright and without mercy by Stalin later on, when non-Russians were set upon by "Great Russian chauvinism" and in some cases, forcibly uprooted and sent to new "homes" far away. In the earlier years, though, Stalin's record on minorities included many positive achievements.

I noted in Chapter 4 that today Russians comprise only one-half of the Soviet Union's population. The Ukrainians are by far the most numerous of the non-Russians, but even they make up only about 15 percent of the total population. Other sizeable minorities, by order of their numbers, include the Byelorussians, Uzbeks, Kazakhs, Tatars, Azeris (or Azerbaijanis), Armenians, and Georgians. There are more than a hundred other national and ethnic groups in the Soviet Union. Because of this diverse composition and the background of oppression against many of these peoples, it is clear why the Party has been vulnerable to attack since *glasnost* opened the way for—as the Chinese would say—"speaking bitterness." It is also understandable why, once this process was underway, national, ethnic, and religious antagonisms among minorities, long suppressed, found expression in violence.

In most of these recent outbursts, it is difficult to separate out national, ethnic, and religious concerns; all three are usually involved. Marx believed that, in the socialist era, not only would nationalism fade away but people's dependence on religion would, too. Capitalist economic development, in his view, entailed the growth of the urban proletariat, organized in ever-larger units, and hence the broadening of workers' understanding of the world around them. When this understanding, built increasingly on a scientific foundation, was far enough along, there would be no need for explanations in terms of gods and spirits. While Marx's conditions for this outcome have not been completely met, it is apparent already that religious beliefs have great staying power in the world generally, and have shown surprising strength in the Soviet Union, as well, especially in view of the efforts of the Communist Party for three-quarters of a century to suppress such departures from what it considers rationalism.

Thus, the two Furies of nationalism and ethnic and religious grievances join the others who are hot on Gorbachev's trail. Their presence was apparent as early as July 1987 when a group of 300 Tatars, calling for the right to return to their Crimean homeland from which they were deported in 1944, staged noisy demonstrations near the Kremlin wall and in Red Square. Stalin deported more than 200,000 Crimean Tatars to Central Asia, claiming that they were Nazi collaborators. There are now about 400,000 of them, living mostly in Uzbekistan.

The violent clashes between the Azeris and the Armenians over Nagorno-Karabakh, a mountainous region within Azerbaijan (and administered, with recent interruptions, by this republic) but inhabited by an Armenian majority, are serious challenges to the entire *perestroika* program. Spurred on by *glasnost*, Nagorno-Karabakh demanded unification with Armenia. In the background of this conflict is the slaughter of Armenians by Ottoman Turks during World War I and the close ethnic relation of Azeris and Turks, but in the foreground is the courage of people throughout the country to speak their minds after years of silence. This has opened long-festering wounds and has led to outright fighting and killing. In February 1988, in this particular dispute, anti-Armenian riots broke out in Sumgait (a city near Baku, the capital of Azerbaijan), leaving 100 dead. Subsequently, Armenians fled from Azerbaijan and the Azeris from Armenia. Still later, the Azeris used the Armenians' dependence on the Azerbaijan rail network to impose an economic blockade on their foes. The special administrator of Nagorno-Karabakh, appointed by Moscow, said that ethnic rivalry "might become the rock against which the ship of *perestroika* is wrecked." (*New York Times*, 9/10/89)

This prediction began to come true during January 1990 when civil war—perhaps better termed anarchy—broke out between Azeris and Armenians, after Armenians were attacked and killed in Baku and elsewhere in Azerbaijan. At about the same time, part of the border between Azerbaijan and Iran was the scene of much violence, and Azeri nationalists throughout the republic challenged the rule of the Communist Party there. To restore order in the republic and to reassert its authority, the Soviet government sent in more than 11,000 troops to join 6,000 already there. In the ensuing clashes, many Azeris and government troops were slain.

During April 1989, 158 militant Georgians—in the republic just north of Armenia, in the Caucasus—began a hunger strike in support of secession of Georgia from the Soviet Union. A few days later, several thousand in Tbilisi, the capital, began demonstrating for this demand. Soviet troops moved in with tanks and armored cars to break up the demonstration; at least twenty people were killed, though Tbilisi estimates ran as high as fifty. At about the same time, people in Abkhazia, which is an autonomous (ethnic) region within Georgia, demanded secession from Georgia and the establishment of a sixteenth republic. The militants attacked a dam that provides half of Georgia's electricity, and there was shooting between armed bands of Abkhazians and Georgians, leaving 21 dead and 400 injured. In fact, Georgians outnumber Abkhazians in the Abkhazia region 240,000 to 90,000. All we need now is a group trying to break away from Abkhazia!

More recently, there was fighting between Soviet troops and people in South Ossetia (an autonomous region in Georgia), who want unification with North Ossetia, which is adjacent but in the RSFSR. In February 1990, dozens of rioters were killed in Tadzhikistan when Soviet troops clashed with local people protesting presumed housing priorities accorded to Armenians, who had been sent to this republic to escape persecution in Azerbaijan.

The Economist (9/23/89) reported yet another ethnic outburst: "The worst ethnic riots in Soviet history occurred in June [1989] in the Fergana valley of Uzbekistan, when Uzbeks began to butcher Meskhetian Turks; 50,000 people were evacuated." These riots may have had their roots in falling living standards and miserable conditions generally.

In another action, 300,000 people demonstrated in August 1989 in Kishinev, the capital of Moldavia (adjacent to Romania), demanding the adoption of Moldavian as the official language. (*New York Times*, 8/28/89) After the fall of Ceausescu in Romania in December 1989, Moldavia, which used to be part of a greater Romania (virtually the same language is spoken on both sides of the border), began further agitation for more autonomy.

Ukrainian Catholics, not affiliated with the Russian Orthodox church, demanded their rights to their own religion in October 1989. The head of the Russian Orthodox Church in the Ukraine, responded: "If—God forbid—the Ukrainian Catholic Church acquires a legal status, its zealots will brew a terrible strife and hinder the effort for beneficial change in Soviet life." (*New York Times*, 10/29/89)

The Baltic republics of Estonia, Latvia, and Lithuania have also been up in arms, demanding everything from independence from the Soviet Union, to the primacy of their own languages, to new voting laws. The Russian minority in Estonia has protested the new language and voting laws, which they claim discriminate against them. (The same type of protest was registered in Moldavia.) In December 1989, the Lithuanian Communists declared themselves independent of Moscow's control, and in March 1990, the Lithuanian parliament voted unanimously for independence from the Soviet Union.

Russian nationalism has also been a growing force, a movement that looks back to the age of the tsars, to the glories of the Russian Orthodox Church, and to the pristine wooded lands that existed before Communist industrialization ravaged them. This movement is not only fervently anti-Communist but anti-Semitic as well. Indeed, some of its leading lights see the two as pretty much the same. (*New York Times Magazine*, 1/28/90)

Many anti-Semitic acts have occurred in the Soviet Union in the past few years. The organization called Pamyat (Memory) has been accused of inciting national and racial hatred and strife and of calling for a program to "de-Zionize" the country. Pamyat urged that "Jews and their ilk" be prevented from overrepresentation in universities, the Communist Party, and government organizations.[2] (*New York Times*, 2/22/90)

The last Fury is also causing trouble, evidenced by the recent expression of workers' long-suppressed grievances. During the summer of 1989, some 300,000 miners in the Ukraine and Siberia went on strike. Gorbachev got them back to work only with promises of pay increases, fresh supplies of consumer goods, a greater voice in the management of their own industries, and other concessions. Similar strikes broke out later in the year. There were riots, too, in Kazakhstan, presumably over the importation of non-Kazakh laborers and environ-

---

[2] Incidentally, anti-Semitism has appeared more strongly and overtly in parts of Eastern Europe since the pro-democracy and anti-Communist movements toppled the Marxist regimes there. I might add that democracy—which is a means, not an end—is capable of producing a majority, in a free and open election, in favor of slaughtering a minority. This, of course, might apply to peoples other than Jews, a recent example being the demonstrators against the new government in Romania who were maligned as "unemployed gypsies." (*New York Times*, 2/20/90)

mental issues. In October 1989, Gorbachev called for a general ban on strikes in all industries for fifteen months—that is, until the end of the present Five-Year Plan. But the Supreme Soviet passed instead a measure to ban strikes in the industries of fuel and energy, transportation, raw materials, chemicals, and metallurgy—pending passage of a law governing labor disputes, which would require arbitration proceedings.

In a strange development—and an ominous one for the Soviet reformers—some Russian workers organized to fight market-oriented economic reforms (that is, *perestroika*) and to oppose nationalist movements in the non-Russian republics. The congress, which took place in Sverdlovsk (in the eastern foothills of the central Ural mountains), was attended by 110 delegates from 29 Russian cities, as well as representatives of Russian groups in Moldavia, Latvia, Estonia, and Tadzhikistan. One U.S. source reported: "A key focus of worker discontent is the cooperatives, essentially private businesses that have boomed under reform. Cooperative restaurants and retail businesses—disproportionately run, at least in popular lore by *non-Russian* nationalities [my emphasis; pause a moment to consider that!]—often charge high prices and have created a class of ruble-rich entrepreneurs who are envied and blamed for inflation." (*San Francisco Chronicle*, 9/14/89) These workers have linked up with some Russian-nationalist groups to form a United Council of Russia, and, in February 1990, they held a protest in Moscow, claiming that rock music, pornography, and other evils were products of *perestroika*.

Thus, the Furies are flying. They threaten to defeat Gorbachev's restructuring program before it has had a chance to raise living standards sufficiently to take the heat out of the many demands now spreading throughout the country. Gorbachev has remained amazingly calm throughout these storms. An example of his cool is his remarks to the Central Committee in July 1989: "If *perestroika* is a revolution—and we agreed that it is—and if it means profound changes in attitudes toward property, the status of the individual, the basics of the political system and the spiritual realm, and if it is to transform the people into a force of change in society, then how can all of this take place quietly and smoothly? And do we really need to be overcome with panic when the revolutionary processes have become a reality?

We have caused them by our policy. Can it be that we didn't understand this when we discussed it all?" Giving the members a moment to absorb that, Gorbachev went on: "The restructuring processes that have unfurled today are enveloping all realms of our life. They are revealing much [that is] unusual and much that is sometimes hard to accept. This is generating additional tension. But that is what these revolutionary years are all about!" (*New York Times*, 7/23/89) I am reminded of Mao Zedong's similar attitude during the cultural revolution in China, when he repeatedly exclaimed how good it all was as everything was crashing down all around him.

Gorbachev's serenity in the face of growing turmoil inside and outside the Soviet Union is based on elements of his philosophy that we have previously discussed: his beliefs that the restructuring now going on is "inevitable," that it is necessarily "revolutionary," and that it is necessarily, leading to a more vibrant socialism for the USSR—to a higher form of society, still another stage beyond capitalism.

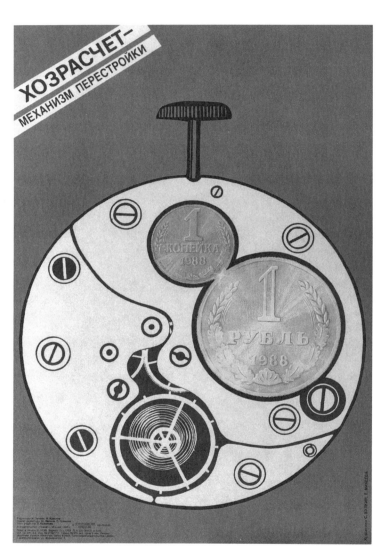

"FREE ENTERPRISE IS A MECHANISM OF *PERESTROIKA*."

THE HARD REALITIES: WHITHER PERESTROIKA?

U p to now, *perestroika* has not been a success. It has failed to raise the average growth rate of Soviet GNP, which has, since 1985, hovered around the low levels of the first half of the decade. From 1980 to 1984, the average annual rate of growth of real GNP was around 2 percent; it has since remained about the same. In the recent period, 1986 and 1989 stand out as above-average years, while the rest were disappointing. Even in 1989, industrial production rose by only 1.7 percent, and in January and February 1990, preliminary data showed a decline of 2 percent. Looking at these and other overall indicators, one cannot see any improvement in the performance of the economy.

The Soviet people cannot see it, either. A survey in the autumn of 1989 found that 94 percent of those interviewed believed that the current economic situation was either critical or bad. Moreover, 75 percent believed that the economic situation in the last two or three years had become slightly or significantly worse (more than half of the interviewees thought the latter), and 86 percent said that supplies of food and other consumer items had diminished over that period.

Still, when these people were asked about their own material well-being, about 70 percent reported improvement (23 percent) or no change (47 percent) in the past two or three years. Apparently, in their perception, the country is running down but they themselves, perhaps through ingenuity or hard work, are able to hold their own. For how long will they be able to do this? Perhaps not long, for most of them have no confidence in the future—except when that future is extended out to their children and grandchildren, in which case a third of the respondents felt that living conditions would be better.

Almost half of those interviewed believed that their leaders had no economic program at all or only a fuzzy notion of one, but most thought, in response to another question, that Gorbachev's program would be blocked by government bureaucracy (44 percent), organized crime and black markets (25 percent), or a general indifference to work (21 percent). Incompetence of leadership as an obstacle to reform garnered only 15 percent. (The respondents gave additional answers; they were evidently allowed more than one answer each.)

Answers to other survey questions suggested that most Soviet citizens wanted prices determined by the government, not the market-place; that they preferred rationing to price increases in dealing with shortages; that they disapproved of cooperatives (which have high prices and enriched owners); that they felt positively about individual farming (leaseholds and privately owned farms), but not about private enterprises; and that they preferred a strong hand at the top to markets at the bottom. The respondents believed that, if the *perestroika* program continued, there would be increases in unemployment, inflation, and disparities between rich and poor. (*New York Times*, 11/5/89)

Taken as a whole, this is bad news for the *perestroika* leaders. Indeed, in October and November 1989, they began to cut back the program of economic reforms. The Soviet legislature gave local authorities the power to place price ceilings on cooperatives and to control their activities in other ways. It also passed a measure assuring the public that price controls would not be removed in the near future. It further approved an emergency package of price controls and production quotas under which state enterprises producing essential goods lost their right to establish their own prices and production plans and were required to produce specified quantities of certain commodities at fixed prices. At the same time, the export of foodstuffs, furs, fish and marine products, electrical appliances, and other goods was restricted so as to increase supplies on domestic markets. In November, Prime Minister Nikolai Ryzhkov outlined the new Five-Year Plan for 1991–95, which ominously resembled the plans of recent decades—detailed production targets for a long list of commodities and, in general, tight reins on state enterprises. Ryzhkov announced this as "a middle way" that avoided plunging the economy "into the abyss of market chaos." These reversals of *perestroika* were described as efforts to buy time for the reform program—a step backward that, it was hoped, would later lead to two steps forward.

Forward to what? According to Gorbachev, who, after the up-heavals in Eastern Europe, reiterated the views he had previously expressed, forward to a richer socialism. "We are expanding the potential of the socialist social system. We shall be advancing on the chosen road, and we shall continue to adhere to socialist ideas," Gorbachev announced. "We don't see any reason to reject the spiritual riches contained in Marxism. The fact that it was distorted, vulgarized . . . incorrectly understood—that should not be the basis for rejecting Marxism." He later said that private property on a large scale was ruled out, though in March 1990 he acceded to small-scale private enterprise. "I do not think the working class will support those authors who want to start making our society capitalist," he said. Prime Minister Ryzhkov added that the Soviet Union would not introduce a system in which hired labor is exploited. (*San Francisco Chronicle*, 11/16/89; *New York Times*, 11/17/89) A few weeks later, Gorbachev insisted that communism was far from dead. It now has the opportunity "for moving toward its just and noble goals, for releasing the enormous humanistic and democratic potential contained in the socialist ideal." (*New York Times*, 12/1/89)

★

CAN THE WORKING CLASS
RISE TO THE OCCASION?

A vigorous socialist system, along Marxian lines, requires the dominance and leadership of a working class, led by the industrial workers. These workers, through their Communist

Party, must have control of the production process, in the sense that they choose their own managers, participate actively in setting the terms of work, and are prominently represented in the formulation of society's goals and its means of achieving them. The Party is their party and belongs to no other social group or class; the Party serves them and does not lead them around by the nose. All of this requires a solid and active organization of working people, workers who take the lead. Nothing less than this will do, if Gorbachev really wants what he says.

If, instead, the Soviet Union were simply out to reform the Stalinist system, the principal order of the day would be to fashion a leaner and more efficient bureaucracy. The leading "class" in this case would be that bureaucracy. It would set the goals, establish the rules, keep labor in its place, and prevent other social classes from developing into a threat against it. The Communist Party would be the vanguard of the bureaucracy; the Party would be part of the bureaucracy.

If the Soviet Union intended, on the other hand, to move to a form of capitalism, then it would have to nurture a capitalist class until it was strong and confident enough to perform the roles described above. Private entrepreneurs and the economic institutions they require would be promoted, and, as these entrepreneurs gained economic power, they would demand political representation through their own party or parties. The Soviet reformers would have to design their reforms to accommodate and encourage these developments.

In keeping with Gorbachev's announced socialist aims, are Soviet workers being strengthened, being groomed for leadership, by the *perestroika* reforms? It hardly seems so. To begin with, strikes have been banned in a number of important industries, and Gorbachev actually campaigned for an even more sweeping measure. Nor do workers seem to have made much progress in becoming masters of their workplaces. Moreover, the working class seems badly split, with some workers actively organizing against the reforms.

If the *perestroika* reforms were to exacerbate inflation, unemployment, and income disparities, it is likely that real wages of workers would fall, although some workers would gain and others would lose—which, in itself, would weaken the basis for solidarity. Those outcomes would not be favorable for the future of the labor movement. (Those outcomes are now in abeyance because one of the key reforms that would help to produce them, price restructuring, has not yet been carried out.)

If the *perestroika-glasnost* combination continues to generate strong separatist movements—within which nationalist, ethnic, and religious battles are fought—would these be conducive to building the hegemony of labor? That hardly seems possible, for such battles would surely divide the labor movement into many parts—Muslim, Christian, Russian, Estonian, Armenian, and so on. *Glasnost*, however, does loosen the chains that have bound Soviet labor, and with that, tongues are loosened as well. It is also possible that the spread of *glasnost* fever to Eastern Europe would produce labor movements, like Poland's, that would serve as an inspiration for the Soviet workers.

When Lenin, in the early years of this century, was analyzing the possibility of a bourgeois revolution against the tsarist regime, he noted that the Russian bourgeoisie was too inconsistent, unstable, self-seeking, and cowardly to carry out the revolution by itself. This overly timid bourgeoisie had to be led, he said, by the proletariat, allied with the mass of the peasantry, if the democratic revolution (to be followed by the socialist one) were to succeed. Today, a new socialist revolution is required in the Soviet Union, but the Soviet workers appear right now to be too backward, too cowed, too disorganized to carry it through. Who is to step into the breach this time? The problem is unique and solutions to it are only now being worked out—as Gorbachev would say—"in life." The Soviet workers themselves could come to life suddenly and alter the perspective radically. At this moment, though, there is little sign of it.

★

WILL SOCIALIST VALUES BE LOST ALONG THE WAY?

Survey results reveal that Soviet people are generally suspicious of others' successes, distrustful of free markets, and more comfortable with government controls over prices and other economic forces. These attitudes complement a general disdain for the single-minded pursuit of material things at the expense of higher principles—a fundamental rejection of the values associated with an intensely competitive society.

These sentiments are expressed repeatedly in Soviet literature. We observed them in Gladkov's novel, *Cement*, when Dasha and others expressed their dismay over the capitalistic features of Lenin's NEP. More recent Soviet stories strike the same chord. The prize-winning Siberian author Victor Suglobov, in his short story "Regardless of Circumstances," voices similar anti-capitalist concerns—yet he also acknowledges the persistant lure of the short-run benefits of certain capitalistic measures.

The hero of this story is young Nikolai Pershin, chairman of the Worker's Committee on a state farm. Restless in his job, Pershin is thinking of leaving the farm, which leads to a confrontation with his boss, Pavel Petrovich. During this encounter, Pershin is blunt in describing his disappointments: "'One day I had a real fright, when I realized that you measured everything in terms of money. Good and evil, people's actions and how important they were—it all came down to rubles! Then all of us who worked alongside you began to slide down the same slope.'"

When Pavel Petrovich argues that his material incentives have improved life on the state farm, Pershin counters that they have killed the cooperative spirit:

> "In the old days people used to come out here from the towns to help at harvest time, for a month or even two. People took them in as lodgers and they lived like members of the family or relatives, eating and drinking with the rest of us and no one thought about money. How interesting it all was! They talked away in the evenings about where they came from and what they had seen; we children often used to stay awake very late, listening to them. And nowadays! Students come out here and we count up what they owe us for food down to the last kopeck. . . . There's no comparison."

A co-worker contributes a story in the same vein:

> "Yesterday evening a lorry was on its way to us from the village store, and it broke down by the bridge outside the village. I

found Petya Anikin and said: 'Start up the tractor and go to help.' By way of an answer I heard: 'If you fill in a duty sheet for a whole day's work then I'll go, otherwise you can set off yourself.'"

In a later extension of this conversation, Pershin argues that people will work hard for non-material incentives, and that there is no need to inspire money-grubbing behavior. This strikes a raw nerve in his boss:

"Pavel Petrovich thundered out: 'You should try sitting it out in my place—just for a couple of years at least! Then I'd watch how far you'd get with your non-material incentives and your high level of political awareness!'" He points out again what good lives people on the farm are now able to fashion for themselves—because they are paid for what they accomplish.

"And is all that just in honour of Tsar Ruble? Just for the sake of profit? Perhaps just for the love of the soil and the work which their fathers, grandfathers and great-grandfathers carried out in the past? Even if it is for the wrong reasons for the moment, never mind. It'll be for the right reasons in the end . . . "

Pavel Petrovich then reveals that he, too, is a dreamer:

"I shall tell you in all honesty what matters to me other than money . . . what I dream about is putting communism into practice here on our state farm. There's no need to look so surprised . . . the food in our canteen is virtually free of charge already, the prices are a formality, no more. No charges are made for the cinema and we'll be bringing the theatre out here, all expenses paid by the farm. Then just think about the living standards people enjoy nowadays. There's no end to the consumer goods an average family can afford. . . . "

Pershin points out that this version of communism seems to be merely a higher material standard of living. You are mixing up ends and means, Pershin admonishes; you are putting the means before the end. Some might make a similar argument about *perestroika*: Will the ultimate socialist goals and values get lost in the interim moves to restore the economy to health? Gorbachev seems to think not, but there are many who worry, just as Pershin does.

★

WHAT WILL HAPPEN
TO MARXIAN SOCIALISM?

E arlier we explored three alternative goals of the current reforms: a reformed bureaucratic (Stalinist) economy, market socialism, and some type of capitalism. None of these qualifies as a Marxian socialist system.

A Stalinist society, reformed or not, is a bureaucratic system in which the working class does not have political power. Nor does it have power, in any real sense, over the principal means of production. The Party-bureaucracy represents itself and manages the economy without significant participation of the workers. That is not Marxism. It is even more obvious that a capitalist system is not a Marxian one.

What about the third choice, market socialism? Socialism, in the Marxian sense, whatever its democratic or market features, has to include central planning. But central planning becomes less viable the more democracy and market activity play important roles in the economic system. To a certain extent, central planning can be improved when planners have access to market prices, but the scope of planning is certainly reduced as free market activity expands. Democracy, too, militates against central planning, for planning cannot be done consistently on a long-term basis when a political party representing the working class (or some of it) can be voted out of power in a few years, to be replaced by a party with different fish to fry. A democratic market socialism, therefore, may be "socialist" in several senses, but it is bound to depart radically from Marx's version.

This conclusion gains greater force when we consider the other requirements for a true Marxian socialism: the working class's hold on political power and ownership of the major means of production. Both become less certain as democracy generates parties representing other classes and other interests. A party representing, say, environmental and consumer concerns is not necessarily interested in protecting the power of the working class, and a party of the entrepreneurial or capitalist class would directly challenge these features of Marxism. Additionally, a market-oriented socialism would undoubtedly contain far more economic and social inequalities than Marxian socialism could countenance.

Finally Marxism is not Marxism if it does not consider socialism to be a transition mode of production from capitalism to the classless society of communism. Needless to say, democratic market socialism would not consider communism as its long-term goal—especially since communism calls for the elimination of all class-based institutions, such as political parties; the distribution of income solely according to need; and the ultimate demise of national borders and supernaturalism. A democratic market socialism would have no interest in proletarian internationalism.

Consequently, my conclusion is that the momentous events of the last few years in the Soviet Union, Eastern Europe, and elsewhere spell the end of Marxian socialism, such as it was. That may be a truism to most readers, but it apparently has not been obvious to Gorbachev, who, while moving with these historical forces, still clings to his vision of a better Marxian socialism emerging from the rubble. What emerges for the Soviet Union may be a more dynamic system that contains some strong socialist (and Russian) features, but it will not be a Marxian one.

★

HOW HAS HISTORY SHAPED SOCIALISM?

Throughout this book I have stressed that the Marxian notion of historical flow is the crucial backdrop for assessing the present and, if it can be done, predicting the future. To understand the meaning of the recent dramatic events, we might put ourselves in Gorbachev's shoes and face the world with his outlook. What is the heart of the matter, as he sees it?

To Gorbachev, all the recent events have been historic ones, in the Marxian sense that they—or something close to them—were bound to happen, given the current of history. It may appear to some that the words and deeds of Gorbachev have been mostly responsible for what has happened, and that these words and deeds were mere accidents in the sense that, if that "great leader" had not come along just when he did, virtually none of this would have occurred. Although it may seem that way, the "great leader" actually considers himself as part of the inevitable historical flow. Thus, his words and deeds were bound to issue forth, and then to call forth the forces leading to the partial breakup of the Soviet empire, the demise of the Stalinist model of economic development, the rejection of Marxism-Leninism by Eastern Europe, the end of one-party rule, and the reunification of Germany—these and other powerful forces of both integration and disintegration. If someone can remain calm, as Gorbachev seemingly has, when things all around are crumbling away, then we can guess that such a person is a Marxist determinist—a person who sees the inevitable march of history as progress, not retrogression. In Gorbachev's view, this means progress in the Soviet Union toward a more dynamic and democratic socialism, eventually another step beyond capitalism.

That vision seems farfetched to many of us, but how strong a case can we make for his point of view? Is history working toward that end? We have to dip into the historical flow somewhere; a relevant place to get our feet wet is in Marx's time, say around the 1840s and 1850s. Were Marx and Marxism mere accidents? Not according to Marxists. The development of capitalism in Western Europe and Britain changed the face of Western society from commercial to industrial, as the industrial revolution spread from Britain to Belgium and France, then through much of Western Europe and North America. For Marxists, this process created an industrial, urban working class—the industrial proletariat—which appeared destined to challenge successfully the dominant class of capitalists. Also destined was that some intellectual would see this and proclaim it. If that analyst had not been Karl Marx, it would have been some John Doe—and so, "Doeism." But it was, after all, Marx, and from him the world heard a thundering denunciation of capitalism's evils and a pronouncement of the revolutionary role of the industrial proletariat. Capitalism, in its maturity—having among other things, a well-developed proletariat—would be ripe for the picking, and a new era of socialism would succeed in Western Europe and North America—and after that, around the rest of the globe. Socialism would spread in a global pattern dictated by the sequence in which capitalism matured first here and then there. In fact, Marxian socialism did not take hold, as expected, among the wealthy capitalist nations. Rather, its landfall was in the less-developed world, and it made its way through impoverished lands, oppressed former colonies—through the back alleys, so to speak, of the metropolitan world. Not the urban proletariat, but peasants, for the most part, waved the Marxian banner.

While Marx was correct in much of his critical analysis of capitalism and in some of his predictions, he did not foresee a crucial direction that capitalism would take after he had finished his major work and that would continue after his death. What Marx failed to predict was the imperialist phase of 1870–1910, during which the major capitalist nations carved out new empires in Africa, the Middle East, Southeast Asia, and elsewhere. Nor did Marx foresee the complex advances of technology that, for one thing, transformed the industrial workers into a more-heterogeneous and less-cohesive class. These two developments combined to raise the revolutionary potential of peasants and workers in the most oppressed areas of the colonial empires and, at the same time, lower it among the workers in the empires' centers, who became increasingly diversified and better off at the expense of the colonies' native populations.

A Marxist like Gorbachev would argue that these developments, or something close to them, were the inevitable outcomes of capitalism's necessary development into a new stage of monopolies and large-scale enterprises, which in turn carried their newly acquired profit-making abilities into even the darkest corners of the globe. Gorbachev, as a Marxist, would also contend that, just as a Marx came along to interpret the earlier stage of capitalist development, someone else had to appear later to intrepret its later stage—and that person happened to be Lenin, who was born at the very beginning of these new capitalist advances. Thus, "history" produced not only the successive stages of capitalist development and their consequences, but also the individuals who best understood what was happening and who would let the world know about it. And what Lenin saw were socialist revolutions in the less-developed areas of the world rather than in the most-advanced ones—in lands of peasants rather than urban industrial workers, in lands of poverty rather than affluence.

Now, Marx was certainly correct in his belief that individuals gain true understanding of their world—its problems and solutions—to the extent that they engage in advanced, cooperative labor. That is why he insisted that the urban working force was the new revolutionary class, while the peasants, stuck in isolated, narrowly circumscribed labor, were basically non-revolutionary. In between, the small shopkeepers, working with few others and squeezed by the bourgeoisie from above and by the proletariat from below, were unstable in their behavior, swinging first toward revolution and then toward reaction. Landlords, capitalists, and trader-speculators were, of course, the enemies.

It was obvious to Lenin and others that, in the absence of a strong proletariat, socialist revolutions could be carried out in the peripheral lands of world capitalism only if especially powerful Communist parties filled the gap—parties that were composed principally of intellectuals who understood the socialist call and could impart such knowledge to the laboring masses. This is the type of party that Lenin fashioned in Russia during the early years of this century. Most of his opponents wanted a more open, democratic party, a type that Marx apparently approved for Western European conditions. But the historical wheel had taken a different turn, and Lenin knew how to move with it.

Lenin's Bolshevik party was composed of professional revolutionaries. It was secretive (to resist tsarist spies), highly disciplined, organized to attain unanimity once a policy was debated and approved, and dedicated to the overthrow of the tsarist regime and its replacement with a Marxian-socialist society. In contrast to the original Marxian scenario, which was to be played out in a mature capitalist society, the Russian script featured a much more powerful role for the party, a weaker and smaller urban proletariat, and a massive presence of peasants. Lenin's drama first centered on whether the party could instill revolutionary juices into a coalition of peasants and workers; Marx's, on how the urban workers, during a capitalist crisis, would arise and overthrow the capitalist class. After tsarism was swept away, the central actors in Lenin's drama were the members of an even stronger party, faced with the enormous task of building socialism from scratch; those in Marx's were members of the urban proletariat, who would take over the industrial wealth of a country—with its huge enterprises, its advanced technology, and ample capital goods—and, with relative ease, establish a functioning socialist society. In Marx's case, capitalism would provide what socialism required as its successor. In Lenin's case, socialism would find the cupboard bare. The contrast between the two dramas couldn't be greater.

A Marxist, in developing this story along historical lines, would also have to remember that the Bolshevik Revolution of 1917 came during a world war among capitalist-imperialist powers and was followed by a civil war in Russia, in which these same imperialists intervened in an attempt to turn back the world's first socialist victory. By the time the Bolsheviks had won their way clear of these murderous entanglements, devastation was everywhere in the Russian landscape, the small urban proletariat had been almost wiped out, and the party was poised to expand and strengthen itself for the tremendous tasks ahead. In the absence of a large and well-developed urban working class, a formidable bureaucracy began to develop, as party and state, to fill in the gap. After all, if there was no legitimate social class to lead the way, the bureaucrats were destined to take over. Later, Stalin's imprint on Soviet development intensified this trend, so that the party-bureaucracy became all-powerful—presumably in the interests of the working class but actually, more and more, in its own interests. Thus did this top-heavy organization come to dominate everything in the land.

This is the way, a Marxist would say, the historical drama had to unfold: Capitalism carried within itself the seeds of its own development from a competitive to an industrial-monopoly stage. Monopoly capitalism generated a new wave of imperialism. This was destined to shift the revolutionary scene away from the advanced center to the oppressed periphery—from the urban proletariat to the peasantry, from a worker's uprising to a Party-led revolution. Imperialism among capitalist powers in various stages of development was bound to lead to war among them, as latecomers found their profit-making opportunities blocked by their predecessors' claims. A capitalist world war was the Leninist setting that substituted for Marx's domestic crisis of capitalism as the necessary backdrop for a socialist revolution. The civil war, Stalin, and all the rest can easily be woven into this historical fabric, which was fated to produce the all-powerful Communist Party of the USSR and its ultimately distorted version of a socialist society.

The second imperialist world war (which grew out of the same compost pile that produced the first one) and its major consequences (including the continuing uneven international balance among the capitalist powers) opened the way for the forcible export of the Stalinist model to Eastern Europe and for its acceptance elsewhere. (It also opened the way for the export of the U.S. model to the vanquished nations of Japan and Germany.) Thus, Stalinist socialism became the socialism of the day, foisting itself off as Marxian socialism, but actually being a socialism of party-bureaucracies, immature working classes, and much poverty.

Several forces weakened and finally destroyed the Stalinist model: the impossibility of socialism's overcoming the initial conditions that were so essential for its triumph in the first place (i.e., poverty, masses of aggrieved peasants, ravages of war); the eventual failure of the institutions that had been crucial for the initial successes of socialist states in backward areas (i.e., the huge bureaucracies holding political and economic power, including the central planning apparatus); other internal failings previously discussed; and the display of capitalist wealth and freedom beyond these socialist islands of economic and political deprivation. In such a climate, within and without, the Stalinist path—broad at first—finally narrowed to hardly a trace.

Such has been the broad course of historical economic development. In which direction will we now be carried by this logical, century-long sequence of events? According to Gorbachev and his Marxian views, we are being swept along within a channel wide enough to permit some room for maneuvering, but a channel, nevertheless, with definite boundaries beyond which we cannot go. Which way does the channel flow?

★

PEERING OVER THE EDGE

In trying to discern the channel's direction, I see four broad possibilities: these are the historical courses that might be described by Smith and von Mises, by Marx, by Lenin and Mao, and by Gorbachev.

The first view harks back to Adam Smith, the founding father of capitalism, and to Ludwig von Mises, the Austrian economist and Nobel Prize winner who, fifty years ago, claimed to prove that socialism was inherently an unworkable system. As I am constructing it through Marxist eyes, this view asserts that the logic of history is to produce increasingly more efficient capitalist systems; there is no economic system beyond capitalism that is superior to it. This main flow developed a side stream of socialism as a result of unusual turmoil and partial blockage in the main flow, an aberration in the historical process. However, socialism is inherently unworkable in that true markets do not exist for capital goods, and true competitive behavior cannot be reproduced among managers of state enterprises. This is so regardless of whether socialism starts in the poorer or richer areas of the world. Therefore, the side stream was bound to return to the main flow—an unending movement along capitalist lines. Capitalism will evolve, but it is the last economic system that we will know.

Another view of the historical process I attribute to Karl Marx. This asserts that socialism could not take root in soils of poverty and capitalist immaturity, especially when forcibly imposed on soils that were hostilely encircled by fertile land. Socialism proved unworkable not because of any inherent flaws, but because a peculiar turn of history placed it in inhospitable environments. The main flow of history still runs from feudalism to capitalism to socialism. Most of the aberrant socialisms will disappear, but, in time, the advanced capitalist countries will develop the fatal symptoms predicted by Marx: growing instabilities, increasing inequalities and inequities, pervasive monopolies that slow development and become ripe for ownership by society, and strong working classes that face debilitated capitalists. When mature capitalism reaches the barriers to further growth inherent in its very nature, a socialist world will succeed it—a socialism growing out of the valuable legacies of capitalist societies that could no longer employ their wealth productively. According to this view, despite the side streams of history and all the false starts, Marx in the end will be proved correct.

A third view I assign to Vladimir Lenin and Mao Zedong. While the main course of history is from feudalism to capitalism to socialism, the imperialist era of capitalism, starting around 1870, changed world capitalism so radically that socialism was established in the peripheral, oppressed areas of the colonial systems, even while capitalism prospered at the center. Although these empires were broken up politically during this century, most of the less-developed countries in the world are still dominated economically, leashed financially, and kept technologically inferior by the leading capitalist nations. Thus, socialism's prospects continue to be in these outlying regions—in China, large parts of the Soviet Union, India, Brazil, Central America, Indonesia, Southeast Asia, and much of Africa. Over time, most of the Third World will lose more and more ground to the wealthier capitalist countries, as the latter organize themselves into powerful trading units, the better to exploit the rest of the world. Therefore, the flow of history, despite some serious retrogressions, continues as before, with socialism eventually expanding extensively in the poorer regions, where most of the world's population resides. China, India, Indonesia, and Brazil, for example, have around half of the world's people—and that, in the end, will tip the scales for socialism in its struggle with capitalism.

Gorbachev's scenario, our final one, is still being formed and reformed, but much of it is clear enough. In his long view, the historical process saw feudalism giving way to capitalism and the latter involuntarily ceding part of its world territory to socialism. During the several decades in which socialism got established, advanced capitalism itself changed from aggressive, dominating colonial systems to more benign and prosperous national units, which no longer actively exploited the Third World and were willing to live in peace with the socialist world. In this view, the main course of history is toward a convergence of capitalism and socialism, though the convergence will be only partial, allowing distinct systems of capitalism and socialism to coexist. The flow of history will eliminate the weaker socialist systems; establish new—more dynamic and more democratic—socialisms here and there, most notably in the Soviet Union; continue to modify advanced capitalism along socialist lines; and leave the Third World to fare as best it can. In Gorbachev's vision, history has already eliminated the Leninist-Maoist story line of Marxist uprisings in the backward regions and continuing confrontation and struggle on a worldwide basis between Marxism and capitalism. History will also not conform to Marx's prediction of the eventual triumph of international proletarianism, with the elimination of nations and social classes. Nor will history treat kindly the Smith and von Mises outlook for the full victory of capitalism. The Soviet Union is destined to fashion a new socialism through *perestroika* and *glasnost* that will combine the central features of socialism with the most progressive ones of capitalist societies; this convergent and dynamic society will serve as a model for other peoples around the world.

Thus, we have four contending visions of where the historical process is leading us: the full triumph of capitalism, the complete victory of socialism the Marxist way, the complete victory of socialism the Leninist-Maoist way, and the partial convergence and coexistence of capitalism and socialism. But not every vision can be true.

According to the vision of Smith and von Mises, while historical forces over more than two millennia have brought forth the economic systems of slavery, feudalism, capitalism, and socialism—roughly in successive waves—history in this sense is now coming to an end. The socialist side stream will curve back into the main one, leaving capitalism as the only game in town—now and forever.

Yet there is nothing in the historical record to suggest such an abrupt termination to the evolution of new forms of society. What is indicated instead is that we can expect continuing societal transformations, even if we are unable to discern the exact form of what comes next. Regardless, capitalism could last for quite some time. Of course, whatever succeeds capitalism can still be called capitalism by those so inclined; but it might well be a system in which political power is held, not by a capital-owning class, but by middle classes of consumers, environmentalists, and peace advocates; or by broad classes of working peoples; or by a technocracy of leading entrepreneurs, scientists, technicians, and financiers.

In the long run, history does not seem to support the vision of Marx. Can anyone any longer identify Marx's urban proletariat in the wealthiest nations of the capitalist world? By virtue of its scientific and professional labor forces, broad middle classes, and social security, medical, and welfare systems, capitalism in the most advanced areas has already changed far beyond the Marxian requirements for socialist revolutions. The gap between capitalist reality and the Marxian conditions for capitalism's overthrow is not only enormous but, apparently, irreversible.

The historical process looks, at first glance, as though it could be consistent with the Lenin-Mao vision, for the Third World has been and continues to be ripe for socialist revolutions against inept, corrupt, and toadyish regimes. However, history has been teaching a valuable lesson to all Marxist-Leninist rebels throughout the Third World: namely that, while revolutions against such regimes might be possible and even easy, Marxian socialism after the revolution is impossible, for the settings are too unfavorable. Thus, in the face of that ongoing lesson, the Lenin-Mao vision looks less and less robust. This does not necessarily mean that all of the so-called Communist countries in the less-developed world are destined to disappear, but most of them probably will; and newly formed ones—whether in India, Indonesia, Brazil, Nigeria, or anyplace else—are quite unlikely. The main flow of history is sweeping past these possibilities.

Gorbachev's vision entails an enriched socialism—a Marxian socialism greatly modified by the most progressive elements of advanced capitalist societies: the use of domestic markets, political democracy, and openness to the rest of the world's economies. The historical current, having carved out both capitalist and socialist societies, has thereby generated a rich assortment of social and economic variations from among which to choose. Thus, a partial convergence of the two systems is certainly a historical possibility.

The main current for the time being, however, would seem to be flowing more or less within the channel whose banks can be called Smith and von Mises: The world is moving the capitalist way. This does not mean that there will be no room for democratic socialism—for Gorbachev's vision. But if he continues to move that way, he must buck formidable tides that may be running against him—including the tide of Soviet opinion.

During January 1990, a poll was taken in the USSR and seven other European countries to determine attitudes toward the various economic-political systems. The Soviet people were highly negative about the system of capitalism but gave fairly good marks to "Communism" (that is, their system) and democratic socialism. Over 40 percent of the Soviets polled believed that Communism with more democratic rights would prevail in Eastern Europe—which probably expressed their preference as much as their prediction. About half looked with any favor on the unification of Germany, and many saw new dangers for conflict and war in the recent events in Eastern Europe. For the most part, the Soviet people's responses to these and related questions were quite different from the attitudes of Poles, Hungarians, and Western Europeans, who had, for example, much less regard for Communism and for its prospects in Eastern Europe. (On the other hand, only the Poles—overwhelmingly—and the British—barely—expressed more positive than negative feelings about capitalism.) From our viewpoint, then, the highlight of the poll was the Soviet people's endorsement— which could be interpreted as only lukewarm, inasmuch as many refused to answer—of their socialist system, provided it was made more democratic.

"Their socialist system" means, according to the poll we discussed at the beginning of this chapter, one in which price controls, rationing, and government guidance play much larger roles than free markets, and in which cooperatives and other forms of private activity are kept within strict bounds. In other words, many favor the Stalinist system modified by political democracy (and perhaps by more private activity in the farm sector). This is not Gorbachev's vision of a socialist economy. The people shy away from the very reforms he proposes.

Recall the Greek Furies, who were placated in the *Oresteia*, a dramatic trilogy by Aeschylus. In the story, Agamemnon, king of Argos, is married to Clytemnestra; they have a son, Orestes, and two daughters. Heading off to the Trojan War, the king sacrifices one daughter to ensure a favorable wind for his sailing vessels. Clytemnestra can never forgive him, and when he returns ten years later, she kills him. Orestes then murders his mother to avenge his father's death. The Furies, grim spirits of vengeance, chase after Orestes; these creatures from the bowels of the earth have come to torment Orestes until his death.

Some years later, Orestes appeals to the goddess Athena to judge him innocent. A jury of Athens' twelve finest citizens is chosen to decide the case. When the jury is split, Athena casts the deciding vote for acquittal. The Furies are outraged, but Athena promises them a home in Athens, a place of perpetual honor where the citizens can make offerings to them. They accept. They are renamed Eumenides ("kind ones"), for they are now benevolent spirits. They have been bought off.

Now consider Gorbachev as Orestes, Stalinism as Clytemnestra, and the Furies as fervent nationalism, ethnic and religious grievances, and the wrath of the working class. (The second set of Furies— inflation, inequalities, and unemployment—has not yet appeared in full force. They are mostly still in the wings because *perestroika* has not yet established free markets extensively enough to activate them.) Gorbachev's monumental task is to tame Furies I, get *perestroika* working to begin producing the new socialism, placate Furies II, and then complete the building of the new Soviet society. Thus far, after five years, very little has been done to fulfill this program. In fact, Furies I are still on the loose and enraged; the economy has made little or no progress (there are even signs of deterioration); *perestroika* has hardly gotten off the ground; Furies II remain to be dealt with; and the new socialism seems farther off than ever.

As history flows rapidly downstream, Gorbachev may well be swept along by the winds of capitalism, despite the allure of stopping at the way station of democratic socialism. But given his own people's present distaste for market economies, he may yet attempt to obstruct history's course with the dam of a kinder and gentler Stalinism. Capitalism and market socialism, however eagerly embraced else- where, have found few welcoming committees among the rank and file here. Many Soviet problems have roots in long-standing Russian traditions, as the country's literature amply demonstrates—and tradi- tions die hard. Indeed, before tranquility is restored to this troubled land, the Soviet people may find themselves swirling in an eddy current of retrograde, religious-nationalistic fanaticism. If Gorbachev's ship of state gets carried too far too fast by the rush of change sweeping the world, he will stir the vengeful spirits of the Furies, who will surely be heard from. The word on their lips will be: "Chaos."

R E A D E R ' S
G U I D E

Group I under each chapter gives the sources for the data, quotations, and literature that appear in the text, listed in order of appearance.

Group II presents additional readings relating to the chapters, much of which I relied on as background material.

★
INTRODUCTION

I

- Vasily Grossman, *Forever Flowing*. New York: Harper & Row, 1972.

★
CHAPTER 1

I

- Gorbachev, Mikhail. *Perestroika: New Thinking for Our Country and the World*. New York: Harper & Row, 1987.

- Abalkin, Leonid I. "The New Model of Economic Management," in *Soviet Economy*. Vol. 3, No. 4, October–December 1987.

- Aganbegyan, Abel. *The Economic Challenge of Perestroika*. Bloomington, IN: Indiana University Press, 1988.

- Marx, Karl. *The Eighteenth Brumaire of Louis Bonaparte*. New York: International Publishers, 1972.

- Tolstoy, Leo. *War and Peace*. New York: Random House, The Modern Library, no date.

- Turgenev, Ivan. *Rudin*. New York: Penguin Books, 1983.

- Turgenev, Ivan. *On The Eve*. New York: Penguin Books, 1987.

- Turgenev, Ivan. *Fathers and Sons*. New York: Penguin Books, 1986.

II

- Tucker, Robert C., ed. *The Marx-Engels Reader*. New York: W. W. Norton, 1972. See especially "Manifesto of the Communist Party" and "Socialism: Utopian and Scientific."

- Berlin, Isaiah. *The Hedgehog and the Fox*. London: Weidenfeld and Nicolson, 1953. A discussion of Tolstoy's theory of history.

- Morrison, Donald, and the Editors of *Time* Magazine. *Mikhail S. Gorbachev: An Intimate Biography*. New York: *Time* Magazine, 1988.

- Wilson, A. N. *Tolstoy*. New York: W. W. Norton, 1988.

- Aganbegyan, Abel. *Inside Perestroika: The Future of the Soviet Economy*. New York: Harper & Row, 1989.

★
CHAPTER 2

I

- Smith, Adam. *An Inquiry into the Nature and Courses of the Wealth of Nations*. Homewood, IL: Richard D. Irwin, 1963. 2 vols.

- Chernyshevsky, Nikolai G. *What Is to Be Done?* Ithaca, NY: Cornell University Press, 1989.

- Lenin, V. I. "On Cooperation," in *V. I. Lenin, Selected Works*, Vol. 3. New York: International Publishers, 1967.

- Tolstoy, Leo. *What Then Should We Do? (What Is to Be Done?)*, *Centenary Edition*, translated by Aylmer Maude. Oxford, England: Oxford University Press, 1928–37.

- Lenin, V. I. *What Is to Be Done?* New York: International Publishers, 1969.

- Lenin, V. I. "Two Tactics of Social-Democracy in the Democratic Revolution," in *V. I. Lenin, Selected Works*, Vol. 1. New York: International Publishers, 1967.

II

- Schumpeter, Joseph A. *Capitalism, Socialism, and Democracy*. New York: Harper & Row, 1942. A classic work that covers, among other things, Marxian theory, the economics of socialism, differences between capitalism and socialism, and the relation between socialism and democracy.

- Fischer, Louis. *The Life of Lenin*. New York: Harper & Row, 1965. An interesting portrayal of Lenin's professional and personal life.

★
CHAPTER 3

I

- U. S. Congress. Joint Economic Committee. *Gorbachev's Economic Plans*. November 23, 1987. 2 vols. Zaslavskaya is quoted in Elizabeth Teague, "Gorbachev's 'Human Factor' Policies," in Vol. 2.

- Schroeder, Gertrude. "Soviet Economic Reform at an Impasse," in *Problems of Communism*. July–August 1987.

- Hewett, Ed A. *Reforming the Soviet Economy*. Washington, DC: Brookings Institution, 1988.

- Pushkin, Alexander. "The Bronze Horseman," in *The Bronze Horseman, Selected Poems of Alexander Pushkin*. New York: Viking Press, 1982.

- Gogol, Nikolai. "The Overcoat," in *The Portable Russian Reader*. New York: Viking Press, 1969.

- Gogol, Nikolai. *The Inspector General (Rezivor)*. Boston: Baker's Plays Publisher, 1937.

- Dudintsev, Vladimir. *Not by Bread Alone*. New York: E. P. Dutton, 1957.

- Mayakovsky, Vladimir. "The Bathhouse" in *The Complete Plays of Vladimir Mayakovsky*, translated by Guy Daniels. Moscow: Progress Publishers, 1972.

- Mayakovsky, Vladimir. "Paper Horrors," translated by Dorian Rottenberg in *Vladimir Mayakovsky, Poems*. Moscow: Progress Publishers, 1972.

II

- Blau, Peter M. *Bureaucracy in Modern Society*. New York: Random House, 1956. Definitions and the ubiquitousness of modern bureaucracies.

- Fainsod, Merle. *How Russia Is Ruled*, Cambridge, MA: Harvard University Press, 1963.

- Gregory, Paul R., and Robert C. Stuart. *Soviet Economic Structure and Performance*. 2nd ed. New York: Harper & Row, 1981. This popular text contains in Part 2 an excellent introduction to Soviet central planning. It also discusses the economic reforms of the postwar period.

★

CHAPTER 4

I

- Mandelshtam, Nadezhda. "Stalin," in *Hope Against Hope*. New York: Atheneum, 1970. Pp. 12-13

- Johnson, D. Gale. "Prospects for Soviet Agriculture in the 1980s," in *Soviet Economy in the 1980s: Problems and Prospects*, Part 2. U.S. Congress, Joint Economic Committee. December 31, 1982.

- U.S. Directorate of Intelligence. *Modeling Soviet Agriculture: Isolating the Effects of Weather*. August 1988.

- Gorky, Maxim. *My Childhood*. New York: Penguin Books, 1983.

- Gorky, Maxim. *My Apprenticeship*. New York: Penguin Books, 1980.

- Gorky, Maxim. *My Universities*. New York: Penguin Books, 1986.

- Chekhov, Anton. "My Life: The Story of a Provincial," in *The Chorus Girl and Other Stories*. The Tales of Chekhov, Vol. 8. New York: Ecco Press, 1985.

- Chekhov, Anton. "Peasants," in *The Portable Chekhov*, edited by Avrahm Yarmolinsky. New York: Penguin Books, 1985.

- Brown, Edward J. *Russian Literature Since the Revolution*. Cambridge, MA: Harvard University Press.

• Abramov, Fyodor. *The Dodgers*. London: Flegon Press in association with Anthony Blond, 1963.

II

• Gatrell, Peter. *The Tsarist Economy 1850–1917*. London: B. T. Batsford, 1986.

• Zelnick, Reginald E. *Labor and Society in Tsarist Russia*. Stanford, CA: Stanford University Press, 1971. This and the above selection offer an excellent background to the economic history of Russia discussed in the text. The book by Nove, cited below under Chapter 5, can be used to extend the background into the 20th century.

• Gorky, Maxim. *Mother*. Secaucus, NJ: Citadel Press, 1975. This is the author's most famous revolutionary novel. It is a story of how a revolutionary son awakened his mother to the injustices in their society.

• Chekhov, Anton. "In the Ravine," in *The Portable Chekhov*, edited by Avrahm Yarmolinsky. New York: Penguin Books, 1985. Another tale of peasant misery and cruelty, written around 1900.

• Troyat, Henri. *Chekhov*. New York: E. P. Dutton, 1986. This is a superb biography of the famous Russian author and playwright, who was constantly moving and constantly wary of commitments until his early death at the age of 44.

★
CHAPTER 5

I

• Lenin, V. I. "Report on the Substitution of a Tax in Kind for the Surplus-Grain Appropriation System," in *V. I. Lenin: Selected Works*, Vol. 3. New York: International Publishers, 1967. Also under the title "Introducing the New Economic Policy" in *The Lenin Anthology*, edited by Robert C. Tucker. New York: W. W. Norton, 1975.

• Lenin, V. I. "Communism and the New Economic Policy," in Tucker, *op. cit.*

• U.S. Directorate of Intelligence. "A Comparison of the U. S. and Soviet Industrial Bases." May 1989.

• Gladkov, Fyodor [Feodor] V. *Cement*. New York: International Publishers, 1929.

• Bedny, Demyan. "Nepman," in *An Anthology of Russian Verse, 1812–1960*, edited by Avrahm Yarmolinsky. Garden City, NY: Doubleday, Anchor Books, 1962.

• Dobb, Maurice. *Soviet Economic Development Since 1917*. New York: International Publishers, 1968.

• Nove, Alec. *An Economic History of the U.S.S.R.* New York: Penguin Books, 1972.

• Deutscher, Isaac. *Stalin: A Political Biography*. 2nd ed. New York: Oxford University Press, 1970.

• Kataev, Valentin. *Time, Forward!* Bloomington, IN: Indiana University Press, 1976.

• U.S. Congress. Joint Economic Committee. *Gorbachev's Economic Plans*, Vol. 1. November 23, 1987.

- Solzhenitsyn, Aleksandr (Alexander) I. *The Gulag Archipelago*, 3 vols. New York: Harper & Row, 1973.

- Gurley, John G. *Challengers to Capitalism:Marx, Lenin, Stalin, and Mao*. New York: Addison-Wesley, 1988.

- U.S. Central Intelligence Agency and the Defense Intelligence Agency. *Gorbachev's Economic Program:Problems Emerge*. June 1988.

- U.S. Central Intelligence Agency and the Defense Intelligence Agency. *The Soviet Economy in 1988:Gorbachev Changes Course*. April 14, 1989.

- Trifonov, Yuri. *Students*. Moscow: Foreign Languages Publishing House, 1953.

- Trifonov, Yuri. "The House on the Embankment," in *Another Life and The House on the Embankment*. New York: Simon and Schuster, 1986.

- Solzhenitsyn, Alexander. *One Day in the Life of Ivan Denisovich*. New York: Bantam Books, 1984.

II
- Deutscher, Isaac. Vol. 1, *The Prophet Armed. Trotsky:1879–1921*. Vol. 2, *The Prophet Unarmed. Trotsky:1921–1929*. Vol. 3, *The Prophet Outcast. Trotsky:1929–1940*. New York: Random House, Vintage Books, 1965. Leon Trotsky was the foremost exponent of central planning and industrialization. For a short time, he was widely considered Lenin's successor, but in the end he was murdered by one of Stalin's hatchetmen.

- Platonov, Andrei. "The Foundation Pit" in *The Fierce and Beautiful World,* translatted by Joseph Barnes. New York: E. P. Dutton, 1970. This novella scoffs at gargantuan projects in Soviet life. In the story, the head engineer of such an undertaking visualizes "a tower at the center of the world into which the whole world would move for eternal, joyous residence."

- Olesha, Yuri. "Envy," in *The Portable Twentieth-Century Russian Reader*, edited by Clarence Brown. New York: Penguin Books, 1985. Another story about gigantic projects. In this one, a huge dining room is being constructed—"the largest kitchen in existence"—which is intended to eliminate all family gatherings in inefficient dining facilities.

★

CHAPTER 6

I
- U.S. Directorate of Intelligence. *Handbook of Economic Statistics 1989*. Table 3. September 1989.

- Lange, Oskar, and Fred M. Taylor. *On the Economic Theory of Socialism*. New York: McGraw-Hill, 1938.

- "A Pragmatist's Approach to the Soviet Economy: A Conversation with Nikolai Shmelev and Ed A. Hewett," *The Brookings Review*. Winter 1989–90.

- Gorbachev, Mikhail S. *Toward a Better World*. New York: Richardson and Steirman, 1987.

II

- Yeltsin, Boris. *Against the Grain: An Autobiography*. London: Jonathan Cape, 1990. The former mayor of Moscow and now chief critic of Gorbachev's *perestroika* efforts discusses crime and extortion in Moscow, the uses of cheap labor, his confrontations with Gorbachev, and much else.

- The Gregory and Stuart book, cited above under Chapter 3, contains an excellent analysis of the Soviet price system and of the function of prices in general. See pp. 154-170. The functions of a price system are explained in all elementary economics textbooks. A particularly good discussion is in Paul A. Samuelson and William D. Nordhaus, *Economics*, 13th ed., Chapters 31 and 32. New York: McGraw-Hill, 1989. However, it takes some knowledge of economic principles to appreciate these chapters.

★

CHAPTER 7

I

- Suglobov, Victor. "Regardless of Circumstances." in *New Voices: A Collection of Soviet Short Stories*. Moscow: Raduga Publishers, 1985.

- Lavoie, Don. *Rivalry and Central Planning*. Cambridge, MA: Cambridge University Press, no date. Contains a discussion of the views of Ludwig von Mises.

- Aeschylus. "Agamemnon," "The Libation Bearers," and "The Eumenides," in *Greek Tragedies*, Vols. 1, 2, and 3, edited by David Grene and Richmond Lattimore. Chicago: The University of Chicago Press, 1968.

II

- Eisen, Jonathon. *The Glasnost Reader*. New York: Penguin Books, New American Library, 1990. This consists of translated articles from Soviet newspapers and journals.

- Pasternak, Boris. *Doctor Zhivago*. New York: Ballantine Books, 1986. Since I began my book with Tolstoy's *War and Peace*, it is fitting that I end it here with reference to Pasternak's Nobel Prize-winning novel, which is the *War and Peace* for this century. Pasternak was concerned with Russia a hundred years after Tolstoy's period, when there occurred three revolutions (1905, February 1917, and October 1917), a world war (1914–18), and a Russian civil war (1918–20). A major difference between the two novels is that Zhivago does not at all approve of the outcome of the Bolshevik Revolution, whereas Pierre Bezukhov, the central character in Tolstoy's work, could not help but be pleased by Russia's defeat of Napoleon.

PHOTO: JOEL SIMON

ABOUT THE AUTHOR

John Gurley's association with Stanford is long and varied. He was an undergraduate economics major (Class of 1942) and a varsity tennis player. He also did his graduate work at Stanford and was an instructor in economics during 1949–50 while working on his doctorate. Having left Stanford during the 1950s, Gurley returned in 1961 as professor of economics. He taught twice at the Stanford campus in Tours, France. Over the years he has addressed many alumni groups; in 1975 and 1979 he was Dean of the Summer Alumni College; in 1975 and 1982 he wrote *Challengers to Capitalism: Marx, Lenin, and Mao* and *Challenges to Communism* for The Portable Stanford book series; for several years he taught in the Stanford Executive Program in the Humanities; and he has participated in other summer programs for the Alumni Association. He and his wife, Yvette, have led alumni groups to China and the Soviet Union.

From 1950 to 1953 Gurley taught economics at Princeton and from 1954 to 1961 was associate professor and professor at the University of Maryland while also serving as senior staff member of the Brookings Institution. From 1963 through 1968 he was managing editor of the *American Economics Review*, the official publication of the American Economic Association; he was vice-president of that association in 1974. He presented the Alfred Marshall lectures at Cambridge University in the autumn of 1976.

Before Professor Gurley's retirement in 1987, he taught courses in elementary economics, Marxian economics, money and banking, and Chinese economic development. He was the initial recipient in 1971 of the Walter J. Gores Award for excellence in teaching, and he was selected several times as one of the Class Day speakers by the Stanford senior class. In the last few years, Gurley has continued to teach now and then, whenever called upon by his department.

As diversions, Gurley reports, he plays tennis, attends the opera, jogs, and heads for warmer weather whenever possible.

Editor-in-chief: Della van Heyst
Series Editor and Manager: Bruce Goldman
Manuscript Editor: Beverly Cory
Production Manager: Amy Pilkington
Business Manager: Edie Filice Barry
Art Director and Cover Designer: Rebecca Taber

POSTERS: Special thanks to Carol Leadenham and Ron Bulatoff of the Hoover
Institution Archives at Stanford University, Stanford, California, for their assistance
in researching and translating the Hoover Institution's poster collection.

The Portable Stanford

This is a volume in The Portable Stanford Book Series published by the Stanford Alumni Association. Portable Stanford Book Series subscribers receive each new Portable Stanford volume on approval. Books may also be ordered from the following list.

$10.95 titles

☐ *Conceptual Blockbusting* by James L. Adams, 3rd. ed.

☐ *Alpha and Omega: Ethics at the Frontiers of Life and Death* by Ernlé W.D. Young

☐ *Ride the Tiger to the Mountain: T'ai Chi for Health* by Martin and Emily Lee and JoAn Johnstone

☐ *This Boy's Life* by Tobias Wolff

☐ *Notable or Notorious? A Gallery of Parisians* by Gordon Wright

☐ *Brief Lessons in High Technology. Understanding the End of This Century to Capitalize on the Next* edited by James D. Meindl

$9.95 titles

☐ *Matters of Life and Death: Risks vs. Benefits of Medical Care* by Eugene D. Robin, M.D.

☐ *Who Controls Our Schools? American Values in Conflict* by Michael W. Kirst

☐ *Panic: Facing Fears, Phobias, and Anxiety* by Stewart Agras, M.D.

☐ *Hormones: The Messengers of Life* by Lawrence Crapo, M.D.

☐ *Wide Awake at 3:00 A.M.: By Choice or By Chance?* by Richard M. Coleman

☐ *Under the Gun: Nuclear Weapons and the Superpowers* by Coit D. Blacker

☐ *50: Midlife in Perspective* by Herant Katchadourian, M.D.

☐ *Cory Aquino and the People of the Philippines* by Claude A. Buss

☐ *The American Way of Life Need Not Be Hazardous to Your Health,* Revised Edition, by John W. Farquhar, M.D.

☐ *The Care and Feeding of Ideas* by James L. Adams

☐ *The Eagle and the Rising Sun: America and Japan in the Twentieth Century* by John K. Emmerson and Harrison M. Holland

☐ *Yangtze: Nature, History, and the River* by Lyman P. Van Slyke

☐ *The Imperfect Art: Reflections on Jazz and Modern Culture* by Ted Gioia

☐ *In My Father's House: Tales of an Unconformable Man* by Nancy Huddleston Packer

$8.95 titles

☐ *Human Sexuality: Sense and Nonsense* by Herant Katchadourian, M.D.
☐ *Some Must Watch While Some Must Sleep* by William E. Dement, M.D.
☐ *Is Man Incomprehensible to Man?* by Philip H. Rhinelander
☐ *The Galactic Club: Intelligent Life in Outer Space*
by Ronald Bracewell
☐ *The Anxious Economy* by Ezra Solomon
☐ *Murder and Madness* by Donald T. Lunde, M.D.
☐ *An Incomplete Guide to the Future* by Willis W. Harman
☐ *America: The View from Europe* by J. Martin Evans
☐ *The World That Could Be* by Robert C. North
☐ *Law Without Lawyers: A Comparative View of Law in China and the United States* by Victor H. Li
☐ *Tales of an Old Ocean* by Tjeerd van Andel
☐ *Economic Policy Beyond the Headlines* by George P. Shultz and
Kenneth W. Dam
☐ *The Politics of Contraception* by Carl Djerassi
☐ *The Touch of Time: Myth, Memory, and the Self* by Albert J. Guerard
☐ *Mirror and Mirage: Fiction by Nineteen* edited by Albert J. Guerard
☐ *Insiders and Outliers: A Procession of Frenchmen* by Gordon Wright
☐ *The Age of Television* by Martin Esslin
☐ *Beyond the Turning Point: The U.S. Economy in the 1980s*
by Ezra Solomon
☐ *Cosmic Horizons: Understanding the Universe* by Robert V. Wagoner
and Donald W. Goldsmith
☐ *Challenges to Communism* by John G. Gurley
☐ *The Musical Experience: Sound, Movement, and Arrival*
by Leonard G. Ratner
☐ *On Nineteen Eighty-Four* edited by Peter Stansky
☐ *Terra Non Firma: Understanding and Preparing for Earthquakes*
by James M. Gere and Haresh C. Shah